HONOR, SHAME, AND THE GOSPEL

When I was in seminary, learning about honor, shame, and the impact of social values on culture and religion was transformative for my understanding of Scripture, theology, and the world. I am delighted to see this interdisciplinary contribution to honor-shame studies bring together influential scholars and practitioners from many backgrounds and contexts. I highly recommend for pastors and students, but also for all who care about the whole church bringing the whole gospel to the whole world.

NIJAY K. GUPTA, PhD
professor of New Testament, Northern Seminary

Honor, Shame, and the Gospel brings afresh an important message and teaching to the attention of the global Church and mission. While in many ways the topic is not new, its renewed attention to the nexus of theology and mission practice today is timely. The richness of this book is in the conversation between different voices as they wrestle with reading scripture and its honor and shame perspective and apply it in a multiplicity of ministry contexts. While the reader can focus on individual chapters, the book is more than individual perspectives and is richer when read in the light of the dialogues that are happening between the individual understandings. It provides an excellent foundation for a much needed, broader, and deeper conversation that gives attention to the differing gendered, religious, and community experiences of honor and shame.

CATHY HINE, PhD
co-founder of When Women Speak: Angelina Noble Women's Mission Research Centre, Australian College of Theology

I am completely convinced that it is high time for a major reframing of the gospel in the West. This is not only because our prevailing articulation of it is indexed to a completely different historic, religious, and cultural era, but also because the culture/s in which we now serve are immeasurably more complex and require a deeper understanding of honor-shame and how the gospel addresses this ubiquitous human experience.

ALAN HIRSCH
author of numerous award-winning books and founder of Movement Leaders Collective and Forge Missional Training Network

Written by leaders and practitioners with diverse missiological experiences, these essays and stories focus on the convergence of honor, shame, and the gospel, at both the theoretical and practical level. This timely volume will further your sensitivity towards honor-shame motifs in Scripture. Additionally, the stories that are drawn from nations as varied as Cambodia, Croatia, and Syria will surely challenge you to consider the strategic importance of such motifs for advancing the gospel in a global context.

TE-LI LAU, PhD
associate professor of New Testament, Trinity Evangelical Divinity School

We are in an era when we need to rethink how we are sharing the Gospel. What worked in earlier decades, or with previous generations, very often is no longer effective. Given the scope of global migration patterns, prior thinking that honor and shame cultures were for "others in a different part of the world" is no longer accurate. In almost any city or context that is not ethnically homogeneous, we now need to understand the concepts in this book if we want to be more effective in leading people to Christ and aiding them in their discipleship journeys.

MARY LEDERLEITNER, PhD
author of *Women in God's Mission*
managing director of the Church Evangelism Institute at the Wheaton College Billy Graham Center

Missiologists have argued for decades that biblical interpretation and theologies emerge from the unarticulated experiences, presuppositions, values, and worldview of theologians and pastor/missionaries engaging scripture. This volume, with its focus on honor-shame, provides substantive documentation of that phenomena, but much more. In Part 1, seven essays explore diverse theological interpretations of scripture, all framed around general and specific questions of honor-shame and the gospel of Jesus Christ. In Part 2, eight essays provide ministry case studies of people who face honor/shame dilemmas and of people who face challenges when seeking to share Christ or make disciples in these communities. The power of this volume lies in its diversity of perspectives—Kärkkäinen with an interdisciplinary reflection on honor, guilt, shame, face, and forgiveness; Georges on historic theology, Steffen with a clothesline theology for the world—which, with the other essays in the volume, embrace the whole of scripture, the diversity of theologies, and a sampling of the broadest range of missional engagement of humanity. This material overflows with rich insight, and provocative application for today's global mission force, providing resources for theological and missiological reflection regardless of one's culture of origin or one's engagement in ministry.

SHERWOOD G. LINGENFELTER, PhD
senior professor of Anthropology and provost emeritus, Fuller Theological Seminary

This compendium highlights an exceptional collection of essays in the ongoing conversation about honor-shame dynamics in biblical, theological, and missiological studies. The wide range of essays contained in this volume will help enrich cross-cultural practice while also equipping the Church to grow as a global family. It is a welcome addition in facilitating understanding and love of neighbor between those in Western and Majority World contexts.

GREG MATHIAS, PhD
assistant professor of Global Studies, associate director of International Missions for the Center for Great Commission Studies, Southeastern Baptist Theological Seminary

In this single volume, God has brought together some of the world's brightest cross-cultural gospel communicators and thinkers to share with us the wisdom they have gleaned about worldview and how it is influenced by guilt, shame, and fear. Armed with this knowledge, missionaries are much better equipped for incarnational ministry than they were a few decades ago.

ROLAND MULLER
WEC International
author of *Honor and Shame: Unlocking the Door*

It's impossible to think about and practice mission today and bypass an honor-shame framework. This new resource offers a deep dive—theological, anthropological, and with case studies—into honor-shame missiological reflection. This will serve as a great resource for colleges, seminaries, and mission training centers equipping God's people for twenty-first-century mission.

ED SMITHER, PhD
president, Evangelical Missiological Society
dean, College of Intercultural Studies, Columbia International University

Christopher Flanders and Werner Mischke in *Honor, Shame, and the Gospel* have brought together an astonishingly diverse selection of essays illuminating the long-neglected dynamics of shame and honor in our understanding of the Christian message. The result is nothing less than a tour de force in exposing the narrow frame of guilt-innocence which has dominated theological and ecclesial discourse for centuries, and, in the process, opening fresh avenues for a deepened understanding of the far-reaching power of the gospel for all peoples. These essays will stir your theological imagination to new heights!

TIMOTHY C. TENNENT, PhD
president, professor of World Christianity, Asbury Theological Seminary

This book presents a collection of presentations of the 2017 Honor-Shame Conference. I recommend the book for reflective practitioners in biblical theology and missions.

HANNES WIHER, PhD
professor of Missiology, French-Speaking World

HONOR, SHAME, AND THE GOSPEL

Reframing Our Message and Ministry

CHRISTOPHER FLANDERS & WERNER MISCHKE
EDITORS

WILLIAM CAREY PUBLISHING

Published by William Carey Publishing
10 W. Dry Creek Cir
Littleton, CO 80120 | www.missionbooks.org

William Carey Publishing is a ministry of Frontier Ventures
Pasadena, CA 91104 | www.frontierventures.org

Cover design: Werner Mischke and Mike Riester
Interior design: Mike Riester
Copyeditor: Andrew Sloan
Indexer: Rory Clark
Managing editor: Melissa Hicks

ISBNs: 978-1-64508-280-4 (paperback), 978-1-64508-282-8 (mobi), 978-1-64508-283-5 (epub)

Printed Worldwide
24 23 22 21 20   1 2 3 4 5   IN

Library of Congress Control Number: 2020946992

DR. DAVID A. DESILVA,

for his lively and influential scholarship
in making honor-shame dynamics a part of New Testament studies,
and his encouragement to many for an honor-bearing gospel
in our lost and broken world, for the glory of Jesus Christ.

"We must start with the basic fact that there is no such thing as a pure gospel if by that is meant something which is not embodied in a culture ... Every interpretation of the gospel is embodied in some cultural form."

—LESSLIE NEWBIGIN

CONTENTS

CONTENTS continued on the next page.

CONTENTS

HONOR, GUILT, SHAME, FACE, AND FORGIVENESS:
A Brief Theological and Interdisciplinary Sketch

VELI-MATTI KÄRKKÄINEN

It is a wonderful joy and privilege for me to write this brief introduction. I find it quite satisfying that the topic of honor and shame is the focus of concentration for this collection of essays. Shame and honor are emerging theological and missiological topics, long studied in anthropology, the behavioral sciences, and also from a philosophical perspective. Certainly those of us who, like me, have lived among peoples of other faiths—I have lived in Thailand and taught theology there for many years—know how honor, shame, and related issues (e.g., face, guilt, dignity, etc.) are key religious and social topics in many faith traditions, particularly from the non-Western world.

These topics deserve considerable attention. In my five-volume series, *Constructive Christian Theology in a Pluralistic World*, I wrote about shame in various settings. Though certainly not comprehensive, I intend this brief foreword to provide encouraging thoughts on these topics from theological, missiological, and interdisciplinary perspectives.

Orientation

Though limited and focused in its orientation, this foreword presents some important aspects of emerging research and discussion on the concepts of honor, shame, and face, as well as the related themes of guilt and forgiveness.[1] I write as a (systematic/constructive) theologian, and approach these topics from an interdisciplinary perspective, engaging also cultural, psychological, and inter-religious perspectives. Additionally,

I approach this compendium's subject as a European who teaches theology in both North America and my native Finland and who has also served as a missionary in Asia (Thailand), while actively engaged in training Christian leaders for the entire global church in my work at Fuller Theological Seminary.

This 2017 Honor-Shame Conference took place during a time when much of the world was commemorating the five hundredth anniversary of the Protestant Reformation. This fortuitous timing offers an opportunity to reflect on the categories of guilt and shame in a world dramatically different from that of sixteenth-century Europe. Similarly, new ecumenical developments in conversations about the doctrine of justification by faith between Roman Catholics and Protestants, as well as about the doctrine of *theosis* (deification, divinization) between the Christian West (Catholics, Protestants, and Anglicans) and Eastern Orthodox churches, bring new resources for thinking about salvation in a global context. Alongside guilt and judgment (typical Protestant categories), concepts such as honor, glory, immortality, and union with God (which are used in Orthodox traditions) may provide fresh and relevant resources to negotiate the nature and conditions of Christian salvation.[2]

Furthermore, the continuing probing into cultural ramifications of the old (and in many ways problematic and even misleading) divide between the so-called shame cultures and guilt cultures could prove a useful task. Finally—and this is the area in which, at least to my knowledge, very little academic work has been conducted so far—the inter-religious dimension of the shame-guilt conversation is urgent in light of this pluralistic world of ours.

Significant questions we must reflect upon more deeply include how the categories of guilt, shame, and forgiveness might be conceived in the increasingly secularized cultures of the Global North. Even if those terms are not religiously framed, they have certainly not lost their importance.

This introductory sketch views the concepts of honor and shame, guilt, face, and forgiveness from a theological perspective in a sympathetic and critical dialogue with interdisciplinary viewpoints. As such, it is an invitation to expand, correct, and take further this highly important query.

Shame and Guilt

According to psychologists (in the Global North), shame[3] is often juxtaposed with pride: "Pride is a positive feeling about the self, and shame is a negative feeling about the self."[4] Shame may block forgiveness,[5] including forgiveness of oneself.[6] Although people seem to differ in how prone they might be to a shame or guilt orientation,[7] all of us have to come to terms with both. Shame makes us liable to the feeling of worthlessness and often elicits defensive mechanisms such as anger, shifting blame, aggression, and self-contempt.

Understandably, shame orientation makes it difficult to forgive both others and oneself. In contrast, guilt proneness[8] allows one "to focus on specific wrong actions one has committed (i.e., 'I did a bad thing') rather than the global negative self-evaluation (i.e., 'I am a bad person')... . [G]uilt proneness is positively correlated with empathy, apology, forgiving others, seeking forgiveness, and other reparative actions in relationships." In sum, research suggests that "guilt-proneness represents certain qualities of humility, while shame-proneness represents a proclivity toward humiliation."[9]

Guilt is both a central religious/theological concept and a psychological/psychiatric phenomenon. Many critics of religions, including not only psychologists but also philosophers and cultural critics such as Nietzsche and Freud,[10] have a hard time acknowledging the health-building value of any concept of guilt, particularly religion-driven guilt. In response, theologians should follow some secular scholars in making a useful distinction between "local guilt," that is, feeling remorse for a specific wrong action one knows is wrong, and "existential guilt," which means "a persistent feeling of imperfection"[11] (approaching the feeling of shame). Some critics of Christianity,[12] particularly Nietzsche,[13] have virtually ignored the first dimension and focused on the latter, and so debunked all notions of guilt. While this kind of naive religious critique (of both Freud and Nietzsche) can be easily defeated by mere appeal to the constructive function of guilt even in a psychological point of view, theologians are often faced with a more serious challenge to guilt: What about the undeniable fact that feelings of guilt seem to be conditioned, at least to some extent, on geographical, cultural, religious contexts?[14] One theological response says, "Of course, guilt, similar to all other human experiences and conceptions, including religiosity itself,[15] is evolving and liable to contextual factors."

What about the most persistent challenge to religious talk about guilt—namely, effects on the conscience? The sick conscience and its many harmful effects on mental well-being are well documented.[16] Evolutionary biology suggests that the "capacity for guilt is innate—we are born with it hardwired into our brain in evolution."[17] Furthermore, it seems that, in the perspective of evolutionary biology, guilt is also societally and culturally beneficial, related to "necessary social emotions," such as shame, embarrassment, regret, and pride. These are also called "moral emotions," as they allow one to make social judgments that are needed for the welfare of the society and culture.[18] Furthermore, guilt and a corresponding concept of "conscience" are universally present among all religions, both Abrahamic[19] and Asiatic.[20] My conclusion, then, is that neither Christian tradition nor other (theistic) traditions should abandon the concepts of guilt and shame but rather should seek to cultivate a healthy, life-affirming, and morality-enhancing sense of these two emotions of self-reference.

Shame and "Face-Work"

Along with guilt and judgment, the twin concepts of shame and honor are present everywhere in the biblical testimonies, as well as in many contemporary cultures of the Global South.[21] Although the old, unnuanced categorization of two kinds of cultures—*shame cultures* (ancient cultures and many cultures in the Global South) and *guilt cultures* (European-American post-medieval cultures)[22]—is in need of revision, there is some justification for the categories.[23] That is, different cultures weight these expressions variably, emphasizing one over the other and creating structures that authorize or prioritize one instead of the other. Every culture, though undoubtedly possessing expressions and experiences of both shame and guilt, often prioritize one over against the other.

A related concept to shame and guilt is that of "face" or "face-work." Face and facing (as well as their opposite, de-facing)[24] seem to be a universal phenomenon across cultures and religions, including all ages of human life.[25] Quite insightfully, physiognomy of old contended that much of human personality inheres in facial expressions.[26] Face/face-work is a lively interdisciplinary topic in anthropology,[27] psychology, primatology,[28] philosophy,[29] theology,[30] missiology, and inter-cultural studies.[31] What is its value for constructive theology?

Face is a familiar theme in the Bible (Num 6:24–26). The face of God denotes divine presence and is highly sought (Gen 32:30; 33:10; Ps 31:16; 67:1–2; 2 Chron 30:9). In the face of Jesus Christ, God has come to be fully revealed to us, and, therefore, Christians look for the day when they see him face to face (1 Cor 13:12; 2 Cor 3:18; 4:6).[32] The Cambridge theologian David Ford states insightfully:

> Christianity is characterized by the simplicity and complexity of facing: being faced by God, embodied in the face of Christ; turning to face Jesus Christ in faith; being members of the community of face; seeing the face of God reflected in creation and especially in each human face, with all the faces in our heart related to the presence of the face of Christ.[33]

Yet, curiously enough, "Both human and divine faces seem to have been almost wholly absent in recent Christian theology and practice."[34]

Because the face of God is narrated in the Old Testament, it is no wonder that some Jewish theologians have also tapped into those resources. Melissa Raphael's *The Female Face of God in Auschwitz* is "a Jewish feminist theology of the Holocaust," to quote her subtitle. It is a profound post-Holocaust theology delving into the mystery of the hiddenness of Yahweh's face in the midst of the horrendous suffering of Yahweh's people. Drawing from the Kabbalistic theology of Shekinah, Raphael reconceives divine presence in female terms and so helps balance the patriarchal post-Holocaust tradition. Whereas Yahweh's face was hidden, the steady and courageous women stood up against the enemy; many female heroes helped keep alive hope.[35]

Much work awaits theologians, scholars of religions, and missiologists in investigating the forms of shame, guilt, and face among living faiths. This compendium is in many ways doing groundbreaking new investigations into this emerging topic. I sincerely trust this volume will make a contribution that will advance these issues in significant ways.

FOREWORD Endnotes

1   This foreword is drawn directly from my book *Spirit and Salvation*, vol. 4 of *A Constructive Christian Theology for the Pluralistic World* (Grand Rapids: Eerdmans, 2016), 385–89 particularly.

2   See further *Spirit and Salvation,* chap. 11, and my book *One with God: Salvation as Deification and Justification* (Collegeville, MN: Liturgical Press, 2004).

3   For a psychological and psychiatric analysis of shame, see Sebern F. Fisher, "Identity of Two: The Phenomenology of Shame in Borderline Development and Treatment," *Psychotherapy* 22 (1985): 101–9.

4   F. LeRon Shults and Steven J. Sandage, *Faces of Forgiveness: Searching for Wholeness and Salvation* (Grand Rapids: Baker Academic, 2003), 54–55 (p. 55); this section is indebted to their work, including finding many sources herein.

5   See further H. Wharton, "The Hidden Face of Shame: The Shadow, Shame, and Separation," *Journal of Analytical Psychology* 35 (1990): 279–99; S. Halling, "Shame and Forgiveness," *Humanistic Psychologist* 22 (1994): 74–87.

6   Mickie L. Fisher and Julie J. Exline, "Moving toward Self-Forgiveness: Removing Barriers Related to Shame, Guilt, and Regret," *Social and Personality Psychology Compass* 4, no. 8 (August 2010): 548–58.

7   J. P. Tagney, "Shame and Guilt in Interpersonal Relationships," in *Self-Conscious Emotions: Shame, Guilt, Embarrassment, and Pride,* ed. J. P. Tagney and K. W. Fischer (New York: Guilford Press, 1995), 114–39.

8   For a psychological definition, see Kugler and Jones, *Journal of Personality and Social Psychology* 62, no. 2 (Feb 1992), "On Conceptualizing and Assessing Guilt," 318; for unhealthy and destructive guilt feelings, see Faiver, O'Brien, and Ingersoll, *Journal of Counseling and Development:* JCD 78, no. 2 (April 2000), "Religion, Guilt, and Mental Health," 155–61; Juha Räikkä, "Irrational Guilt," *Ethical Theory and Moral Practice* 7 (2004): 473–85.

9   Shults and Sandage, *Faces of Forgiveness,* 54–55 (including references). For an important current essay, see Sangmoon Kim, Ryan Thibodeau, and Randall S. Jorgensen, "Shame, Guilt, and Depressive Symptoms: A Meta-analytic Review," *Psychological Bulletin* 137, no. 1 (2011): 68–96.

10   See Herman Westerink, *A Dark Trace: Sigmund Freud on the Sense of Guilt* (Leuven, Belgium: Leuven University Press, 2009); Roberto Speziale-Bagliacca, *Guilt: Revenge, Remorse, and Responsibility after Freud* (Hove and New York: Brunner-Routledge, 2004).

11   Mathias Risse, "On God and Guilt: A Reply to Aaron Ridley," *Journal of Nietzsche Studies* 29 (2005): 46–53 (p. 46).

12   See further Kelly Murray and Joseph W. Ciarrochi. "The Dark Side of Religion, Spirituality, and Moral Emotions: Shame, Guilt, and Negative Religiosity as Markers for Life Dissatisfaction," *Mental Health, Religion and Culture* 1, no. 2 (1998): 165–84.

13 See particularly Friedrich Wilhelm Nietzsche, *On the Genealogy of Morality,* ed. Keith Ansell-Pearson, trans. Carol Diethe (Cambridge: Cambridge University Press, 2006).

14 Elisabeth J. Albertsen, Lynn E. O'Connor, and Jack W. Berry, "Religion and Interpersonal Guilt: Variations across Ethnicity and Spirituality," *Mental Health, Religion and Culture* 9, no. 1 (March 2006): 6784; S. E. Asano, "Cultural Values, Ethnic Identity, Interpersonal Guilt and Shame: A Comparison of Japanese Americans and European Americans" (PhD diss., Wright Institute, 1998).

15 For the complex relationship between evolution and the rise of religion (including the theme of evolutionary epistemology), see chap. 10 in my *Creation and Humanity*, vol. 3 of *A Constructive Christian Theology for the Pluralistic World* (Grand Rapids: Eerdmans, 2015).

16 An up-to-date interdisciplinary study on conscience from evolutionary, behavioral, sociological, cultural, and religious sciences' viewpoints is Herant Karchadourian, *Guilt: The Bite of Conscience* (Stanford: Stanford University Press, 2010).

17 Ibid., xiii.

18 Ibid., chap. 1 (p. 7).

19 See ibid., chap. 8.

20 See ibid., chap. 9.

21 See David deSilva, "Turning Shame into Honor: The Pastoral Strategy of 1 Peter," in *The Shame Factor: How Shame Shapes Society*, ed. Robert Jewett, Wayne Alloway Jr., and John G. Lacey (Eugene: Cascade Books, 2011), 159–86.

22 Rightly critiqued in Gerhart Piers and Milton B. Singer, *Shame and Guilt* (New York: Norton, 1971 [1953]).

23 Robert H. Albers, *Shame: A Faith Perspective* (New York: Haworth, 1995).

24 What many Asian and some African cultures call "losing face" is named by some contemporary behavioral scientists "defacement"; for a highly useful and richly documented current discussion, see chap. 3 in Stephen Pattison, *Saving Face: Enfacement, Shame, Theology* (Surrey, UK: Ashgate, 2013).

25 For the importance of face to the child and its relation to divine Presence, see James E. Loder, *The Transforming Moment*, 2nd ed. (Colorado Springs: Helmers and Howard, 1989), 163.

26 See the classic modern work by Swiss pastor John Caspar Lavater, *Essays on Physiognomy: For the Promotion of the Knowledge and the Love of Mankind*, trans. Thomas Holcroft (London: G. G. J. and J. Robinson, Paternoster-Row, 1878); see Pattison, *Saving Face*, 16–17.

27 For basic guidance to the key insights and vast literature concerning various dimensions of face in contemporary research (with a view to theologians, particularly practical theologians), see Pattison, *Saving Face*, 19–24 and chap. 2 particularly.

28 Primatologists raise questions about whether higher animals, such as mammals (chimpanzees), may be able to discern facial expressions; see Marc D. Hauser, *Wild Minds: What Animals Really Think* (New York: Holt, 2000), 96–103.

29 As is well known, for the Jewish theologian Emmanuel Levinas, the "Other" is a key concept; face plays an important role in the reciprocal encounter between I and the Other; see his *Totality and Infinity: An Essay on Exteriority,* trans. Alphonso Lingis (Pittsburgh: Duquesne University Press, 1969), 50–51.

30 Jean-Luc Marion, "The Face: An Endless Hermeneutics," *Harvard Divinity Bulletin* 28, no. 2 (1999): 9–10.

31 Christopher L. Flanders, "About Face: Reorienting Thai Face for Soteriology and Mission" (PhD diss., Fuller Theological Seminary, 2005); R. Lienhard, "Restoring Relationships: Theological Reflections on Shame and Honor among the Daba and Bana of Cameroon" (PhD diss., Fuller Theological Seminary, 2000); Taesuk Raymond Song, "Shame and Guilt in the Japanese Culture: A Study of Lived Experiences of Moral Failures of Japanese Emerging Generation and Its Relation to the Church Missions in Japan" (PhD diss., Trinity International University, 2009).

32 A fine study on the face of God in the Bible is Pattison, *Saving Face,* chap. 5; historical and contemporary developments are discussed in chaps. 6 and 7 (this paragraph is indebted to Pattison's work). Also useful is Shults and Sandage, *Faces of Forgiveness*, 105–24.

33 David F. Ford, *Self and Salvation: Being Transformed* (Cambridge: Cambridge University Press, 1999), 24–25; see also his "God's Power and Human Flourishing: A Biblical Inquiry after Charles Taylor's *A Secular Age*," *Yale Center for Faith and Culture Resources,* n.d., 1–28; https://faith.yale.edu/sites/default/files/david_ford_-_gods_power_and_human_flourishing_0_0.pdf (5/22/2017).

34 Pattison, *Saving Face*, 2. The English philosopher Richard Scruton's *The Face of God: The Gifford Lectures* (London: Continuum, 2012) issues a bold diagnosis of the turning away from the presence and reality of God by the atheistic and secular cultures of the Global North.

35 Melissa Raphael, *The Female Face of God in Auschwitz: A Jewish Feminist Theology of the Holocaust* (London and New York: Routledge, 2003). For an insightful Christian appropriation, see Pattison, *Saving Face*, 141–43.

The Inaugural Conference

The Honor-Shame Conference, held June 19–21, 2017 at Wheaton College, gathered 285 persons from some one hundred organizations to learn and work together for the sake of the gospel. The conference theme was "Honor, Shame, & the Gospel: Reframing Our Message for 21st-Century Ministry." Six plenary sessions were held. The presenters were David A. deSilva, Steven Hawthorne, Jayson Georges, Paul R. Gupta, Brent Sandy, and Jackson Wu. Plus, twenty-eight workshops provided a variety of additional learning opportunities. Christopher Flanders served as moderator. This compendium incorporates sixteen articles from conference participants.

The conference succeeded most notably in bringing together ministry practitioners and leaders from different disciplines and nations. Everyone was interested in some aspect of the intersection of honor, shame, and the gospel. Innumerable connections were made. New initiatives were birthed. Among the most significant initiatives birthed were the Patronage Symposium, held October 3–5, 2018, at Arab Baptist Theological Seminary in Beirut, Lebanon;[1] and Cru's "Honor Restored" evangelistic presentation for their GodTools app.[2]

How the Seed Was Planted

The seed idea for the Honor-Shame Conference was planted at Houston Baptist University when a consultation of the International Orality Network (ION) brought sixty-five leaders together July 7–10, 2014. The conference theme was "Beyond Literate Western Contexts: Honor & Shame and Assessment of Orality Preference."[3] Some of those who gathered had begun writing, blogging about, or studying honor-shame in theology and missions. Some had corresponded by email. Most had never met face to face.

Samuel Chiang, director of ION at the time, was asked to recall for this volume what motivated him to convene the consultation in Houston. He noted, "Biblical worldview is predominately filled with honor and shame; the orality movement recognized *the syncing of this century to that of the first century.* This necessitated deep recovery of the biblical worldview, reflective practices in missiology, and renewed understanding in both theology and praxis; thus, the inclusion of honor and shame in the International Orality Network's 2014 global consultation." *Thank you, Samuel, for your catalytic role in this journey.*

Definitions

The following definitions summarize various descriptions of shame and honor.

Shame is the feeling or condition of being unworthy or defective. It is the negative valuation of one's worth or adequacy. This can occur in public or relational contexts (e.g., embarrassment, social stigma, or scorn); it may also be the private experience of the individual without any audience (simply feeling ashamed or harboring a sense of inadequacy).

- "Shame is the fear of disconnection—the fear that we're unlovable and don't belong."[4]
- "The fundamental difference between shame and guilt centers on the role of the self. Shame involves fairly global negative evaluations of the self (i.e., 'Who I am'). Guilt involves a more articulated condemnation of a specific behavior (i.e., 'What I did')."[5]
- "Disgraceful shame is a humiliating or dishonorable experience of one's socially or morally inappropriate behaviors, but discretionary shame is a cautionary or self-protective sense toward possible wrongdoings."[6]

> At its core, shame is about the defective, unattractive self—'an inner experience of self as an unattractive social agent, under pressure to limit possible damage to self via escape or appeasement... . It does not matter if one is rendered unattractive by one's own or other people's actions; what matters [is] the sense of personal unattractiveness—being in the social world as an undesired self, a self one does not wish to be.'[7]

Honor refers to positive recognition of or by a group or individual based upon some type of excellence or norm. A person acquires honor by following norms (group or individual).

- "Honor is fundamentally the public recognition of one's social standing."[8]
- Honor is "the esteem in which a person is held by the group he or she regards as significant others—it is the recognition by the person's group that he or she is a valuable member of that group. In this regard, it is having the respect of others."[9]
- Honor is "the worth or value of persons both in their eyes and in the eyes of their village, neighborhood, or society."[10]
- "Honor is a claim to positive worth along with the social acknowledgment of that worth by others."[11]
- "The psychology of honor is deeply connected with walking tall and looking the world in the eye."[12]

An Overview of "Honor-Shame" for Christian Ministry

"Honor-shame" is a growing body of knowledge gained in recent decades with intersections across various disciplines—theology and biblical scholarship, anthropology and the social sciences, missiology and inter-cultural ministry, psychology and neuroscience, and more. These intersections have given rise to an informal Christian learning community around the moniker "honor-shame." Although several websites offer resources about honor-shame, the main website of the Honor-Shame Network is HonorShame.com, which Jayson Georges founded in 2013.

This introductory article is an overview of recent efforts to understand and engage with honor-shame issues. Toward that end, we provide below a list of *top ten statements* concerning honor-shame (hereafter, often "HS") in Christian ministry and their significance for the gospel.

These statements have three functions: 1) to identify assumptions and some of the scholarship which ground these recent efforts; 2) to provide a general framework through which readers may understand the compendium articles; 3) to serve as a catalyst for further thought and action about honor-shame and its meaning for Christian ministry and the gospel.

"Top Ten Statements" Concerning Honor, Shame, and the Gospel

1. Honor-shame is a foundational cultural dynamic.

This is true not just of contemporary "honor-shame cultures," but especially of the societies in which the Bible's various authors wrote the Scriptures.[13] Moreover, HS is found in every culture—East and West, North and South—although varying in style and degree. *Writers and leaders are increasingly prioritizing HS as a growing and prominent part of hermeneutics, missiology,[14] biblical studies, and theology.[15] They are seeing honor significantly related to the gospel.[16]*

2. There is no culturally neutral gospel.

The gospel contains essential truths—e.g., Christ died for our sins; he was buried and rose again on the third day—all in fulfillment of the Scriptures (1 Cor 15:3–5). But just as true is this: Every gospel presentation is articulated using a particular language and media, and is carried by persons who themselves are cultured beings who communicate in culturally specific ways. Accordingly, every articulation of God's good news contains assumptions that relate first of all to the worldview of the person presenting the gospel.[17] Therefore, all theologies are contextual.[18] Western theology, with all its diversity, benefits, and blessings, may be nonetheless influenced by various Western values of guilt, law, and justice[19]—along with individualism, consumerism, and different types of reductionisms.[20] The typical Western gospel focuses on salvation for individuals as a pardon for sin and guilt,[21] a forensic solution.

The Western legal-framework gospel is true; it is nevertheless informed in part by Western values. And "we compromise the gospel when we settle for the truth."[22]

3. Humanity's longing for honor is part of God's design.

Humans are made in God's image and given regal honor as God's vice-regents.[23] Humanity's fall is the loss of innocence; the Fall also resulted in the loss of regal honor and glory.[24] Contrary to the popular belief that humanity's longing for honor is essentially prideful and innately wrong, the longing for honor exists in the human heart by God's design.[25] *Humanity's hunger for honor is positive, not negative; it is biblically faithful to speak of the re-glorification of humanity in Christ as one aspect of the gospel.*[26]

4. Honor-shame is both old and new.

On the one hand, HS is as old as humanity; it is conventional; it is rooted in human history and present in all cultures.[27] HS is in continuity with historic Christian orthodoxy; a variety of theologians throughout Christian history have incorporated HS dynamics into their theology.[28] As the truism goes, "We stand on the shoulders of giants." HS is first of all about hermeneutics—getting closer to the way the original authors and hearers of Scripture understood the Word of God in their own cultural context. On the other hand, HS may be considered new; it addresses some acute problems better than conventional Western theology— and thus may be considered paradigmatic. "Paradigms gain their status because they are more successful than their competitors in solving a few problems that the group of practitioners has come to recognize as acute."[29] *A gospel rooted in honor-shame is a biblically faithful, problem-solving gospel in continuity with historic Christian orthodoxy.*

5. Shame is often honorable.

Various studies in the West point out the negative (even pathological) aspects of shame—whether psychological or social.[30] However, the idea that shame is universally negative or pathological belies a Western bias and is too simplistic. Billions of people in the world are part of cultures with multifaceted, highly nuanced views of shame—cultures that include positive, constructive shame, reinforce social harmony, and encourage moral excellence. Confucian philosophy (common in East Asia) sees shame in this way.[31] The Bible reinforces the view that shame can be an appropriate response to moral violation and sin—and that shamelessness is the grossest immorality.[32] The Christian world at large, and Western Christians in particular, can broaden their understanding of shame and honor by learning from non-Western scholars, thus mitigating simplistic views. *The recognition of "healthy shame" or "honorable shame" in culture and Scripture can be vital for serving effectively in the global mission of God and for contextualizing the gospel.*

6. Honor-shame is "one among equals," as well as "one above others."

On the one hand, HS may be understood as merely one value among a variety of cultural values that characterize the broad diversity of human societies; others commonly mentioned in the literature are innocence-guilt and power-fear.[33] Other examples are purity-pollution, peace-hostility, and educated-ignorant. It is instructive to see how the gospel can "speak in the language" of each of these values. *On the other hand*, none of these cultural values exist like silos, wholly distinct from the others; indeed, each may intersect with the other dynamics in varying ways and degrees.[34] Plus, HS can be seen as a factor in all the others. It may be appropriate to view HS as a kind of meta-value under which all the other values are subsets.[35] Moreover, the glory of God may be considered the crux of all biblical theology,[36] and glory is (obviously) an HS reality. Could it be that HS is worthy of a privileged status among the array of cultural values? If so, *we should understand HS as a pivotal cultural dynamic—in God's Word, his world, and his gospel.*

7. The Bible incorporates many facets of honor and shame.

The Bible is an array of various kinds of literature, including stories and characters both tragic and heroic. The Bible describes positive (healthy) and negative (toxic) aspects of honor; likewise, the Bible describes positive (healthy) and negative (toxic) aspects of shame. Honor and shame are both *subjective* (originating within the self)—and *objective* (originating outside the self).[37] Shame in Scripture can be found to be psychological (inward), social (horizontal), or sacred (vertical).[38] These HS dynamics in Scripture are within an epic narrative of God blessing all the earth's peoples for his glory. *The Bible, authored in the social context of HS cultures, is saturated with HS dynamics; it is the story about the regal Savior-King and his honorific gospel to bless all peoples.*

8. Toxic shame is a global epidemic.

The Fall has corrupted humanity's longing for glory. Across history, this has given rise to all manner of sin, idolatry, brokenness, suffering, and other shame pathologies in every corner of the human race.[39] This fallen longing for honor, this sin-laced "desire for recognition"—and the corresponding obsession to avoid a decline in status or to avenge shame—drives human history.[40] Issues of core identity (honor and shame, inclusion and exclusion) are at the crux of global crises, such as the refugee crisis, various forms of terrorism and violence, and racism (and racism's cousins, tribalism and nationalism). *Since toxic shame and honor competition between groups of every kind—families, tribes, religions, ethnicities, nations*[41]—*seems to be an incurable plague, it is strategic and compassionate to examine the cure offered by a shame-covering, honor-bearing gospel.*[42]

9. The gospel is inherently honorific.

Scriptures about salvation, the gospel, and the atonement of Christ overlap with a variety of HS dynamics.[43] The cross of Jesus Christ dramatically and specifically represents the epitome of shame.[44] The crucifixion of Christ took place in the Roman Empire, which was socially ordered by HS values held in common from the top to the bottom rungs of society.[45] The resurrection and exaltation of Jesus Christ are dramatically and specifically honorific and regal to the nth degree.[46] *Jesus Christ is the only truly good King.*[47] *He fulfills Israel's story. He died for the glory of God to atone for humanity's sin, cover humanity's shame, and restore humanity's honor. The gospel is already contextualized for HS cultures in a broad variety of ways.*[48]

10. Honor-shame reveals the gospel as ever new.

HS offers believers a double blessing: When the gospel is framed in the Bible's own ancient "language" and concepts of honor and shame, Christians deepen their ability to be both biblically faithful and culturally relevant.

- *Hermeneutics—being biblically faithful—deepens:* Incorporating HS into the interpretation of the Bible in general and the gospel in particular gets one closer to how the original authors and hearers of Scripture understood the Word of God.
- *Cultural relevance increases:* An honorific gospel offers new points of resonance with communities where shame and honor are critical values, including most unreached peoples; this resonance extends to secular peoples where issues of relational pollution, inclusion/exclusion, and social status are vital concerns.[49]

Linked with its ancient HS cultural roots, the gospel, paradoxically, is ever new—offering fresh wisdom and optimism to the church in its quest to expand Christ's kingdom and serve the global mission of God.

Overview of Chapters on Honor-Shame

The following contributors to this volume have given abundant time, energy, resources, experience, and scholarship to make these chapters what they are. We are profoundly grateful for the wonderful work of all the authors in this volume.

Section 1: Honor-Shame in General Contexts

STEVEN HAWTHORNE: "The Honor and Glory of Jesus Christ: Heart of the Gospel and the Mission of God." The glorious person of Jesus Christ is the crux and destiny of mission. The beauty of Christ includes this astounding reality: He who suffered great shame and rose in exalted honor shares his glory with all who call him Lord. Accordingly, believers endure hardship and suffer gladly for his name's sake among the nations.

JAYSON GEORGES: "Honor and Shame in Historical Theology: Listening to Eight Voices." Significant theologians, from Ignatius to Anselm to Edwards to C. S. Lewis, have explained biblical truth in honor-shame terms. Honor-shame theology is in continuity with Christian orthodoxy.

TOM STEFFEN: "A Clothesline Theology for the World: How a Value-Driven Grand Narrative of Scripture Can Frame the Gospel." A unifying story of Scripture is an antidote to fragmentist and specialist tendencies in theology—and vital for ministry among all of story-oriented humanity. The value system of honor-shame functions as a major theme in the Bible's grand narrative.

JACKSON WU: "Saving Us from Me: Cultivating Honor and Shame in a Collectivist Church." Scripture depicts the church as a collectivist body, which yields a particular Christian way of living based on honor-shame dynamics. This counters the self-centered, lonely individualism of much of Western Christianity.

E. RANDOLPH RICHARDS: "The Shaming of Jesus in John." Understanding honor-shame dynamics in the social world of the New Testament clarifies the meaning and integrates various stories in John's Gospel—for example, Jesus cleansing the temple.

MAKO A. NAGASAWA: "Empowering Personal Healing through the "Medical Substitutionary Atonement."" Christians throughout history have articulated different views of the atonement of Christ. An early Christian approach to the atonement and resurrection (namely, recapitulation) connects to modern concerns of identity, sacrifice, and justice—along with sin and shame.

STEVE TRACY: "Abuse and Shame: How the Cross Transforms Shame." Sexual abuse and wartime rape horribly defile millions in our world. Early church fathers addressed the problem of rape and sexual-abuse shame. Jesus Christ—in his scandalous crucifixion and honorific resurrection—absorbs and conquers the subjective and objective dimensions of sexual-abuse victimhood and shame.

Section 2—Honor-Shame in Various Mission Contexts

LYNN THIGPEN: "The Dark Side of Orality." Christian workers can unwittingly marginalize "adults with limited formal education" (ALFE). Billions of people in the world are oral-preference learners. Many ALFE suffer from toxic shame. Cross-cultural workers must acquire new skills and develop learner-centered, dignity-enhancing ministry among non-readers.

ARLEY LOEWEN: "Must Honor Clash with Humility? Transformed Honor within the Emerging Church in Muslim Societies." Honor competition was common in the early church; it is common today for Christian leaders around the world—including those in Muslim societies. Leaders can move toward a servant-based honor willing to relinquish position—by experiencing Christ as their unlimited source of honor.

STEVE HONG: "Sharing God's Love in an Urban, Pluralistic Context." The practices of vulnerability, listening, creativity, inclusion—and intentionally dignifying others—lead to deep relationships with secular moderns. They awaken to the gospel of the kingdom whose King is Jesus.

CRISTIAN DUMITRESCU: "Discipleship in Asian Honor Cultures." Making disciples is not a culturally neutral endeavor. In the Asian context, attention to honor-shame issues is critical for effective discipling.

RICH JAMES: "An Honor-Shame Gospel for Syrians Displaced by War: Jesus Christ as Good Shepherd and Honorable Patron." A culturally relevant and biblically faithful gospel for Syrian refugees involves not just a morally good Shepherd but the honorable Shepherd and Patron who gives his life for the good of the flock.

KATIE RAWSON: "A Gospel That Reconciles: Teaching about Honor-Shame to Advance Racial and Ethnic Reconciliation." Attention to honor-shame issues and terminology can have a profound impact upon efforts to mend relational rupture and bring about reconciliation in contexts of conflict.

NOLAN SHARP: "The Book of Samuel: A Reconciling Narrative." Cycles of blood violence, nationalism, even ethnic cleansing—as was the case in the wars of Yugoslav succession (1991–95)—are often driven by honor and shame. The stories of Saul and David in 1 and 2 Samuel are a fountain of insights to help reconcile peoples, tribes, or nations in honor-bound conflicts.

AUDREY FRANK: "The Muslim Woman's Journey from Shame to Honor." For women from Muslim backgrounds, barrenness or abuse can be sources of shame, exclusion, and defilement. The gospel of Christ covers the shamed and cleanses the defiled—thereby restoring honor.

Introduction

We, the editors, together with the organizers of the 2017 conference, humbly submit the following chapters with at least two goals. First, we expect that readers will find in these pages significant help for current practice. These chapters contain helpful resources to positively impact the theological, missiological, and ministry efforts of the global church. Second, we pray this volume will add energy to the ongoing honor-shame conversation. We believe this conversation is significant for the global church and missiological community—the profoundly good work of these scholars and practitioners deserves widespread attention.

Together with the readers of this volume, we are fellow travelers in this learning journey about honor, shame, and the gospel. May every reader be nourished by these pages to know Christ better—and for more effective ministry. May the gospel be advanced among all the peoples of the world. To God be the glory.

—Christopher Flanders, PhD, and Werner Mischke, DD, editors
May, 2020

INTRODUCTION Endnotes

1 For the presenter list of the Patronage Symposium, see: http://honorshame.com/patsym-presentations.

2 See https://godtoolsapp.com/tools/honor-restored.

3 The compendium from the 2014 ION Consultation is *Beyond Literate Western Contexts: Honor & Shame and Assessment of Orality Preference*, ed. Samuel E. Chiang and Grant Lovejoy (International Orality Network, 2015). See https://orality.net/library/beyond-literate-series/beyond-literate-western-contexts.

4 Brené Brown, *Daring Greatly: How the Courage to Be Vulnerable Transforms the Way We Live, Love, Parent, and Lead* (New York: Gotham Books, 2012), 109.

5 June Tangney and Ronda Dearing, *Shame and Guilt* (New York: Guilford Press, 2002), 24.

6 Bongrae Seok, *Moral Psychology of Confucian Shame* (London: Rowman & Littlefield International, 2017), 35.

7 Christopher Flanders, *About Face: Rethinking Face for 21st Century Mission* (Eugene, OR: Wipf and Stock, 2011), 64; quoting Paul Gilbert, *Shame: Interpersonal Behavior, Psychopathology, and Culture* (New York: Oxford University Press, 1998), 22.

8 Halvor Moxnes, "Honor and Shame," in *The Social Sciences and New Testament Interpretation*, ed. Richard L. Rohrbaugh (Grand Rapids: Baker Academic, 2010), 20.

9 David A. deSilva, *Honor, Patronage, Kinship & Purity: Unlocking New Testament Culture* (Downers Grove, IL: InterVarsity Press, 2000), 25.

10 Jerome H. Neyrey, *Honor and Shame in the Gospel of Matthew* (Louisville: Westminster John Knox Press, 1998), 15.

11 Bruce J. Malina and Jerome H. Neyrey, "Honor and Shame in Luke-Acts: Pivotal Values in the Mediterranean World," in *The Social World of Luke-Acts*, ed. Jerome H. Neyrey (Peabody, MA: Hendrickson Publishers, 1991), 25–26.

12 Kwame Anthony Appiah, *The Honor Code: How Moral Revolutions Happen* (New York: W. W. Norton, 2010), xvii.

13 See, for example, deSilva, *Honor, Patronage, Kinship & Purity*; Bruce J. Malina, *The New Testament World: Insights from Cultural Anthropology*, rev. ed. (Louisville: Westminster John Knox Press, 1993); Jerome H. Neyrey, *Honor and Shame in the Gospel of Matthew* (Louisville: Westminster John Knox Press, 1998); Jerome H. Neyrey and Eric C. Stewart, eds., *The Social World of the New Testament: Insights and Models* (Peabody, MA: Hendrickson, 2008).

14 See Jayson Georges and Mark D. Baker, *Ministering in Honor-Shame Cultures: Biblical Foundations and Practical Essentials* (Downers Grove, IL: InterVarsity Press, 2016); and Georges, *Ministering in Patronage Cultures: Biblical Models and Missional Implications* (Downers Grove, IL: InterVarsity Press, 2019). See also Jackson Wu, *One Gospel for All Nations: A Practical Approach to Biblical Contextualization* (Pasadena, CA: William Carey Library, 2015).

15 Examples of theological works that significantly incorporate the literature of the Greco-Roman/Hebrew world and the social world of the New Testament include John M. G. Barclay, *Paul and the Gift* (Grand Rapids: Eerdmans, 2015); Matthew Bates, *Salvation by Allegiance Alone: Rethinking Faith, Works, and the Gospel of Jesus the King* (Grand Rapids: Baker, 2017); Joshua Jipp, *Christ Is King: Paul's Royal Ideology* (Minneapolis: Fortress, 2015).

16 See, for example, Flanders, *About Face*; Jayson Georges, *The 3D Gospel: Ministry in Guilt, Shame, and Fear Cultures* (Timē Press, 2017); Werner Mischke, *The Global Gospel: Achieving Missional Impact in Our Multicultural World* (Scottsdale, AZ: Mission ONE, 2015); Jackson Wu, *Saving God's Face: A Chinese Contextualization of Salvation through Honor and Shame* (Pasadena, CA: WCIU Press, 2012).

17 "We must start with the basic fact that there is no such thing as a pure gospel if by that is meant something which is not embodied in a culture.... Every interpretation of the gospel is embodied in some cultural form." Lesslie Newbigin, *The Gospel in a Pluralist Society* (Grand Rapids: Eerdmans, 1989), 144. See also David J. Bosch, *Transforming Mission: Paradigm Shifts in Theology of Mission* (Maryknoll, NY: Orbis, 1991). Bosch's chapter "Mission as Inculturation" (447–57) is an excellent overview about the problem of an "assumed" gospel and unwitting cultural bias in the mission enterprise.

18 Mark Noll writes, "The contrast between the West and the non-West is never between culture-free Christianity and culturally embedded Christianity, but between varieties of culturally embedded Christianity." *The New Shape of World Christianity: How American Experience Reflects Global Faith* (Downers Grove, IL: InterVarsity Press, 2009), 44.

19 In turn, Western values of guilt, law, and justice have been influenced by the Bible. The relationship between Western culture and its theology is a two-way street; "the pollination goes both ways" writes Adonis Vidu in *Atonement, Law, and Justice: The Cross in Historical and Cultural Contexts* (Grand Rapids, Baker Academic, 2014), xiv.

20 Timothy Tennent writes, "Since Western systematic theology has been almost exclusively written by theologians from cultures framed primarily by the values of guilt and innocence, there has been a corresponding failure to fully appreciate the importance of the pivotal values of honor and shame in understanding Scripture and the doctrine of sin." *Theology in the Context of World Christianity: How the Global Church Is Influencing the Way We Think About and Discuss Theology* (Grand Rapids: Zondervan, 2007), 92.

21 "It is no exaggeration to state that for much of Protestant theology, personal guilt and salvation from sin have come to function symbiotically, existing in a theological tandem at the core of much evangelical soteriology." See Flanders, *About Face*, 31.

22 See Jackson Wu, "We Compromise the Gospel When We Settle for the Truth: How 'Right' Interpretation Leads to 'Wrong' Contextualization," *Global Missiology* 2, no. 10 (January 2013), http://ojs.globalmissiology.org/index.php/english/article/viewFile/1130/2613.

23 See chap. 6.3, "A Reglorified Humanity in Romans 8:30," in Haley Goranson Jacob, *Conformed to the Image of His Son: Reconsidering Paul's Theology of Glory in Romans* (Downers Grove, IL: InterVarsity Press, 2018), 223–27.

24 Ibid., 93.

25 C. S. Lewis, "The Weight of Glory" in *The Weight of Glory and Other Addresses* (New York: HarperCollins, 1976), 25–46. See also Mischke, chap. 2.1, "Honor/Shame Dynamic #1: The Love of Honor," in *The Global Gospel*, 84–92.

26 Goranson Jacob, *Conformed*, 237.

27 See, for example, Kwame Anthony Appiah, *The Honor Code: How Moral Revolutions Happen* (New York: W. W. Norton & Co., 2010); and Tamler Sommers, *Why Honor Matters* (New York: Basic Books, 2018).

28 See the chapter in this volume by Jayson Georges, "Honor and Shame in Historical Theology: Listening to Eight Voices."

29 Thomas Kuhn, *The Structure of Scientific Revolutions* (Chicago: University of Chicago Press, 1962), 24.

30 See, for example, June Tangney and Ronda Dearing, *Shame and Guilt* (New York: Guilford Press, 2002); Brené Brown, *Daring Greatly: How the Courage to Be Vulnerable Transforms the Way We Live, Love, Parent, and Lead* (New York: Gotham Books, 2012); Donald Nathansan, *The Many Faces of Shame* (New York: Guilford Press, 1987).

31 "Early Confucian philosophers believe that shame is a great moral disposition. In early Confucian texts such as the *Analects,* the *Mencius,* and the *Xunzi,* there are many passages where shame is praised and emphasized as a major moral virtue." Bongrae Seok, *Moral Psychology of Confucian Shame: Shame of Shamelessness* (London: Rowman & Littlefield International, 2017), 4.

32 In Ezekiel 16, the prophet tells the story of God's relationship with his people; it is a passionate story of honor and shame, disloyalty and adultery. God calls his people (who are in exile) to recover their sense of morality—to "be ashamed" (vv. 52, 54, 61) because they had been shamelessly sinful. This accords with the Confucian sense of shame noted above.

33 See Eugene Nida, *Customs and Cultures: Anthropology for Christian Missions* (Pasadena, CA: William Carey Library, 1975); Roland Muller, *Honor & Shame: Unlocking the Door* (Bloomington, IN: Xlibris Corporation, 2000); and Georges, *3D Gospel.*

34 When examining Scriptures related to Christ as Messiah-King, the overlap of cultural dynamics of innocence-guilt, honor-shame, and power-fear can be clear. Psalm 110 is instructive. Christ as King will "rule in the midst of [his] enemies" (v. 2) to "execute judgment" (v. 6); this reflects *innocence-guilt.* Christ as King will "Sit at [God's] right hand, until [he makes his] enemies [his] footstool" (v. 1; cf. v. 5), and he has an honorific "mighty scepter" (v. 2); this reflects *honor-shame.* Christ as King conquers all his enemies (v. 1) and "will shatter kings on the day of his wrath" (v. 5) and "shatter chiefs over the wide earth" (v. 6); this reflects *power-fear.*

35 This idea of honor-shame as "one above others" requires further study. In a panel discussion with Brent Sandy at the 2017 Honor-Shame Conference, David A. deSilva asked whether honor-shame might be considered a meta-value in the Bible (June 20, 2017).

36 John Piper, *God's Passion for His Glory: Living the Vision of Jonathan Edwards* (Wheaton, IL: Crossway, 1998).

37 Jackson Wu, "Have Theologians No Sense of Shame? How the Bible Reconciles Objective and Subjective Shame," in *Themelios* 43, no. 2 (August 2018): 205–19. http://themelios. thegospelcoalition.org/article/have-theologians-no-sense-of-shame.

38 Ibid., 207–12.

39 For a survey on the pathology of shame from a Christian psychiatrist who incorporates discoveries from the field of neurobiology, see Curt Thompson, *The Soul of Shame: Retelling the Stories We Believe About Ourselves* (Downers Grove, IL: InterVarsity Press, 2015).

40 "The desire for recognition is the motor of history." This assertion from philosopher Friedrich Hegel is developed by Francis Fukuyama in *The End of History and the Last Man* (New York: Free Press, 1992) and *Identity: The Demand for Dignity and the Politics of Resentment* (New York: Farrar, Strauss and Giroux, 2018).

41 See Amy Chua, *Political Tribes: Group Instinct and the Fate of Nations* (New York: Penguin Press, 2018).

42 See Werner Mischke, "An Honor-Bearing Gospel for Shame-Fueled Crises," presented at the 2019 EMS annual conference, http://missiodeijournal.com/issues/md-11/authors/md-11-mischke.

43 For a survey of how honor-shame dynamics overlap with the atonement of Christ, see Mischke, *The Global Gospel*, 205–78. See also Flanders, *About Face*, 210–62.

44 See Philip D. Jamieson, *The Face of Forgiveness: A Pastoral Theology of Shame and Redemption* (Downers Grove, IL: InterVarsity Press Academic, 2016); his chapter "The Shame of the Cross" (pp. 89–104) is a concise and compelling overview. See also Jerome H. Neyrey, "Despising the Shame of the Cross: Honor and Shame in the Johannine Passion Narrative," *Semeia* 69 (1996): 113–37. https://www3.nd.edu/~jneyrey1/shame.html.

45 J. E. Lendon, *Empire of Honour: The Art of Government in the Roman World* (New York: Oxford University Press, 1997).

46 See Scot McKnight, *The King Jesus Gospel: The Original Good News Revisited* (Grand Rapids: Zondervan, 2011); and N. T. Wright, *How God Became King: The Forgotten Story of the Gospels* (New York: Harper Collins, 2011).

47 See Jipp, *Christ Is King*.

48 The assertion, "The gospel is already contextualized for honor-shame cultures," is from Jackson Wu, "Rewriting the Gospel for Oral Cultures: Why Honor and Shame are Essential to the Gospel Story," in *Beyond Literate Western Contexts: Honor & Shame and Assessment of Orality Preference*, eds. Samuel E. Chiang and Grant Lovejoy (International Orality Network, 2015), 65.

49 See Alan Mann: *Atonement for a Sinless Society* (Eugene, OR: Cascade Books, 2015), and Andy Crouch, "The Return of Shame," *Christianity Today* 59, no. 3 (March 2015): 32–43.

HONOR-SHAME IN GENERAL CONTEXTS

THE HONOR AND GLORY OF JESUS CHRIST:
Heart of the Gospel and the Mission of God

STEVEN C. HAWTHORNE

To understand honor-shame dynamics amid the inter-cultural complexities of mission, one must consider the honor and glory of Jesus Christ. And here's why: Behind, beneath, and above all human shames and honors is the singular glory of Jesus. In this chapter, we will affirm the glory that Jesus is worthy to receive. But we will also consider the "praise and glory and honor" (1 Pet 1:7)[1] that the living God bestows upon people in Christ.

Following some introductory remarks, we will explore what I call "true glory," the glory that God gives to people in and with Christ. Then we will identify a few highlights of the great biblical narrative of God's glory. Finally, we'll look at three occasions when God spoke from heaven in the Gospels, each of them increasing our understanding of how we are called to share in the suffering and joy of Christ's glory.

Why Glory Matters

To consider the honor and glory of Jesus Christ, it's helpful to recognize, by contrast, how honor and glory usually work among humans in the flow and go of cultures.

Creatures and Cultures of Glory

Two things seem to be at work in honor-shame dynamics within every culture. First, honor and shame are known and practiced in every culture. Although practices are endlessly varied, every society functions with customary ways of offering respect and recognition, as well as opprobrium and disgrace. In some cultures, honor and shame dominate most interactions, so that we can refer to them as honor-shame cultures. But in reality honor-shame dynamics are a human universal.

Second, every culture, including every honor-shame system, is broken by sin. It's not too much to say that every honor-shame system is somehow defective and damage-dealing. Paul claims that not a few but "many walk" so that their "glory is in their shame" (Phil 3:17–19). The very things that should be disdained and rejected are instead exalted. This inversion, this flip, to exalt what is detestable is so endemic to humanity that we are not wrong to trace it back to the Fall.

In Romans 1, Paul pinpoints just how we became such reckless shame shifters. When humanity ceased to honor God in accord with what they clearly knew, "their foolish heart was darkened" (Rom 1:19–22). They made a horrific exchange. They—let's identify with this in the first person and say *we*—we traded "the glory of the incorruptible God for an image in the form of corruptible" humanity and animals (1:23). Why this trade? What motivates the human heart to make this exchange?

We desire glory. Actually, God made us that way—as creatures of glory. Three features mark humans as creatures of glory: We perceive glory, we celebrate glory together, and we desire glory. People, as well as angels, perceive glory.[2] Not only do humans recognize splendor, excellence, and beauty,[3] but we also instinctively know that we must point out that beauty to others. Anything truly worthy is also praiseworthy. That is, we don't just behold what is beautiful or exceptional. We call for the attention of others to see and celebrate it together. There is something deeply satisfying about celebrating, with others, someone or something of worth. Perhaps the only thing we find even more satisfying is to be the object of praise and celebration. We are formed with an intrinsic yearning, an essential desiring, to be named, to be recognized, to be loved.

This yearning for glory is the hunger that drives us, in the heart-darkened foolishness seen in Romans 1, to keep making the exchange that Paul describes, so that we glory in the very things that are, in reality, our shame. Our self-created objects of adoration, our precious idols, are nothing more than an assemblage of exaggerated human abilities—glamorized ideals of what we see in ourselves. Idolatry is usually denounced as wrong because false gods are not real. But because idols are grotesque exaggerations of creaturely powers, in reality, the heart of our folly is the absurdity of self-given honor.

I mention the universality of broken honor systems because our goal in this broad conversation about honor-shame is not merely to learn tips for using honor-talk in some face-saving cultures. We want to explore how to better follow our Lord in fulfilling the mission of God. The heart of that mission is the glory and honor of Jesus. In his glory is the only hope of glory for the nations.

Our Greater Creator and the Conflict of Cultures

The world seems to be shrinking, with growing technologies, globalized interactions, and ever-shifting social-group identities. In this crush and clash of cultures we hope to resolve the chaos by embracing egalitarian ideals. We like the equanimity of the fictional community of Lake Wobegon, where "all the children are above average." But in reality, present-day postmodern societies are often confused by brash demands for dignity, outlandish virtue signals, and shame campaigns.

Ironically, the rules of multiculturalism call for a rigorous equalizing of all cultures, races, and genders. Ideas of beauty, excellence, or prestige, along with any kind of all-encompassing metanarrative—supposedly all of these are mere social constructs that are inherently oppressive. The earth must be flattened into a morass of coexistent sameness.

I describe this postmodern, post-truth environment in order to highlight a huge operative presumption behind all the phony equivocation about equalization: There is no one greater to bestow honor. Without a creator God, there is no greater God—someone who can regard and recognize people, or who can prize and praise their cultural endeavors. Without someone higher and greater who transcends all cultures, then honor and shame are indeed mere social constructs. The only remaining hope, then, is to find or fabricate ways to gain or sustain fleeting moments of respect.

But there is someone greater! The God of glory. In his sight we are not merely equal. We are much more than merely equal. In his sight we are precious. The living God values and treasures people.

Many of us have known this since childhood days. In Sunday school we sang:

Jesus loves the little children, all the children of the world.
Red and yellow, black and white, they are precious in his sight.
Jesus loves the little children of the world.

The key words are "in his sight." We are not objects of pity. Since God gazes upon us as his beloved, we are precious.

We are known and named by our greater Creator. We are truly honored by his love. This God-given honor-in-love is what I will call "true glory."

Loving Glory: From People or from God

By the words "true glory," I am speaking of the honor, acclaim, and praise that come from God himself to people. I am not referring to the marvel of God's "intrinsic glory," a term we use to speak of the eternal, inherent worth and splendor of the uncreated, triune God.

Biblical authors often use the same words (Hebrew *kavod*, Greek *doxa*) to refer both to the glory of which God is utterly worthy as well as to the honor and praise that God gives to people. *Glory* is not a word that is reserved for God alone. *Glory*, as used by biblical authors, can also refer to the beauty, the brightness, the weight, and the worth of created things or persons.

Having celebrated in 2017 the anniversary of the Protestant Reformation,[4] understand that I'm not trying to undermine the fifth "sola," *Soli Deo gloria*: "glory to God alone." That slogan was designed primarily to controvert the practice of crass veneration of saints and angels. Paul mentions more than once God's "riches in glory in Christ Jesus" (Phil 4:19).[5] God does not demean himself by condescending to bestow honor upon his people. His infinite glory can never be diminished in the slightest.

Jesus called people to abandon the habit of receiving "glory (*doxa*) from one another" and instead to "seek the glory (*doxa*) that is from the one and only God" (John 5:44). Later John notes that "many even of the rulers" believed in Jesus, but they were not openly "confessing Him" (12:42). Why do we so often see more believers than followers? John offers a penetrating insight as to why. The leaders were fearful of being ousted from their society. They remained crypto-believers "for fear that they would be put out of the synagogue" (12:42). John gets to the heart of the matter. This fear was based on a love: "for they loved the approval [or glory] (*doxa*) of men rather than the approval [or glory] (*doxa*) of God" (12:43).

John contrasts two different kinds of glory. First, there is "the glory of men": the applause, the status, the fame, that humans seek to gain and retain from other people. Second is what I call "true glory"—that is, the praise or honor that people can hope to receive from God himself. Only the living God can give this honor. He has made us to yearn to be named, celebrated, and prized. And he delights in giving such glory.

As we examine the honor-and-shame dynamics in various societies, we must first consider the honor and glory of Jesus Christ. Here's why—the best honors bestowed in any culture can only lightly satisfy our yearning for glory. Jesus himself calls us to "seek the glory that is from the one and only God" (John 5:44). The "one and only God" reveals his glory in "the only begotten Son of God" (John 3:18). We only experience this authentic glory as we know, and are known by, the person of Jesus—the crucified Lamb, the risen One, the exalted Son of Man.

True Glory from God with Christ

We will approach the glory of Christ by exploring the great facts of the gospel. The power of the gospel is that *in* one man, *by* God's doing, there is the creation of a new humanity. This new humanity shares in the death, the life, and the glory of the singular Son of God. There is glory for humankind only *in* and *with* the crucified, risen, and exalted One. Let's consider four aspects of how people are joined with Christ.

True Glory with Christ in His Death and Resurrection

The gospel is not some self-esteem bromide, urging us to try to be a little bit more like Jesus. The gospel declares that we can be joined *with* Jesus, somehow letting his death become our death so that his life can be our life. The familiar lines of Romans make it clear that all "who have been baptized into Christ Jesus have been baptized into His death" (Rom 6:3). Paul says that "Christ was raised from the dead through the glory of the Father" so that those joined in his death "might walk in newness of life." Paul's logic is simple: "If we have become united with Him in the likeness of His death, certainly we shall also be in the likeness of His resurrection" (6:3–5). To be "in Christ" is to be joined with Jesus in his life and in his death.

True Glory with the Exalted Christ, Revealed at His Coming

We rightly hold the death and rising of our Lord as central. But as our creeds and liturgies declare, Christ was not merely raised from the dead. He was lifted from the earth into the sky while his followers watched (Luke 24:51; Acts 1:9–11). They became convinced by the Scriptures that Jesus had been exalted to the right hand of God. On Pentecost they declared his death and his resurrection (Acts 2:23–32). But the high point of Peter's message was not that Jesus was somehow alive, but that Jesus had "been exalted to the right hand of God" (2:33). Peter's outrageous claim of what was unseen in the heavens was demonstrably true because Jesus had "received from the Father the promise of the Holy Spirit." And that was evident to all because, as Peter said, "He has poured forth this which you both see and hear" (2:33), referring to the many people prophesying in languages from "every nation under heaven" (2:5).

Christ had been enthroned at God's right hand. But his glory was not seen. Jesus had been inaugurated as King, but his kingdom was hidden. Followers were urged to focus their hope on his coming, when the glory of the Messiah-King would be revealed.

Writing to the Colossians, Paul announced that they could live very differently because they had "died with Christ" (Col 2:20). Paul had also urged them to realize that they had been "raised up" with Christ (Col 2:12). We could easily hear those words as referring to the resurrection. But he actually used the words "raised up" to refer to the exaltation of Christ: "Therefore if you have been raised up with Christ, keep seeking the things above, where Christ is, seated at the right hand of God" (Col 3:1). Why should ordinary people seek such otherworldly matters? Because, although the risen Lord may be hidden now, he *is* coming. And he is coming with glory: "When Christ, who is our life, is revealed, then you also will be revealed with Him in glory" (3:4).

In his letters, Peter taught something similar about Christ's exaltation. Peter claimed that because of the resurrection of Jesus, Christians have already been given an unfading but unseen inheritance "reserved in heaven" until it is "revealed in the last time" (1 Pet 1:4–5). At that time their faith will "be found to result in praise and glory and honor at the revelation of Jesus Christ" (1:7). Until that day of global revealing, even though they had "not seen Him," their love for Jesus would deepen as their faith proved strong, with a relational joy that was "full of glory" (1:8).

Following similar logic, Paul assured the Thessalonian believers that the purpose of their "salvation through sanctification" was that God had called them "through our gospel, that [they] may gain the glory of our Lord Jesus Christ" (2 Thess 2:13–14). That glory would become clear on the coming day "when the Lord Jesus will be revealed from heaven" (2 Thess 1:7). At that time, he will be "glorified in His saints … to be marveled at among all who have believed" (1:10). Until that day they could count on his strength to endure many "persecutions and afflictions" (1:4).

True Glory with Christ in His Suffering
Jesus' teaching had prepared the first believers for some of the hostilities that came soon after Pentecost. As the governing powers' opposition increased, the believers found courage as they prayed the Scriptures, which had prophesied long ago that there would be all-out war against the Messiah (Acts 4:25–28).

After enduring humiliation in court, they rejoiced "that they had been considered worthy to suffer shame for His name" (Acts 5:41). Soon after, Stephen stood accused of the same crime for which Jesus had been accused, that of planning to destroy the temple (Acts 6:13–14). He stood in the very same courtroom, testifying before the very same rulers. When he responded with the same declaration as Jesus—that the Son of Man would be seen at the right hand of God—they moved swiftly to kill him. Stephen's witness and execution made it clear that Jesus Christ was still on trial. Paul, who witnessed Stephen's death, would later hear the risen Lord identify himself: "I am Jesus whom you are persecuting" (Acts 9:4–5; 22:7–8; 26:14–15). They were all his witnesses in a continuing global trial of Jesus by the nations. They were not merely suffering shamefully for the name of Jesus. They were suffering *with* Jesus.

The Christian movement came to expect and to endure such suffering, recognizing God's greater gospel purpose. Peter urged believers to "not be surprised at the fiery ordeal among you" because many of those hardships could be considered "the sufferings of Christ" (1 Pet 4:12–13). Certainly, Jesus had already accomplished the sacrifice necessary for atonement. But it became clear that Christ himself was continuing to suffer as his followers lived and labored for the glory of his name: "If you are reviled for the name of Christ, you are blessed, because the Spirit of glory and of God rests on you" (4:14). In the midst of horrendous shame for Christ's name, they would experience the surpassing joy of Spirit-revealed glory.

This suffering was clearly connected to Christ's mission. Suffering would not be pointless, endless, or random, but something to be *accomplished*. Peter assured them that "the same experiences of suffering are being accomplished by your brethren who are in the world" (1 Pet 5:9). Paul saw the sufferings he endured to be "on behalf of His body, which is the church, in filling up what is lacking in Christ's afflictions" (Col 1:24). He did this gladly to "fully carry out the preaching of the word of God," or the work of evangelization, among the nations (1:25–27).

Paul described the reality of knowing Christ as an experience of both "the power of His resurrection and the fellowship of His sufferings" (Phil 3:10). Suffering to further God's mission was not for apostles alone, but for all who serve him. Present-hour suffering with Christ was profoundly linked to glory with Christ in the age to come: "The Spirit Himself testifies with our spirit that we are children of God … heirs of God and fellow heirs with Christ, if indeed we *suffer with Him* so that we may also be *glorified with Him*" (Rom 8:16–17).

True Glory with Christ in Intra-Trinitarian Joy
Consider one occasion when Jesus gave honor to his Father. In fact, all three persons of the Trinity were involved. Luke reports that Jesus "rejoiced greatly" (Luke 10:21). I don't think we can find a time when the joy of Jesus was any greater. He rejoiced "in the Holy Spirit," as he gave praise to the Father for how the Father had revealed—or glorified—himself. Jesus was jubilant in what had pleased the Father.

This text points us to the heart, soul, and center of true glory: the glory that is everlastingly given and received in the Trinity. Biblical indicators, like this text in Luke, point toward a relational model of the Trinity, which speaks of community with unity—a mutual and reciprocal indwelling of three interpenetrating persons.

In some models of a relational or social Trinity, the perichoretic dance of distinct but interpenetrating persons can veer into pantheistic confusion. We can avoid this mistake. I like J. Scott Horrell's proposal of "an eternally ordered social model." Horrell presents biblical evidence that supports a relational Trinity with eternal order in the Godhead. In this model, he sees "the Trinity as the one divine Being eternally existing as three distinct centers of consciousness, wholly equal in nature, genuinely personal in relationships, and each mutually indwelling the other."[6] There is order without subordination. In this communion, the inseparable persons are differentiated without being divided in all they are and do.

The great beauty of the relational Trinity is the unceasing exchange of love, joy, and honor. Each person speaks. Each person listens. Intra-trinitarian generosity abounds. Each person is constantly giving and receiving.

Miroslav Volf affirms the constant exchange of love within the Trinity using the analogy of an incessant exchange of gifts:

> Each divine person gives, receives, and returns. Each loves and glorifies the other two, and each receives love and glory from them. One does not give first, with the result that the others would be indebted, but all give in an eternally moving circle of exchanges…. Their eternal bliss is the delight of this loving gift exchange.[7]

How is it possible for people to enter or experience this glory? God created humans with the capacity to recognize his intrinsic, or essential, glory. But in Christ he has re-created humanity to recognize and celebrate his excellence in a relational way. To glorify God is not only to comprehend his glory, but also to offer celebratory recognition and honor directly to him in the company of others who also recognize and honor him.

This way of glorifying, or honoring, is commonplace between humans, and not only from those considered lesser to those who are greater. For example, children are often rightly praised by their parents. When this happens, they receive *glory*, or shall we say *honor*, from persons who are greater than they are. And children can, of course, give expressions of honor to their parents in return. In such transactions of honor, when there is self-giving love, we are never surprised that there is joy. This relational glory can be mutual and at the same time also asymmetric—that is, exchanged between greater and lesser entities.

The goal of God's purpose and mission has ever been for himself—that he would be loved and served. Within the Trinity is mutual delight in the giving and receiving of glory. In leading "many sons to glory" (Heb 2:10)—in presenting to himself a bride, "the church in all her glory" (Eph 5:27)—Christ has accomplished God's purpose of bringing people into the relational glory of God. Joined with Christ, as people offer themselves to God in the magnificent priest Jesus, they are profoundly honored as God condescends to receive them with their gifts of worship and love. In and with the Son of God, God's people are never deified, but they are glorified, welcomed into the relational joy of the Trinity.

The Story of Self-Made Glory

The glory of Christ is best grasped in the framework of the great biblical story. We will look at the end of the story in light of some events near the beginning that are sometimes overlooked.

Honor from God: God's Gaze and Cain's Face

Look again at the very first worship event. It may be more significant than you've previously realized. Consider the following three noteworthy points regarding the offerings Cain and Abel willingly offered.

First, both gifts came from their distinctive labors. Abel was a shepherd. Cain was a crop-raising farmer. This suggests that their worship gifts were in some way tokens of themselves, representing the work of their hands and their respective cultures.

Second, both offerings were described with a Hebrew word (*minkhah*) that was exclusively used for grain offerings and never used for any kind of sacrifice that was intended to be efficacious for forgiveness or atonement.

Third, there is no reference to blood sacrifice. There's not a hint of expiation or atonement. In spite of all the sermons that we have heard or preached, this worship event was a straightforward occasion of thanks and celebration.

The account says that God looked, or gazed, favorably upon Abel and his offering (Gen 4:4). The word for God's gaze (*sha'ah*) conveys intensity and interpersonal immediacy.[8] The word order makes it clear that God was primarily looking upon the *giver* rather than his *gift*. But there was no such regard for Cain, who became angry and his face, or countenance, fell (4:5).

God's response to Cain in verses 6–7 uses a Hebrew expression: "If you do well, uplifting." The word for uplifting, when combined with the word for face, was an idiom in that day, describing significant honor. Someone with a "lifted face" was someone of high reputation.[9] God was telling Cain, "I want to exalt you just as much as I delight in honoring Abel. Do well. Do worthily. And there will be an uplifting of your face as well." This honor-shame language reveals that God's gaze was showing favor, joy, and honor to Abel that God would *also* gladly show toward Cain.

Then comes the grim warning in verse 7. God uses animal imagery to portray sin as a monstrosity that desired to consume him. Instead of Cain obtaining what he desired, the desire was about to overcome him. Why is this significant? I think we can identify the sin-monster as jealousy, a competitive desire that is a malignant twisting of God-created yearnings for honor. The entire event reveals God's readiness to honor both brothers and Cain's runaway jealousy to be honored as much as, or more than, his brother.

The Pursuit of Self-Made Glory

After Cain murders Abel, he flees God's presence, fearing that he will be a vagrant, without identity or place (Gen 4:13–16). Then Cain builds the first city, naming it after his son (4:17). Naming the city after his son was Cain's way of establishing his own reputation, his own renown, his own glory. This self-given glory would become a recurring reality among the passing generations, and eventually among the nations. The monstrosity of jealousy foments lasting honor competition. This quest to be best will eventually drive and devour and corrupt humankind. One philosopher of history describes the animating impetus among all nations to be "the desire for recognition." Another refers to this desire as "the motor of history" that drives societies and nations into conflict and war.[10]

As the story is told, just after the flood comes the building of another city. Among several things that go awry in building the city of Babel, we see humankind collectively motivated to "make for [themselves] a name" (Gen 11:4). The perverse desire for self-made honor had become pervasive.

Abrahamic Honor: God-Gifted Greatness

In the Genesis account, immediately following God's response to Babel's bid for self-made glory, we see the stark contrast of his promise to Abram: "I will bless you, and make your name great" (Gen 12:2). To receive blessing is an honor. But the one who blesses holds even greater honor (Heb 7:7). The magnitude of God's promise to cause Abraham's family to become his gift of blessing to all peoples should be seen as an almost unimaginable God-wrought honor (Gen 12:3; 18:18; 22:18; 26:4; 28:14). God fulfilled the promise of blessing by redeeming Abraham's family in ways that established God's name and glory in all the earth (2 Sam 7:23). In Christ, that family would become "a people for His name" from and amid all the peoples (Acts 15:14). Abraham's honor would become God's glory.

The Glory of the Nations Illumined by the Glory of the Lamb

In this limited overview, we must jump from the primordial days of Babel all the way to Babylon near the end of the book of Revelation. The whore of Babylon symbolizes the hideous degradation of all nations and kingdoms. She has seduced "the kings ... and the merchants of the earth" (Rev 18:3). They drank of her passion—compromised desiring.

Her "sins have piled up as high as heaven" (18:5), but the measure of her judgment, in part, is commensurate with her self-given glory. She is to be punished "to the degree that she glorified herself" (18:7). Many kings of the earth stand exclaiming their shameful lament: "Woe, woe, the great city, Babylon, the strong city!" (18:10).

In utmost contrast to this horrific vision of shame on self-made greatness, we hear God declare that he is "making all things new" (Rev 21:5). We behold "the bride, the wife of the Lamb" (21:9) descending from heaven, "having the glory of God" (21:11). The bride? Were it not in the Bible, the very idea of the matrimony of God's people with the Son of God would be utterly obscene. But this great honor culminates the Bible. No greater honor can be imagined.

This heavenly city needs no sun or moon, "for the glory of God has illumined it" (21:23). The kings of the earth continually "bring the glory and the honor of the nations into it" (21:26). This is not the language of conquered vassal states coerced to bring tribute. The language does not suggest nation states as much as it highlights ethnic or linguistic peoples. It is a grand spectacle of the tribes, languages, and ethnicities with generational depth and cultural substance. The best of every one of the cultures and peoples of the earth has been redeemed. Distinctive music and literature, diverse artistry, various inventions and industries, gorgeous and soul-stirring human creations of culture—all have been purged and redeemed by the Lamb. You would think that the glory of God shining in full brilliance would eclipse all human glories. But they shine! And they are all received! The nations do not bring the treasures as trophies to express subjugation. No, they bring their glories in celebratory gladness.

These wonders are not only received by the Lamb. People from every tribe and tongue are also receiving each other. And there is joy as they all behold the ever-escalating party. The monstrous jealousy is gone. Honor and glory abound in the light of the Lamb.

The Glory of the Father

The Gospels record three occasions in which God spoke from heaven so that people heard his words. As we'll discover, each of these events reveals something significant about the honor and glory of Jesus.

The Baptism: Love Abounding in Joy

The first time we hear God speak from heaven is at the Jordan River, presumably with some of the throngs that came to the revival meetings of John the Baptizer. Jesus disregarded his cousin John's protest that he did not need to be baptized, saying something about fulfilling all righteousness. By being baptized, Jesus was identifying with sin—but not his own.

As Jesus emerged from the water, a great voice sounded. It was clear and firm, without being loud: "This is My beloved Son, in whom I am well-pleased" (Matt 3:13–17).

The voice startled the entire crowd. There was awe. And a hush. People looked up and around. All that was visible was what—or who—usually was invisible: the Spirit of God, hovering as a dove over the water. Everyone who heard the voice could hear the smile on the Father's face without seeing it.

It was clear: God himself was thoroughly pleased and joyously proud. And it was stunning: The living God of heaven was delighted with a man. It was so clean, bright, and good. By announcing his love and delight, the Father had bestowed immense honor upon the Son.

The Father said something about a "beloved Son" and being "well-pleased." We all know how difficult it can be when we try to get or earn another person's love. The rationale usually goes something like this: "If I please him, then he will love me." This universal performance formula—well known, but practiced differently in every culture and generation—is reversed by the Father's words: "This is My beloved, and therefore I am pleased." God's love—a constant, never contingent love—precedes his being pleased. By announcing to all the magnitude of his joy, the Father, with the Spirit, honored the Son.

This, then, is the purpose of living righteously: that God himself would be glad in those he loves. This is what it meant for Jesus "to fulfill all righteousness" (Matt 3:15).

The point of a righteous life is not to earn, but to enter, the relational glory of the God of joy.

The declaration from heaven reverberated in the hearts of those who heard. It may have revealed more about the Father than it said about the Son. Might the Father also say of others who are his beloved what he said of the Son? Might the Father extend such perfect pride to the daughters and sons who have joined themselves with the Son? Make no mistake, the God of all the earth is to be feared and revered, but his love inclines him to be pleased. Because his love is so vast, he is not hard to please. He may be the easiest person in the universe to please.

We do not strive to somehow link ourselves with Jesus, or to imitate him, so as to win the Father's honor. By stepping into that river, Jesus entered humanity, into the depth of human evil in order to bring "many sons and daughters to glory" (Heb 2:9–10). By being baptized into his death, we are also raised, not like him, but with him, "through the glory of the Father" (Rom 6:4). And in "this grace … we stand; and we exult in hope of the glory of God" (Rom 5:2).

The Transfiguration: Greater Glory in Suffering

The second time God speaks from heaven we know as "the transfiguration." Days before this event, Jesus brought up a topic he rarely discussed—his reputation and public identity. "Who do people say that the Son of Man is?" (Matt 16:13). Jesus affirmed Peter's answer, "You are the Christ" (16:16). But then, to their surprise, Jesus immediately urged the disciples to "tell no one that He was the Christ" (16:20).

If that wasn't perplexing enough, "from that time Jesus began" to make it vividly clear to his disciples that he would suffer, be killed, and then be raised from the dead (16:21).

With an obvious face-saving move, Peter took Jesus aside to speak with him privately. He counseled Jesus to not allow himself such dreadful, pessimistic ideas about his future. We usually focus on Peter's appeal as a satanic temptation— "Get behind Me, Satan!" (16:23). But consider Jesus' analysis of Peter's ideas about how Jesus should build his renown: "You are not setting your mind on the things of God, but on the things of man" (16:23 ESV). Jesus distinguishes two opposing schemes or worldviews: God's ways and human ways.

Peter may not have been alone among the disciples in seeking ways to get Jesus the glory and recognition they thought he deserved. Could this be why Jesus told them, "If anyone wishes to come after Me, he must deny himself, and take up his cross and follow Me" (16:24)? The enigmatic call to "deny [one]self" certainly involves renunciation of any practice of giving oneself glory. To underscore that honor was the issue, either self-made or God-given, Jesus immediately assures them that "the Son of Man is going to come in the glory of His Father with His angels" and reward with honor those who suffer shame and pain in serving him (16:27). The reward described here is not a payback for performing good deeds.[11] Instead, it is a grand celebration in the greatest possible venue of honor, that of magnificent angels, with the glory of—and from—the Father himself.

Days later, Jesus took Peter, James, and John to a mountaintop. Luke tells us it was one of Jesus' times of extended prayer. How long he prayed we don't know, but it was long enough that the three disciples fell asleep (Luke 9:32). Perhaps the brilliant light woke them. Or the voices. Now awake, they saw Jesus, whose garments had changed color to a brilliant, glowing white. And his face had changed. He was shining somehow. Light radiated from his face, as bright as the sun, but somehow without glare, so their eyes could look on him. "They saw His glory" (9:32).

The voices they heard upon waking belonged to two men talking with Jesus. Without introduction, the disciples knew who they were. Moses was speaking with the prophet Elijah. They too were shining in glory. The three disciples overheard them discussing something about Jesus departing. They marveled as they listened, hearing Elijah speak, and Moses respond. The Law and the Prophets, in the flesh.

But then the conversation ended. Moses and Elijah were leaving. Peter stepped forward with an idea: "Master, it is good for us to be here; let us make three tabernacles" (Luke 9:33). Peter hadn't thought it through, but he may have imagined the awesome credibility of their movement with Moses and Elijah affirming and confirming everything Jesus said. The booths, or tabernacles, might have been a way to establish a kind of holy headquarters for Jesus' teaching. Every other important rabbi had a teaching center. But Jesus had resisted such a thing.

Jesus said nothing. But as Peter spoke, a cloud formed. On this perfectly clear day, a cloud began moving and rapidly expanding. It shone with a bright, unearthly radiance. And it seemed massively heavy, as if all of heaven bore down on them. And then the voice—immense, vast, and passionate: "This is My beloved Son, with whom I am well-pleased; listen to Him!" (Matt 17:5). They dropped to the ground, trembling (Matt 17:6).

They had not only glimpsed Jesus in glory; they had also heard the Father giving him glory and honor. How do we know? Because Peter wrote his eyewitness account of what happened on "the holy mountain": "For when he received honor and glory from God the Father, such an utterance as this was made to him by the Majestic Glory, 'This is my beloved Son with whom I am well-pleased'" (2 Pet 1:17–18). This word is identical to what the Father said at Christ's baptism, except for the additional command: "Listen to Him!"

In the risen, enthroned Messiah is the final and full revealing of God. He is the fulfillment of the Law and the fullness of the Prophets. This is not some guru supporting his ideas by quoting respectable sources. The Father declared the sufficiency and the supremacy of Jesus. In the days coming, he would not make a spectacle of his glory with bright lights or on high mountains. Instead, the voice of Jesus, once he is raised from death to reign, will be heard by all who follow him.

But would these disciples listen to him? Would they deny themselves to follow him? Yes, but not easily. Two events highlight the challenge and the hope of hearing and following Jesus.

Shortly after they beheld Jesus' glory on the mountain, Jesus' band of disciples set out with him for Jerusalem. Jesus sent a few followers ahead to make overnight arrangements in a Samaritan village. They returned with the bothersome news that not only had the Samaritans refused, they had also insulted them. They didn't want Jews desecrating their town (Luke 9:51–56).

James and John, the same disciples so recently on the mountain with Jesus, were so offended by this Samaritan insolence that they approached Jesus with an idea: "Lord, do You want us to command fire to come down from heaven and consume them?" (Luke 9:54). Jesus did not quibble with them about their ability to do that trick. Instead, he expressed a terse rebuke, with an assessment of their motives: "You do not know what kind of spirit you are of" (9:55). They were oblivious to the arrogance, anger, and jealousy that drove them.

Not long after this, these same brothers, James and John—still working out their honor issues—approached Jesus with another idea. Surely this time He would be impressed. What they had seen on the mountain matched the teachings of many rabbis. The long-expected Messiah would be enthroned in glory, and others would be seated in honor with him. They saw themselves as candidates for such an honor. Thus, their request: "Grant that we may sit, one on Your right and one on Your left, in Your glory" (Mark 10:37). To this audacious suggestion Jesus replied, "You do not know what you are asking" (10:38).

These stories reveal Jesus' assessment of our foolhardy ambitions for glory—our propensity for setting our minds on "the things of man"—the human habit of self-made glory. Most likely we are every bit as ignorant as James and John. We may not realize how we presumptively arrange for thrones of glory. We may not know what "spirit we are of."

But these stories also give us hope. Jesus went on to ask them if they were able to drink the cup of suffering that he would drink and to endure the baptism of his death. The brothers glibly responded, "Sure." Here's the hope we can embrace—Jesus assures them they will indeed willingly deny themselves and follow him in the way of the cross for his glory (Mark 10:38–39; Matt 20:22–23).

Palm Sunday: Following Christ for the Father's Glory

The third time God spoke from heaven occurred on Palm Sunday as Jesus was thronged by a cheering crowd. It may have been the largest crowd ever surrounding

Jesus without him trying to escape it. Jesus refused to shut down the loud exclamations of praise. From a public relations point of view, it was a tremendous boost to his fame and favor.

Some wealthy God-fearing Gentiles (Greeks from a city such as Athens) approached Jesus' inner circle to request a special audience. Philip and Andrew had to wonder what Jesus would say. He usually turned down opportunities to hobnob with rich and well-connected people. But he was also interested in Gentile inquirers, so they brought the matter to Jesus. His response stunned them: "The hour has come for the Son of Man to be glorified" (John 12:23). Whoa! Was Jesus going to go for glory? On an international scale?

But it turned out to be yet another "Truly, truly" moment when he grabbed their attention and then said something unexpected. This time Jesus said something about a seed dying in the sand and bearing fruit (John 12:24). Then he repeated the bit about losing your life or saving it (12:25). They had heard this before. They must have wondered, "How does this relate to the Greek leaders?" But Jesus continued: "If anyone serves Me, he must follow Me; and where I am, there My servant will be also; if anyone serves Me, the Father will honor him" (12:26).

Then came the real surprise. Jesus said, "Now my soul has become troubled" (12:27 NASB). The word for "soul," sometimes translated "life," is the very same word he used two sentences earlier to describe one's "life in this world" (12:25 NASB). The word for "troubled" means shaken, distressed, or conflicted. This was not what popular teachers would say to win followers.

Then Jesus identified the trouble—a choice he was facing. He described it as a fork in the road before him. He could pray either "Father, save Me from this hour," or "Father, glorify Your name" (12:27–28).

To pray "save Me from this hour" would effectively ask God for a comfortable and pleasant, trouble-free life. The other prayer for God's glory was familiar to them. Asking God to glorify his name was a condensed way of calling on God to accomplish something great for his praise in the earth. This single phrase summed up the entire global purpose of God: *to be famous among all so that he would be worshipped and loved by many.*

Recognize this: The Father would have answered either prayer. In Matthew 26:53, Jesus says he could have asked the Father for "legions of angels" to escape the cross. So why did he pray the second prayer, effectively offering his life to see God glorified on earth? It was a simple matter of purpose: "But for this purpose I came to this hour" (John 12:27).

Jesus paused. After a moment, he prayed, as he often did, with his face toward heaven: "Father, glorify your name" (12:28 NASB). For a few seconds, the crowd maintained polite quiet. And then they all heard it—a sound from somewhere high in the cloudless sky—loud and deep and rumbling. "I have both glorified it, and will glorify it again" (12:28). Many in the crowd swore it was the sound of thunder. Others were sure they could make out some syllables and words, so they said, "An angel has spoken to Him" (12:29). But the scores of Jesus' followers standing nearby heard every word. Even though the voice was full and loud, the words seemed to settle deeply within them, as if they heard it with their hearts.

Then Jesus said, "This voice has not come for My sake, but for your sakes" (12:30). For most of them, months would pass before they would realize why the Father had addressed those words ("I have both glorified it, and will glorify it again") to them and not to Jesus. Wasn't Jesus the one who prayed? Surely the Father intended to encourage and comfort him for the coming ordeal. What did Jesus mean by saying the voice was for them?

Weeks later they would piece things together (12:16). They recalled that just moments before his prayer, Jesus had summoned them yet again to follow him: "If anyone serves Me, he must follow Me" (12:26). After he was exalted, they would discover that anyone who followed Jesus would eventually follow him to the same fork in the road. Every follower would eventually come to the same choice that Jesus himself had faced. They could either seek God's help to live a pleasant, trouble-free life, or they could offer their life to God for his greater glory in the earth.

What amazing assurance they found in the Father's words: "I have both glorified it, and will glorify it again" (12:28). Their lives might seem wasted, lost, or squandered, like a seed in the sand. But no. Anyone who prays this prayer, offering their life for the purpose of the Father's glory, will see God advance his purpose in history yet "again."

Still today, the Father's voice confirms Jesus' call to follow him. Jesus made it clear: To serve Jesus, one must follow him (12:26). To anyone who serves in this way—choosing the Father's glory instead of their own—Jesus says the Father himself will honor him. The Father himself will honor her.

And this, my fellow followers, is true glory. This is the glorious gladness of the Father. This is the blessing of the Spirit of glory, resting on those who endure with Christ. This is the singular glory of Jesus Christ, the worthy Lamb who was slain. If we suffer with him, we shall also be glorified with him.

A Prayer

Father of glory, we rejoice to behold, through the eyes of our expectant hearts, the abounding glory that you have given your Son. You have raised him from death, exalted him to your right hand, and now, by your Spirit, you are drawing people from every nation to lavish obedient love upon him. In these days, in which Christ is both hated and praised as never before, we aspire to follow him fully, tasting the honor of bearing shame for his greater glory. We call on you to subdue our wayward, jealous ambitions. Guide us in your ways so that the gospel would swiftly bear the fruit of Christ's beauty amid each of the peoples.

For Further Reflection

1. The surpassing glory of Jesus Christ is the crux and destination of the biblical narrative. Humanity's longing for honor—indeed, every people group's longing for honor—will ultimately be fulfilled in glorious union with Christ. Why might this hope of glory be an effective entry point for the gospel among unreached peoples?

2. Hawthorne ends this chapter with the statement, "If we suffer with him, we shall also be glorified with him," an allusion to Romans 8:17. To what degree is suffering essential to authentic glory? Why? What does this imply for the gospel?

CHAPTER 1 Endnotes

1 All Scripture quotations in this chapter, unless otherwise noted, are from the New American Standard Bible (NASB).

2 There is abundant biblical support for the idea of angels recognizing and celebrating glory (Isa 6:3; Ps 29:1; 1 Pet 1:11–12; Rev 4:9–11; 5:12–13; and many more).

3 The idea of "glory" has a wide range of meaning in its biblical usage. Of course, glory can refer to God's intrinsic glory that is uniquely his. But glory can also describe the beauty and worthiness of what God has formed in creation. Paul mentions different created glories (Greek *doxa*) of the sun, moon, and stars in 1 Cor 15:40–41. The idea of glory also frequently refers to works or designs produced by human endeavor. For example, "the kingdoms of the world and their glory" (Matt 4:8), and "Solomon in all his glory" (Matt 6:29).

4 Mention of the Reformation may also call for clarification about what Luther called a "theology of glory." Luther and many others used this phrase, since his day, as a catch-all category to denounce theologies that were about gaining prestige and wealth, along with salvation in the world to come. Instead, Luther called for a "theology of the cross," something we must embrace in recognizing "true glory" as coming from God.

5 See also Rom 9:23; Eph 1:18; 3:16; Phil 4:19; Col 1:27.

6 J. Scott Horrell, "Toward a Biblical Model of the Social Trinity: Avoiding Equivocation of Nature and Order," *Journal of the Evangelical Theological Society* 47 (2004): 405.

7 Miroslav Volf, "Being As God Is: Trinity and Generosity," in *God's Life in Trinity*, ed. Miroslav Volf and Michael Welker (Minneapolis: Fortress, 2006), 9.

8 Hermann Austel, "sha'ah," in *Theological Wordbook of the Old Testament*, ed. R. Laird Harris (Chicago: Moody, 2004), 533.

9 The Hebrew verb "to lift up" (*na'as*), with the noun for "face" (*panh*), is an idiom usually indicating favor or public honor. For example, in 2 Kgs 5:1: "Naaman ... was a great man in the sight of his master and highly regarded", the idiomatic Hebrew can be more literally rendered: "Naaman ... was a great man before the face of his master and lifted up with respect to the face."

10 Francis Fukuyama refers to Hegel's idea that "the desire for recognition" drives history as "the motor of history." See Fukuyama's *The End of History and the Last Man* (New York: Perennial, 2002), xix.

11 In Matthew 16:27, Jesus quotes the last line of Proverbs 24:11–12. In these verses, God is concerned about those being taken away to death. The idea of keeping "your soul" aligns with Matthew 16:25 regarding losing or finding life. The emphasis is not on payback for exploits or what moderns might consider performance orientation. Both the Proverbs and Matthew passages are about how thoroughly God cares for and honors his servants who suffer death.

HONOR AND SHAME IN HISTORICAL THEOLOGY:
Listening to Eight Voices

JAYSON GEORGES

Theologians throughout church history have explained biblical truth in honor-shame terms. So that we can stand on the shoulders of giants instead of starting at ground zero, this article examines the honor-shame contributions of the following eight prominent theologians, summarizing each author's theology regarding honor and shame, using their own words as much as possible:

1. John Chrysostom–*Hermeneutics*
2. Jonathan Edwards–*God*
3. Thomas Watson–*Sin*
4. Athanasius–*Salvation*
5. Anselm–*Atonement*
6. Dietrich Bonhoeffer–*Ethics*
7. Ignatius–*Suffering*
8. C. S. Lewis–*Eschatology*

This historical survey of theology provides ideas and inspiration for theologizing in contemporary contexts.

John Chrysostom—*Hermeneutics*

John Chrysostom, the archbishop of Constantinople (353–407), was famous for his eloquent preaching. (The moniker *Chrysostomos* means "golden-mouthed.") His eighty-eight exegetical homilies on the Gospel of John read much like a social-science commentary, wherein honor and shame shaped his interpretation of Scripture.[1] I will mention three areas in which honor and shame influenced Chrysostom's hermeneutics.[2]

One, Chrysostom references honor-shame dynamics to expound the theology of the incarnation in John 1:1–14. Chrysostom says that John opens with the preexistence of God's Word because "he knows that men most honor the eldest of beings which was before all" (2:7).

Chrysostom was adamant that the term "son" does not imply inferiority to the Father. John used the expression "son" because he was "very confident that between Father and Son there was an equality of honor" (5:2).

Chrysostom describes the incarnation in John 1:14 ("the Word became flesh") as a king conferring honor upon the lowly.

> For the high when it associates with the low touches not at all its own honor, while it raises up the other from its excessive lowness; and even thus it was with the Lord. He in nothing diminished His own Nature by this condescension, but raised us, who had always sat in disgrace and darkness, to glory unspeakable. Thus it may be, a king, conversing with interest and kindness with a poor mean man, does not at all shame himself, yet makes the other observed by all and illustrious. (11:1)

Chrysostom uses the metaphor of a wedding (cf. Matt 22 and 25) to explain John 1:13 ("who were born, not of blood nor of the will of the flesh nor of the will of man, but of God"; NASB). The wedding invitation is "so great an honor," but we behaved with insolence (10:3). God "honored us with all other honor; but we … have offered insult to Him" (10:3). Because we acted unworthily and defiled our garments as invitees, "It is to honor the marriage and guests, that [God] drives off those bold and shameless persons" (10:3).

Chrysostom read John as stories about people honoring or shaming Jesus. He says the opponents "use every artifice to destroy the honor of the Son of God … seeking eagerly to pull down Him whom they say they worship." But their opposition to Christ will "fill their faces with shame and their souls with punishment" (3:2). In contrast, the apostle John was "not ashamed of the dishonor of his Teacher" (10:2).

Two, Chrysostom interprets Jesus' miracle at the wedding in Cana (John 2) in light of honor and shame. He notes how the wedding hosts failed to properly respect Jesus—they "invite[d] Him not as some great one, but merely as an ordinary acquaintance" (21:1). Nevertheless, the famous Jesus attended the wedding not looking "to His own honor, but to our benefit" (21:1).

Chrysostom says that Jesus' comment to his mother ("Woman, what have I to do with you?") was not disrespectful or insulting. "Though [Jesus] was careful to honor His mother, yet He cared much more for the salvation of her soul," which comes through giving honor to Jesus. Had Mary expected to "always be honored by Him as by a son," then Jesus could not change his mother's thoughts from "His present lowliness to His future exaltation."

And why did Jesus say, "My hour has not yet come," but then perform the miracle? Chrysostom proposes, "He did it to honor His mother, that He might not seem entirely to contradict and shame her that bare Him in the presence of so many" (22:1). After the wedding, Jesus escorts his family home to Capernaum where he spent a few days "to honor His mother" (23:1).

Finally, Chrysostom's homilies exhort listeners to appropriate God's honor. The God who assigns honor is more honorable than mortals. For Chrysostom, the text of John (especially in passages where people reject Jesus) should refashion our "honor code." These quotes illustrate Chrysostom's reflection on the nature of honor in discipleship and morality.

> Beloved, let us ... be sensible of the nobility which has been given to us by God; let us despise vulgar applause. For nothing is so ridiculous and disgraceful as [vainglory], nothing so full of shame and dishonor. One may in many ways see, that to love honor is dishonor; and that true honor consists in neglecting honor, in making no account of it, but in saying and doing everything according to what seems good to God. (3:6)

> Look up straight to God: He will praise you, and the man who is approved by Him must not seek honor from mortals. (4:4)

> If an earthly king approve you, you make no account of the many, though they all deride you; but if the Lord of the universe praise you, do you seek the good words of beetles and gnats? For this is what these men are, compared with God, or rather not even this, but something viler, if there be anything such. How long do we wallow in the mire? How long do we set sluggards and belly-gods for our judges? (76:3)

Chrysostom's homilies on John provide a historical model for hermeneutics and homiletics from an honor-shame perspective.

Jonathan Edwards—*God*

Jonathan Edwards (1703–58) was a Puritan pastor and Reformed theologian in early New England. His book, *The End for Which God Created the World* (hereafter, *The End*), provides a radically God-centered view of the world. Edwards argues, philosophically and biblically, that the ultimate end of God and of history is the magnification of God's supreme glory.

The notion of honor pervades Edwards' vocabulary. He repeatedly mentions *glory* (500 instances), *name* (169), *value* (115), *regard* (114), *praise* (93), *esteem* (61), *worthy* (51), and *honor* (30). He could speak of honor eight different ways in one sentence: "If God's own *excellency* and *glory* is *worthy* to be highly *valued* and delighted in by him, then the *value* and *esteem* hereof by others is *worthy* to be *regarded* by him" (p. 172). A rich variety of language was necessary for Edwards "to express things of so sublime a nature" as God himself (p. 242).

Edwards claims, "All that is ever spoken of in the Scriptures as the ultimate end of God's works, is included in that one phrase, *the glory of God*" (p. 242). God does all things for his glory (pp. 191–210), for his name's sake (pp. 210–14), for displaying his excellencies (pp. 210–14), and for his praise (pp. 218–20)—all synonyms of God's chief end. *The glory of God* signifies "the emanation and true external expression of God's internal glory and fullness" (p. 242).

For Edwards, God is morally disposed toward his own glory. God "loves and esteems his own excellence," "values the glory of his own nature," and "testifies a supreme respect to himself" (pp. 150, 158, 159). This self-glorification is morally right because God "is worthy in himself to be so [respected], being infinitely the greatest and best of beings" (p. 140).

God's innate disposition toward honor is not "dishonorable to him" or "unworthy of God," for "he should value himself infinitely more than his creatures" (pp. 168–71). His holiness "consist[s] in giving due respect to that Being to whom most is due; for God is infinitely the most worthy of regard. The worthiness of others is as nothing to his" (p. 141).[3] His honor is neither ascribed nor achieved; his honor simply *is*, for all of eternity. God *should*, and *does*, seek his own glory.

God's glory is not static, but actively overflowing into creation for eternity; the full manifestation of God's glory necessitates a full process. Edwards explains the pervasive extent and full course of God's self-glorification: "The beams of glory come from God, are something of God, and are refunded back again to their original. So that the whole is *of* God, and *in* God, and *to* God; and he is the beginning, and the middle, and the end."

Edwards explains how the Hebrew *kabod* and Greek *doxa* are used in each of these ways. *Glory*, the common translation of those words, involves three aspects: (1) internal excellency or worthiness for regard, a possessed value, (2) the public exhibition of his gracious goodness, a visible effulgence, and (3) the honor he receives from creatures—that is, praise (pp. 229–39). In sum, God has glory, displays glory, and gets glory—forever.

God's own joy in his glorious fullness disposes him to exhibit his glory in creation, so that his glory is further known and cherished by others. God "loves to have himself valued and esteemed" (p. 150). "God's glory should be *known* by a glorious society of created beings" and esteemed according to its dignity (p. 149). This recognition of divine supremacy is God's aim in creation and redemption. As the sun radiates light, God's supreme glory overflows (p. 246). God's internal glory and fullness are communicated; he externalizes his innate excellency. God's own delight in his internal glory disposes him to exhibit that glory in all things: providence, creation, redemption, and eternity (pp. 191–210).

Edwards argues how God's glory and human happiness are one and the same. Our joyous praising of God acknowledges and exhibits his glory (p. 246). Or, "God is most glorified in us when we are most satisfied in him." Salvation is receiving and returning the effulgence of divine radiance (pp. 246–47). Our delight and praise perfect the fullness of divine glory.

Our chief end as humans is to glorify God, as Edwards repeats in multiple ways. Our knowledge and happiness consist in regarding, esteeming, respecting, and exalting God as the chief good (p. 249). Christian holiness means "the heart exalting, magnifying, or glorying God" (p. 158). God is "pleased with the proper love, esteem, and honor of himself" (p. 173).

The magnification of God's supreme glory continues unabated into eternity. Edwards viewed the eternal state as "increasing union and conformity through eternity" (pp. 159–61, 249). Our knowledge and magnification of God's glory will infinitely progress. God's desire for his glory leads to "increasing communication of himself through eternity." The end for which God created the world has no end. His glory abounds forever.

Edwards, like no other theologian, offers a radical vision of God's supreme honor in all things. From eternity past to eternity future, the ultimate end of all things is the glory of God.[4] Edwards provides a philosophical and biblical anchor for a Christian theology of God in honor-shame terms.

Thomas Watson—*Sin*

Thomas Watson was a Puritan pastor in seventeenth-century England. He became a famous preacher and author, he was ejected from the Church of England for dissenting against Charles II. His book, *The Doctrine of Repentance*, includes an extensive shame-based hamartiology. Watson explains the centrality of shame in both sin and repentance, summarized here in five points.[5]

One, sin brings shame upon God.

> Sin is an offense to God. It violates his laws. Here is *crimen laesue majestatis* ("grievous high treason"). What greater injury can be given a prince than to trample on his royal edicts? A sinner holds the statutes of heaven in contempt: "They toss your law behind their backs" (Neh 9:26), as if they scorned to look at it. Sin robs God of his due (p. 51).

See how Scripture has penciled [sin] out: it dishonors God (Rom 2:23); despises God (1 Sam 2:30); enrages God (Eze 16:43). (p. 21)

Two, sin belittles Christ. Our iniquity is the reason Jesus bore the shame of the cross. But also, our perpetual unbelief undercuts the glory of the cross.

We have affronted and disparaged [Christ's] blood by unbelief. (p. 18)

Did our sins put Christ to shame, and shall they not put us to shame? Did he wear the purple, and shall not our cheeks wear crimson? (p. 17)

Sin, when acted to its height, crucifies Christ afresh and puts him to open shame. (p. 21)

Three, sin makes people shameful before God. Sin brings disgrace into our lives.

Sin is a debasing thing. It degrades a person of his honor: "I will make your grave; for you are vile" (Nah 1:14). This was spoken of a king. He was not vile by birth but by sin. Sin blots our name and taints our blood. Nothing so changes a man's glory into shame as sin. It is said of Naaman, "He was a great man and honorable, but he was a leper" (2 Kgs 5:1). However great a man may be with worldly pomp, if he is wicked, then he is a leper in God's eye. (p. 52)

[Sin] has made us naked and deformed in God's eye. (p. 17).

Adam never blushed in the time of innocence. While he kept the whiteness of the lily, he did not have the blushing of the rose; but when he had deflowered his soul by sin, he was ashamed. Sin has tainted our blood. (p. 17)

Four, true repentance requires "holy shaming." Healthy shame is essential for believers, but impossible for unbelievers.

When the heart has been made black with sin, grace makes the face red with blushing: "I am ashamed and blush to lift up my face" (Ezra 9:6). The repenting prodigal was so ashamed of his excess that he thought himself not worthy to be called a son any more (Luke 15:21). Repentance causes a holy bashfulness. If Christ's blood was not at the sinner's heart, there would not be so much blood in the sinner's face. (p. 17)

How far from being penitent are those who have no shame? Many have sinned away shame: "the unjust knows no shame" (Zeph 3:5). It is a great shame not to be ashamed.... Those who cannot blush for sin too much resemble the beasts. (p. 19)

There are some so far from this holy blushing that they are proud of their sins.... Others are so far from being ashamed of sin that they glory in their sins: "whose glory is in their shame" (Phil 3:19). Some are ashamed of what is their glory: they are ashamed to be seen with a good book in their hand. Others glory in what is their shame: they look at sin as a piece of gallantry. The swearer thinks his speech is most graceful when it is interspersed with oaths. The drunkard considers it a glory that he can drink to excess (Isa 5:22). (p. 19)

Five, repentance repairs the problems of shame (i.e., God's reputation, our shame, and our shamelessness).

> We have wronged God by sin. There is a great deal of equity in requiring that we repent. By sin, we have wronged God. We have eclipsed his honor. We have infringed his law. And we should reasonably make reparation. By repentance we humble and judge ourselves for sin. We stamp our seal that God is righteous if he were to destroy us. Thus [by repentance] we give glory to God, and we do what lies in us to do in order to repair his honor. (p. 27)

> Let us show our penitence by a modest blushing…. O let us take holy shame to ourselves for sin. Be assured, the more we are ashamed of sin now, the less we will be ashamed at Christ's coming. If the sins of the godly are mentioned at the Day of Judgment, it will not be to shame them, but to magnify the riches of God's grace in pardoning them. (p. 19)

> The sooner we repent, the more glory we may bring to God. (p. 40)

In Watson's theology, shame is foremost a spiritual and theological concept—it defines our vertical relationship with God. Also, he offers a profound explanation of the role of shame in repentance: Our "holy shame" repairs the honor of God.

Athanasius—*Salvation*

Athanasius (297–373), the bishop of Alexandria and leader at the Nicene Council, famously said, "God became man, so that man might become God" (*On the Incarnation*, 54.3). This quote summarizes the orthodox soteriology of *theosis*, which means "divinization" or "deification."[6] In this view, salvation involves becoming like God and sharing his divine nature (2 Pet 1:4). Athanasius explains, "The Word was made flesh in order that *we might be made gods*…. Just as the Lord, putting on the body, became a man, so also *we men are both deified through his flesh*, and henceforth inherit everlasting life" (*Against the Arians*, 1.39, 3.34; emphasis added).

The Arian controversy surrounding the Nicene Creed spurred Athanasius' teaching on theosis. For Athanasius, soteriology explained Christology; theosis underscores the divinity of Christ. For only if Jesus is of one divine essence (*homoousios*) with the Father could those who united with him become deified.

Athanasius links deification with the New Testament themes of adoption and sonship (John 1:12; 8:42; Rom 8:15–17, 23; 9:4; Gal 4:5; 1 John 3:2).[7] He says that Jesus Christ "glorifies creation and presents it to the Father by divinizing it and granting it adoption" (*Ad Serapion*, I.26). This sonship implies an entirely new mode of being (not only a new legal status). However, theosis is never a matter of actual substance; Athanasius himself contrasts the *natural* sonship of the Logos with our *adoptive* sonship given to us by grace (*A Defense of Nicene*, 1).[8]

Deification is about illumination and eternality—"He, indeed, assumed humanity that we might become God. He manifested Himself by means of a body *in order that we might perceive the Mind of the unseen Father.* He endured shame from men *that we might inherit immortality*" (*On the Incarnation,* 54.3). Christ assumed mortality so that we might become incorruptible for eternity. As "co-heirs with Christ," we are united *in God* and *with God.* Theosis involves deliverance from mortality and corruption, participation in the life of God, renewal to the original *imago Dei,* and appropriation of divine status.[9]

Many early church fathers assumed and advocated theosis.[10] For example, Augustine of Hippo said, "But he himself that justifies *also deifies,* for by justifying he makes sons of God…. If then we have been made sons of god, *we have also been made gods*" (*Expositions on Psalms,* 50:2). And the purpose of Jesus' incarnation was "to make human beings gods" (Sermon 192.1.1).

Ephrem the Syrian (fourth-century father of Syriac Orthodoxy) links deification with honor and shame. His poetic theology portrays salvation as God raising humanity to the honorable position of divinity.[11] At the fall, Adam lost his original "Robe of Glory" and his "name became loathsome" (*Hymns on Paradise* 15:8–10). Adam blushed, "because, in place of such splendor, a man who is naked is filled with shame" (*Hymns on Paradise* 2.7). Then, to restore human glory, Jesus stripped himself of divine glory and put on Adam's body. In Christ, believers "become a god" (*Hymns of Virginity* 48.18) and "put on the very likeness of God's majesty" (*Hymns of Virginity* 9.20–21). Concerning salvation, Ephrem explains:

> Among the saints their nakedness is clothed with glory, none is clad with leaves or stands ashamed, for they have found, through our Lord, the robe [of glory] that belongs to Adam and Eve. (*Hymns of Virginity* 6.9)

So how does theosis relate to honor and shame? Theosis perceives sin as a fall from honor, stripping of glory, and loss of communion. Salvation is "a re-honoring that is accomplished by a restoration of that image and the accompanying honor that comes from being included in the fellowship of Trinitarian life"[12]—i.e., theosis, divinization. Becoming "like God" involves regaining our original status of honor and appropriating God's face. We share his glory (John 17:22).

As Cyril of Alexandria (fifth-century patriarch of Alexandria) explains, to be sons and gods by grace is to be "brought to this wonderful and supernatural dignity" (*On the Unity of Christ*). In Christ and through the Spirit, God draws us into the divine life characterized by reciprocal and eternal glorification. We become truly human as we join in the trinitarian honor of giving and receiving glory.[13]

Theosis is the salvific process of fully participating in God's honor. One might consider a doctrine of theosis "honorification." Despite some Western skepticism of Eastern theology, the doctrine of theosis offers a potential soteriology for honor-shame cultures today.

Anselm—*Atonement*

Anselm (c. 1033–1109) was a Benedictine monk and the archbishop of Canterbury. His greatest work, *Cur Deus Homo* ("Why God Became Man"), employs scholastic rationalism to explain the necessity and atonement of Jesus Christ, the God-man.[14]

Reformed scholars in the seventeenth through the nineteenth centuries repackaged Anselm's satisfaction theory into the penal substitutionary atonement (PSA) model. For this reason, contemporary evangelicals often misinterpret Anselm through a legal and penal paradigm. (An honor-shame atonement theory does not necessarily deny the PSA model. The two approaches are not mutually incompatible.) However, we must read *Cur Deus Homo* in light of the medieval feudal values of honor and shame, not the legal values of latter Reformers. As Baker and Green explain,

> Anselm's understanding of the atonement reads as a kind of allegory, with the lord as the Lord and the serfs as the human family. "Satisfaction" for us, in our criminal-justice system, has to do with the apprehension and punishment of the guilty, while for Anselm and his contemporaries, satisfaction hinged on the fulfillment of certain obligations related to loyalty and honor.[15]

For Anselm, all creatures must "be subordinate to the will of God" (I:11). "When a rational nature wills what it ought to, it honors God. A person honors God when he "keeps his proper place" under the Lord's rule (I:15).

Man owes glory and honor to God, but fails in this obligation. "Whoever does not pay to God this honor due Him dishonors Him and removes from Him what belongs to Him; and this removal, or this dishonoring, constitutes a sin" (I:11).

And so, "everyone who sins is obliged to repay to God the honor which he has stolen" (I:11). Honor repayment is essential because God could never tolerate "that the creature remove the honor owed to the Creator and not repay what he removes" (I:13). To be clear, human sin does not diminish God's honor. "Nothing can be added to or subtracted from His honor, considered in itself. For His honor is, in itself, incorruptible and altogether immutable.... No one can honor or dishonor God as He is in Himself" (I:15). So, technically, human sin fails to give God the glory that is always his, and this creates an obligatory debt.

God's honor must be satisfactorily repaid because "God keeps nothing more justly than the honor of His dignity" (I:13). God is morally just because he rightly demands honor (not because he legally appeases his anger or satisfies his wrath). God is "constrained" to save us for his own sake (not for our sake) because he is "under the necessity of maintaining His honor. Indeed, this necessity is nothing other than the immutability of His honor—an immutability which He has from Himself and not from another" (II:4).

God cannot forgive sin "apart from any repayment of the honor stolen from Him" (I:12). God is just and righteous because he requires the restoration of his honor (not because he punishes wrongs). Justice for Anselm is when God rightly honors.

We humans are incapable of repaying our own honor debt. Our good deeds and worship are what we always owe God anyhow, so they cannot be used as a back payment for previous insults. "If even when I do not sin I owe to God—in order to keep from sinning—myself and whatever I can do, I have nothing with which to make payment [of honor] for my sin" (I:20). For this reason, the coming of Jesus Christ, the God-man (i.e., *Deus homo*) "was necessary for man's salvation" (I:20). "This debt [of man] was so great that only God was able to pay it, although only a man ought to pay it; and, thus, the same [individual] who was divine was also human" (II:18).

Jesus Christ is a "complete satisfaction for sin" (II:4). For Anselm, this means Jesus' sacrificial life repays our debt of honor (not appeases the Father's wrath). "His life is paid to God for the sins of men" (II:18) as a gift that brings honor to God (not as a victim who absorbs punishment). Because Jesus was sinless, he could "make payment for what is owed for the sins of the whole world" (II:18). So he freely "gave Himself over to death for the honor of God" (II:18).

Jesus was not required to die because his perfect obedience fulfilled his own duty of honoring God. Therefore Jesus could voluntarily give to God his very own life as an above-and-beyond honor payment (II:11). "He paid on behalf of sinners that which He did not already owe for Himself" (II:18)—namely the honor debt due to our Master. The giving of his own life was the highest honor he could offer to God. "A man cannot at all give himself to God to any greater extent than when he hands himself over to death for the honor of God" (II:11). Jesus' life was an infinite gift of honor.

When the honor debt is not satisfied (in the case of unbelievers), then God must punish. But punishment is not itself the repayment or "satisfaction." Repayment of our honor debt happens *so that* the punishment does not happen. In the realm of banking, for example, a debtor who repays does not face consequences. In Anselm's words, "It is necessary *either* for the honor that has been removed to be repaid *or else* for punishment to result" (I:13; emphasis added). "*Either* satisfaction *or* punishment must follow upon every sin," Anselm asserts (I:15; emphasis added).

Punishment does not satisfy or save anything. Punishment only happens because man's obligation of honor is not satisfied. For Anselm, the cross is not God's punishment, but a gift that satisfies our debt *so that* man is not punished. Louis Berkhof notes, "Anselm looks upon satisfaction as an [honor-restoring] gift rather than as a [wrath-appeasing] punishment."[16]

God is most honored when man "exhibits due subjection to God" by obeying or repaying honor (I:14). However, when that honor is not properly paid, then

God resorts to punishing the sinner by taking away his happiness. Such a natural punishment for sin is neither salvific nor punitive, but a public demonstration that God is the honorable Master. "What God takes away conduces to His honor simply by virtue of His taking it. For by taking it away He shows that the sinner and his possessions are subject to Him" (I:14).

God's punishment is honorable because it proves God's power and ownership (not because it fulfills the punitive requirements or appeases his wrath). In other words, punishment does justice to God's honor only when man fails to rightly honor God. But fortunately, the God-man has justly honored God for us.

Anselm's satisfaction theory explains the atonement in terms of honor-shame. His model can be helpful for explaining the saving significance of the cross.

Dietrich Bonhoeffer—*Ethics*

Dietrich Bonhoeffer (1906–45), a German dissident and theologian, speaks about shame in his book *Ethics*. The context of Bonhoeffer's reflection was World War II–era Germany, a time when the church lost its prophetic and moral vision.[17]

Bonhoeffer first analyzes the role of shame in the divine-human relationship. People perceive their disunion from God, and this causes shame. "Shame is man's ineffaceable recollection of his estrangement from the origin; it is grief from this estrangement, and the powerless longing to return to unity with the origin... . Man is ashamed of the loss of his unity with God and with other men" (p. 24).

The human response of covering and concealing shame is actually redemptive. "Covering is necessary because it keeps awake shame, and with it the memory of the disunion with the origin, and also because man, disunited as he is, must now withdraw himself and must live in concealment. Otherwise he would betray himself" (p. 25). Bonhoeffer thought shame was a necessary reminder of our longing to be reunited with God, not an artificial mask to be stripped away. Because man is disunited, solitude is where we experience our true self as estranged and isolated.

The shame of isolation is overcome through reunion and restoration. "Shame can be overcome only when the original unity is restored, when man is once again clothed by God" (p. 27). But to overcome that shame, we must endure the ultimate shame—making ourselves fully exposed to God by confessing sins.

Because shame is a primal element of human theology, it must be central in our social ethics (pp. 28–29). Bonhoeffer was skeptical about human conscience (i.e., the internal conviction of wrongdoing), for it is "concerned not with man's relation to God and to other men but with man's relation to himself." While shame indicates our disunion from God, "Conscience is the sign of man's disunion with himself." Since rules are always defined as either "permitted" or "forbidden," our conscience defines morality as legal and illegal as defined by the state—not good or bad.

Bonhoeffer notes how for the conscience "permitted is identical with good, and conscience does not register the fact, that even in this, man is in a state of disunion with his origin [God]. It follows from this also that conscience does not, like shame, embrace the whole of life; it reacts only to certain definite actions" (p. 28). Conscience pretends to be the voice of God, defining morality. The internal conscience becomes the new origin of good and evil. This makes man "judge over God and men, just as he is judge over himself" (p. 29). The result is utter narcissism; man's life becomes simply understanding himself, and not God.

Such a moral system of individual conscience fails because, for Bonhoeffer, our conscience is not "God's law written on human hearts," but an echo chamber of idolatrous humans. He witnessed the Nazi regime hijack the Lutheran Church and German Protestants condone the atrocities of World War II. Perhaps this explains why Bonhoeffer lost faith in the role of human conscience for guiding Christian morality. Shame, he proposed, was a better moral force. For one, "Shame is more elemental [primal, original] than remorse" (p. 24), as it goes back to our fundamental disunion with God. And two, shame affects the whole of life, not just certain actions regulated by legality.

In a later discussion on exploitation and torture, Bonhoeffer frames immoral behavior as dishonoring. In torture, "The body is misused, and therefore dishonoured." Violent humiliation perpetuates sin. "Any physical torture inflicts the most extreme dishonour of the human being.... Bodily dishonour seeks to avenge itself on the body of the infamous tormentor. In this way the violation of man's bodily freedom once again destroys the foundations of society" (p. 183).

Offenses against people are immoral because the victim "is deprived of the honour which is associated with bodily liberty." For Bonhoeffer, the act was immoral because it stripped away honor.

Shame plays a prominent role in Bonhoeffer's ethics, as is needed in global Christianity.

Ignatius of Antioch—*Suffering*

Ignatius was the bishop of Antioch around AD 100. En route to his execution in Rome, Ignatius wrote seven letters about his looming martyrdom.

Ignatius redefines martyrdom for the sake of Christ as honorable. About his circumstances, he said, "I have been judged worthy to bear a most godly name" (Magn 1:2).[18] Ignatius asked the believers in Trallia to pray "that I may be thought worthy of the lot to which I press forward to attain" (Trall 12:3; cf. Rom 1:1; 2:2).[19] His own execution demonstrates that "I have been judged worthy of serving the honor (*timē*) of God" (Eph 21:2)[20]. Ignatius sought to follow the footsteps of the Apostle Paul, who was approved and "worthy of honor" (Eph 12:1–2). In Ignatius' mind, to be publicly executed for Christ's sake was more honorable "than to rule over the ends of the earth" (Rom 6:1).[21] In fact, he wrote to the church in Rome so that they would not interfere with his martyrdom because he suspected that some might envy his honor as a martyr (3:1; 7:2). For Ignatius, suffering was a great honor, and martyrdom demonstrated he was worthy of that honor.

Also, the Christians who helped Ignatius on his way to Rome were equally honorable. Ignatius said to the believers who visited him in prison, "You did not despise [my chains], nor were you ashamed of them. Nor will the perfect hope, Jesus Christ, be ashamed of you" (Smyrn 10:1).

When the Ephesian church sent a deacon (Burrhus) to accompany Ignatius, he considered that gesture as a "mark of honor" (*eis logon timēs*) for which "the Lord Jesus Christ would honor them" (Phil 11:2).[22] Ignatius asked the Ephesians to let the deacon Burrhus "remain with me, to the honour of yourselves and of your bishop" (Eph 2:1).[23] Ignatius recognized honor as a proper motivation for the entire church and its leader.

The believers did not fear the shame of associating with the condemned bishop, but eagerly extended support and hospitality. Helping Ignatius "in his march toward martyrdom was honorable because such a death brought honor to God."[24]

Ignatius makes two important points about suffering: Martyrdom for Christ brought honor, and believers who extended hospitality to martyrs enjoyed similar honors. Ignatius' redefinition of suffering and persecution offers pastoral encouragement to global Christians who face similar shame today.

C. S. Lewis—*Eschatology*

C. S. Lewis (1898–1963) was a literature professor and Christian apologist who explained Christianity to modern Westerners. His essay-sermon "The Weight of Glory" speaks of the eschatological realities of honor and glory.[25]

Lewis first observes how honor and glory are central in biblical salvation. "There is no getting away from the fact that this idea [of glory] is very prominent in the New Testament and early Christian writings. Salvation is constantly associated with palms, crowns, white robes, thrones, and splendor like the sun and stars (p. 32)."

Lewis also identifies five salvific promises in Scriptures, all of which relate, in some fashion, to honor. "It is promised, firstly, that we shall be with Christ; secondly, that we shall be like Him; thirdly, with an enormous wealth of imagery that we shall have 'glory'; fourthly, that we shall, in some sense, be fed or feasted or entertained; and finally, that we shall have some sort of official position in the universe (p. 31)." The Bible describes the eschatological inheritance of Christians in terms of honor.

Nevertheless, these biblical realities of our glory confounded Lewis. His intellect wanted to explain away these puzzling, and even repulsive, promises of divine glory.

"Glory suggests two ideas to me, one seems wicked and the other ridiculous." And he acknowledges his modern bias against honor. "All this makes no immediate appeal to me at all, and in that respect I fancy I am a typical modern" (p. 32).

But Lewis came to understand honor as the very gift we humans covet the most. "Glory, as Christianity teaches me to hope for it, turns out to satisfy my original desire and indeed to reveal an element in that desire which I had not noticed" (p. 35). Salvation history climaxes with the full revelation of God's face, which could only confer glory or inflict shame. Honor and shame define the end of history. "In the end that Face which is the delight or terror of the universe must be turned upon each of us either with one expression or with the other, either conferring glory inexpressible or inflicting shame that can never be cured or disguised (p. 34)."

As Lewis grasped such eschatological honor, he wrestled at a personal level to fathom the seemingly impossible "weight or burden of glory which our thoughts can hardly sustain (p. 34)." God's majestic glory created a dreadful awe in his earthen vessel. Mortals ought not possess such honor.

In the end, such glory captured Lewis' heart and mind. The eschatological glory satisfies the deepest groaning of our souls.

> Apparently, then, our lifelong nostalgia, our longing to be reunited with something in the universe from which we now feel cut off, to be on the inside of some door which we have always seen from the outside is no mere neurotic fancy, but the truest index of our real situation. And to be at last summoned inside would be both glory and honour beyond our merits and also the healing of that old ache. (pp. 36–37)

Eschatological glory climaxes with divine approval. "The promise of glory is the promise, almost incredible and only possible by the work of Christ, that some of us, that any of us who really chooses, shall actually survive that examination, shall find approval, shall please God (p. 34)."

Lewis' eschatology avoids current events and timelines. He instead features the beauty of glory and terror of shame. "The Weight of Glory" captures the essence of Christian eschatology—the full revelation of God's glorious honor to his people.

Analysis of Historical Theologians

This brief tour through historical theology shows that honor-shame is clearly not "new." Theological reflection on this topic has spanned the centuries. Regrettably, these reflections were largely independent. Theologians did not build on the work of previous authors. There was no intergenerational conversation among them.[26] Without any such collaboration, most of these historical gems have remained hidden.

Nevertheless, their reflections show remarkable depth and insight. The theologians articulate key Christian doctrines in terms of honor and shame. This testifies to the centrality of honor-shame in biblical truth and in the human experience. Moreover, all of their reflections were notably *theological* (not psychological or anthropological) in orientation. They perceive honor and shame in light of God's glory.

For Further Reflection

1. Select one or two of these historical figures and think of ways their ideas might connect with your own ministry context.

2. As Georges notes, all these important figures view honor and shame as theological (not psychological or anthropological) issues. They largely perceive honor and shame in light of God's glory. What might a God-centered gospel of glory look like in your context?

CHAPTER 2 Endnotes

1 H. R. Stander, "Honour and Shame as Key Concepts in Chrysostom's Exegesis of the Gospel of John," *HTS* 59, no. 3 (2003): 899–913.

2 All citations from John Chrysostom, "Homilies on the Gospel of John," in *From Nicene and Post–Nicene Fathers,* ed. Philip Schaff, trans. Charles Marriott, revised and edited by Kevin Knight, vol. 14 (Buffalo, NY: Christian Literature Publishing Co., 1889), http://www.newadvent.org/fathers/2401.htm.

3 All citations of *The End* are from John Piper, *God's Passion for His Glory: Living the Vision of Jonathan Edwards (with the Complete Text of* The End for Which God Created the World) (Wheaton, IL: Crossway, 2006).

4 For contemporary theologies of God's glory, see John Piper, *Desiring God, Revised Edition: Meditations of a Christian Hedonist* (Colorado Springs: Multnomah Books, 2011); Daniel I. Block, *For the Glory of God: Recovering a Biblical Theology of Worship* (Grand Rapids: Baker Academic, 2014).

5 All citations are from Thomas Watson, *The Doctrine of Repentance*, originally published in 1668, edited and modernized by William Gross (2011), http://www.onthewing.org/user/Watson%20 -%20Repentance%20-%20Modern.pdf.

6 Though Athanasius himself used the word *theopoiesis* (Αὐτὸς γὰρ ἐνηνθρώπισεν, ἵνα ἡμεῖς θεοποιηθῶμεν), in this section I am using the conventional term *theosis*.

7 Early theologians appealed to Psalm 82:6, cited by Jesus in John 10:34–36, to explain deification: "You are gods, children of the Most High, all of you" (Ps 82:6 CEB).

8 Saint Maximus the Confessor clarifies this tension: "In theosis, man (the image of God) becomes likened to God, he rejoices in all the plenitude that does not belong to him by nature, because the grace of the Spirit triumphs within him, and because God acts in him (Letter 22)." From http://oca.org/saints/lives/2013/01/21/100249-st-maximus-the-confessor.

9 Christopher L. Flanders, *About Face: Rethinking Face for 21st Century Mission* (Eugene, OR: Wipf & Stock, 2011), 246, traces the theme of sharing in divine life through strands of Western theology. He concludes, "Due to its presence in all major theological traditions, *theosis* may legitimately be termed a catholic teaching of the church that has been preserved by Orthodox theology."

10 Irenaeus, Clement of Alexandria, Justin Martyr, Theophilus of Antioch, Hippolytus of Rome, Gregory of Nyssa, Maximus the Confessor, Cyril of Alexandria, and Gregory of Nazianzus. For a list of primary quotes, see https://en.wikipedia.org/wiki/Divinization_(Christian).

11 St. Ephrem, *St. Ephrem the Syrian: Hymns on Paradise,* trans. Sebastian Brock (Crestwood, NY: St. Vladimir's Seminary Press, 1997), 72.

12 Flanders, *About Face,* 252.

13 Ibid., 254–55.

14 All quotes from Anselm, *Cur Deus Homo,* trans. Jasper Hoskins and Herbert Richardson (Minneapolis: The Arthur J. Banning Press, 2000), http://jasper-hopkins.info/CurDeusI.pdf and http://jasper-hopkins.info/CurDeusII.pdf.

15 Mark D. Baker and Joel B. Green, *Recovering the Scandal of the Cross: Atonement in New Testament and Contemporary Contexts,* 2nd ed. (Downers Grove, IL: InterVarsity Academic, 2011), 22.

16 Louis Berkhof, *History of Christian Doctrines,* rev. ed. (London: Banner of Truth, 1996), 175.

17 All citations from Dietrich Bonhoeffer, *Ethics* (New York: Touchstone, 1995).

18 Unless otherwise noted, all citations from Michael W. Holmes, ed., *The Apostolic Fathers: Greek Texts and English Translations* (Grand Rapids: Baker Academic, 1999).

19 Peter Kirby, "Historical Jesus Theories," *Early Christian Writings,* 2020, http://www.earlychristianwritings.com/text/ignatius-trallians-hoole.html.

20 "Eph" refers to Epistle of Ignatius to the Ephesians.

21 "Rom" refers to Epistle of Ignatius to the Romans.

22 "Phil" refers to Epistle of Ignatius to the Philadephians.

23 Peter Kirby, "Historical Jesus Theories," *Early Christian Writings,* 2020, http://www.earlychristianwritings.com/text/ignatius-ephesians-lightfoot.html.

24 Drake Levasheff, "Jesus of Nazareth, Paul of Tarsus, and the Early Christian Challenge to Honor and Shame Values" (PhD diss., UCLA, 2013).

25 C. S. Lewis, "The Weight of Glory," in *The Weight of Glory and Other Addresses* (New York: Harper Collins, 1976), 25–46.

26 Three of the above doctrines have not remained in complete isolation: Orthodox *theosis,* Anselm's satisfaction atonement theory, and Edwards' "the glory of God." However, these three positions have not been broadly accepted. Western Christianity has largely misunderstood and rejected Orthodox soteriology, even despite a resurgence in some circles; Anselm's satisfaction theory was distorted by later Reformed theologians who added a penal element; and regarding Edwards' theology, historian Mark Nolls says, "There were no successors to his God-entranced worldview or his profoundly theological philosophy" ("Jonathan Edwards' Moral Philosophy, and the Secularization of American Christian Thought," *The Reformed Journal* [February 1983]).

A CLOTHESLINE THEOLOGY FOR THE WORLD:
How A Value-Driven Grand Narrative of Scripture Can Frame the Gospel

TOM STEFFEN

Western Christians tend to be parts specialists, focused on fragments.[1] Many from the West have never heard a sermon that covers either Testament in entirety during the sermon—fewer yet the entire Bible. Most have never heard a book or letter covered in a single sermon. Westerners tend not to be "people of the Book"; rather, they are people of the New Testament who feast on parts.

Most sermons in the West originate from the New Testament, the last third of the Bible. Most are topical, bunny-hopping from one verse to another, paying little attention to context.

Most of us have been asked, "What is your favorite Bible verse?" Fewer have been asked, "What is your favorite book of the Bible?"

Most of us have memorized Bible verses; few have memorized entire books or letters.[2] Fewer still the entire New Testament.

Most of us have learned the Bible from cherry pickers, snackers, Scripture surgeons, fragmentists—who believe real theology derives primarily from the New Testament. Since we tend to teach as we were taught—i.e., Bible bits learned through systematic theology—we create more of the same. Is it any wonder that a grand narrative,[3] the big picture, the metanarrative of the Scripture story, is so foreign to pastors and people in the pews? To cross-cultural Christian workers and those they serve at home and abroad? And those reaching post-modernists and post-truthers? Have we made the Bible one of the worst-taught books in the world?

Is it time to provide a clothesline (linear or circular) for all the individual pieces of clothing that comprise the wardrobe?

The grand tour question for this chapter is this: *Why is it important to view Scripture as a grand narrative?* To begin to answer this question, I will define a grand narrative of Scripture, provide reasons for its necessity, offer ways to identify it, and note some assumptions that drive it. I will conclude by presenting the grand narrative of the Scripture story that integrates four value systems—legal, relational, control, and hygienic—and provide two checklists to evaluate the author's comprehensiveness.

Meta What?

An assignment I give in classes is to write the theme (thesis) of the Bible in three or four sentences. *Impossible and unnecessary!* some students say. Note the responses of two seminarians:

> Why is it necessary in the first place to find a metanarrative in Scripture? Wouldn't it be enough to say, "The Psalms teach us one thing, the Prophets teach us a different thing, and the Gospels another, and the Epistles another?" They could all be inspired and yet nonconnected, couldn't they?

> I have been a Christian for twelve years; I have read my Bible from cover to cover; I have studied the Bible formally in Bible college, and informally in many small-group Bible studies. However, I have never, in all of my time as a Christian studying the Bible, heard of a method for teaching through God's story in a chronological way so that it is easier to understand. The only exceptions to this reality in my life were the Old and New Testament survey classes that I have taken. Despite the way that those classes attempted to teach somewhat chronologically, the classes were often more structured around different genres of the content of different biblical books, and the survey courses never actually intended to teach Scripture chronologically.

An insightful Indian seminarian, taught by Westerners, recognized that the pieces had to be placed into a unified whole to make sense. "For me, I began my life with Christ with a vague understanding of Truth, and then spent the next fifteen years picking through sermons and books, trying to get the pieces put together into the right places." A similar story from China:

> I'll never forget my second year in China. I was working with about four girls on Bible study tools/practices. I met with one of them for lunch; she was the oldest in the group and therefore the de facto leader. I asked her what she thought would be helpful to study in our next session (as I wanted it to meet their needs). She said, "I want to learn the Bible."

> Upon further conversation, I discovered she wanted to understand the metanarrative of the Bible, how it all fits together. I was able to explain on a chart the timeline of all the Bible stories and how they fit together that way. But I had no practice with or concept of a metanarrative in Scripture before she asked me that question, despite sixteen years of Christian schooling, each year with a Bible/theology class.

The Need for a Grand Narrative of Scripture

A grand narrative serves as a totalizing framework[4] for all the individual pieces, tying them into and expressing them as a unified whole; it is the narrative of narratives.[5] In relation to Scripture, the grand narrative answers the question, "What is this book all about?" It unpacks "the purpose of God in all its dimensions" (Acts 20:27 VOICE). And it transcends all other metanarratives.

Reflecting on how I initially learned the Bible, I realized that the sixty-six pieces of the puzzle were virtually scattered over the tabletop by my dedicated instructors, Sunday school teachers, and pastors—not unlike seminary curricula. Theologian David Wells concludes:

> Subjects and fields develop their own literatures, working assumptions, vocabularies, technical terms, criteria for what is true and false, and canons of what literature and what views should be common knowledge among those working in the subjects. The result of this is a profound increase in knowledge but often an equally profound loss in understanding what it all means, how the knowledge in one field should inform that in another. This is the bane of every seminarian's existence.[6]

Can sixty-six books written by multiple authors in different geographical locations over centuries actually produce a unified story? Philip Yancey writes:

> I find it remarkable that this diverse collection of manuscripts written over a period of a millennium by several dozen authors possesses as much unity as it does. To appreciate this feat, imagine a book begun 500 years before Columbus and just now completed. The Bible's striking unity is one strong sign that God directed its composition. By using a variety of authors and cultural situations, God developed a complete record of what he wants us to know; amazingly, the parts fit together in such a way that a single story does emerge.[7]

While definitely an untidy landscape of hills, valleys, deserts, bodies of water, lush fields, and forests, it is possible for a grand narrative to emerge. The sixty-six pieces of the puzzle can come together in a picture that closely resembles that which the Creator designed.[8]

Fragmentation can easily result in the loss of the big picture. Both the parts and the whole are necessary for true meaning to prevail. Flannery O'Connor reminds us that "the whole story is the meaning."[9] To lose the grand narrative is to lose the meaning that the totalizing framework is designed to provide and protect. T. Desmond Alexander concludes,

> Each book contributes something special to the metastory and, in turn, the metastory offers a framework within which each book may be best interpreted. In this regard, the longstanding principle of interpreting Scripture by Scripture makes considerable practical sense.[10]

Part of our hermeneutic must be to analyze the grand narrative. Why? Because "meanings emerge from literary *wholes*."[11]

If the grand narrative is lost, the possibility of misinformed interpretations increases. Michael Goheen suggests, "If the story of the Bible is fragmented into bits (historical-critical, devotional, homiletic, systematic-theological, moral) it can easily be domesticated by the reigning story of culture."[12] Jackson Wu posits a possible outcome:

> Lacking a framework inherent to the Bible, one inadvertently imposes a structure onto the narrative. Thus, many Western missionaries will naturally select and organize stories in ways that tacitly reflect Western culture. Even though they are using a "storying" methodology, their narrative becomes a "Trojan horse" for their systematic theology.[13]

Another reason for the necessity of a metanarrative is because one's understanding of the sweep of Scripture is the heart hermeneutic that interprets every other part that is heard, read, or seen. This is true whether one has articulated the grand narrative or not.

The psalmist reminds us, "The entirety of Your word is truth" (Psalm 119:160 VOICE). For a more complete understanding of *the Author and his Story*, our hermeneutic must encompass the sweep of Genesis through Revelation.[14]

Ways to Identify the Grand Narrative of Scripture

How do you decide which foods to choose first at an all-you-can-eat buffet? Do you automatically skip over some? How do you place them on your plate? Segregated parts? Overlapping piles? All mixed together? In what order do you eat them? What is your buffet-culture philosophy? What assumptions drive your samplings and selections? Are you a vegan? A carnivore? Have a sweet tooth?

Before going to a buffet, you might discuss the types of food offered at different locations—Italian, Brazilian, Chinese, Japanese—but you might rarely review your sampling, selection, and stacking philosophy. This does not mean you do not have one. Everyone has a foundational sampling, selection, and stacking philosophy, whether articulated or not. Moving the discussion from the buffet to the Bible, Wu raises some pertinent questions:

> Certainly, many missiologists rightly stress the need to tell the "grand story" of the Bible; yet, what framework are people using to shape that overarching narrative? What implicit theology underlies our story selection? On what basis have we chosen one story thread and not another?[15]

The seven-mile Emmaus-road trip is instructive in discovering the grand narrative of the Sacred Storybook. Roy Gingrich makes this astute observation about that eventful two-and-a-half hour walk down "Review Lane":

It cannot mean just a few scattered predictions about the Messiah. It means the Old Testament as a whole, encompassing all three of the major divisions of the Old Testament that the Jews traditionally recognized.... The Old Testament as a whole, through its promises, its symbols, and its pictures of salvation, looks forward to the actual accomplishment of salvation that took place once for all in the life, death, and resurrection of Jesus Christ.[16]

To discover the grand narrative of Scripture, it will be necessary to consider "the Old Testament as a whole"[17] (the Emmaus-road discussion) as well as a sweep of the New Testament. Here's how.

Compare the Bookends

Alexander rightly suggests that "a story's conclusion provides a good guide to the themes and ideas dominant throughout."[18] We can go further. Any well-written book or movie has strong ties between its prologue and epilogue. The Bible is no exception. Major matching themes, symbols, and rituals can be identified in Genesis 1–3 (prologue) and Revelation 21–22 (epilogue). Identifying these will aid in discovering the grand narrative of Scripture.

Identify Controlling Stories and Characters
The Bible contains around eight hundred stories.[19] Is the Bible a grab bag of stories? Of course not! Jennifer Jagerson astutely asks,

> Is it possible to teach a paradigmatic story from each book of the Bible that makes clear to the oral learner what the big picture of the book is about? Might these paradigmatic stories be used to knit together the larger picture of God's overarching historical work to help insure a strong understanding of the meta-narrative?[20]

This calls for identifying the controlling stories, those that serve as turning points to advance the storyline of the grand narrative, such as creation, fall, flood, Abrahamic covenant, building the temple, Jesus' life. *No, the Bible is not a grab bag of stories.*

What is true for story inclusion follows for characters. Glenn Paauw concludes, "If I can't tell you who Moses, Paul, Abraham, Jesus and David are, and in what order they appear in the Bible's drama, I can't possibly know much about what's really going on there."[21] *No, the Bible is not a grab bag of characters.*

Identify the Controlling Symbols and Rituals
Is the Bible a grab bag of symbols and rituals? Just as there are controlling stories and characters that help advance and define the grand narrative, so there are controlling symbols and rituals. Symbols like trees, doors, covenants, light, darkness, temples, rainbows, ark, dove, altars, blood, water, wind, circumcision, clothing, sheep, soap,

oil, temple, and others can be traced across the rugged landscape of Scripture, giving meaning to, and being defined by, the grand narrative. The same is true of controlling rituals—washings, offerings, communal meals, assembling together, baptisms. Identifying the controlling symbols and rituals will help bring clarity to the grand narrative.

Survey the Summary Verses

Good authors know that readers require periodic summaries, including authors of Scripture. Richard Bauckham notes, "The summaries are themselves part of the story and even contribute to the story's own development,"[22] which would include the grand narrative. Kevin Vanhoozer summarizes, "The rule of faith was not an invention of the church, but a 'construal' of Scripture as a unified narrative … nothing less than a summary of Scripture's own storyline."[23]

Some Old Testament summary statements include Exodus 3:15–17; 4:29–31; 6:6–9; 15; Deuteronomy 1:6–3:29; 6:10–25; 26:5–9; 32:7–43; Joshua 24:2–15; 1 Samuel 12:6–13; 1 Chronicles 16:14–22; Job 38; Psalms 76; 78; 105; 106:6–12; 136; Jeremiah 2:1–19; Nehemiah 9:5–37. New Testament summary statements include the genealogies in Matthew and Luke; Luke 24:27; Acts 7; 13; Romans 5–8; 9–10; Hebrews 11.

Determine the Acts of the Bible

A grand narrative of Scripture assumes that there are acts that connect the dots—the Bible bits—from Genesis through Revelation. It assumes all stories are embedded in other stories.[24] N. T. Wright concludes,

> Everything Paul says about Jesus belongs *within one or more of the other stories*, of the story of the creator and the cosmos, of the story of God and humankind and/or the story of God and Israel…. There really is, in one sense, a Pauline "story of Jesus," but it is always the story of how Jesus *enables the other stories* to proceed to their appointed resolution.[25]

How do various authors perceive the acts of the Scripture drama? The titles of these acts not only help discover how the authors perceive the grand narrative, they also spotlight the Hero of the document.[26]

Give Narrative Theology a Seat at the Table

I often ask students if they have taken classes in systematic theology. Every hand goes up. Biblical theology? Fewer hands go up. Historical theology? A few hands show, maybe. Narrative theology? A virtual unknown! How can that be if narrative is the predominant genre of Scripture? Why does systematic theology (pulling threads out of a weaving) reign as queen of the sciences in the seminaries taught by surgeon specialists?

In relation to theology, the Enlightenment was instrumental in replacing narrative with philosophy,[27] events with ideas, characters with concepts. Paauw posits:

> The abandonment of story in the modernist attempt to make sense of the Bible is one of the biggest mistakes God's people have made with the Scriptures in the entire history of the church... . It is precisely the narrative character of the Bible that allows us to make an authentic connection between these ancient writings and our own lives.[28]

Sadly, if there is little or no focus on narrative, certainly there will be *less focus still* on the grand narrative. But there is hope. Hannes Wiher notes, "The analytic, conceptual, guilt-oriented thought patterns of the Enlightenment made the narrative disappear, and their failure made it reappear again. The development of narrative theology has to do with the rediscovery of shame orientation in theology."[29]

Gabriel Fackre defines narrative theology as "discourse about God in the setting of story."[30] Since the predominant genre of Scripture is narrative, evangelicals must give narrative theology its rightful role in the hermeneutic process.[31]

The Bible did not arrive as Western systematic theology. Rather, systematic theology evolved over time from the multiple narratives comprising it as Western theologians teased out the answers to *their* questions. This often resulted in philosophical ideas being separated from characters and events. I call this "The Great Bifurcation." Most people who grew up on Western systematic theology will have to learn how to *re-story, re-narrate, re-drama, re-event, re-character, re-symbol, re-ritual, re-metaphor, and re-mystify* theology laundered of her earthiness so that abstract, philosophical concepts can be interfaced with concrete characters and events.

Narrative theology, which focuses on the entire text, determines the theologies. Both the whole and the parts are necessary. "Story is the ring that provides a setting for the precious gems of propositions."[32]

Consider Character Theology

What if there are other theologies that could paint different perspectives of the face of God? Could "character theology" add to existing theologies? With more than 2,900 characters in Scripture, how could they teach abstract doctrines? Ruth Tucker advocates pushing personalities to the front page:

> For many publishers and preachers and ordinary people, the Bible is largely a manual of propositions. The colorful personalities pushing their way out of its pages are seen as secondary—if that. But any attempt to turn this incredible chronicle into a theological dissertation destroys the very essence of its message. We learn how to live and how to die by putting ourselves into the narrative. Indeed, we recognize these characters by looking in the mirror.[33]

Here's how I define character theology:

> By character theology I mean utilizing some of the more than 2,900 human characters in the Bible, including groups, such as the Pharisees or Sadducees, along with those associated with the spirit world, such as the Holy Spirit, Satan, angels and demons, to teach abstract doctrines, morals, and ethics. Character theology relies on earthy, concrete characters to frame abstract truths and concepts, thereby giving ideas a home. It does so even as it retains God as the center of the story, and the individual story's place within the broader sweep of Scripture… . For example, rather than teach the abstract doctrine of justification by faith, let the earthy lives of Abraham and David define this abstract doctrine (Romans 4). Or, review the life of Moses to teach the doctrine of adoption… . Dogma without spiritual and human characters defining it is on the fast track to coldness. Bringing Bible characters out of the closet will heat up the conversation.[34]

Character theology, which should precede concept studies, provides a concrete way to redraw the face of God and break the bifurcation.

Character theology has the potential to paint a different picture of the face of God. That is because, as John Goldingay contends, the "story-shapedness of Scripture corresponds to the story-shapedness of human experience."[35] The lives of Bible characters speak to the lives of all peoples as they contain slices of life—family feuds, sickness, sexual sins, warfare, barrenness, birth, curses, death, power abuse, persecution, poverty, executions, making a living, making love, mishandling finances.[36] A cast of biblical characters makes it easy for us to identify with their choices, the resulting consequences, the implications they have for abstract doctrines, and the role they play in delineating the grand narrative of the Scripture story. Bible characters provide a rich reservoir from which to draw a more complete and correct picture of the face of God.

Discern and Develop Value Systems

When residing among the Ifugao of the Philippines, I intuitively presented the verbal gospel predominantly from my preferred value system expressed through the *legal language* of guilt and innocence (G-I).[37] As I unceremoniously discovered, "suitcase theology" has its limitations.

If I showed you a PowerPoint slide that pictured well-known Western evangelism models—*The Four Spiritual Laws, The Romans Road, Evangelism Explosion,* Chronological Bible Storying (Firm Foundations), Simply the Story—and asked you what all these models have in common, how would you respond?

All are based on legal language (G-I).[38] Nothing is wrong with that unless G-I is not one of the culture's preferred value systems. Timothy Tennent tells us why:

Since Western systematic theology has been almost exclusively written by theologians from cultures framed primarily by the values of guilt and innocence, there has been a corresponding failure to fully appreciate the importance of the pivotal values of honor and shame in understanding Scripture and the doctrine of sin. Even with the publication of important works such as *Biblical Social Values and Their Meaning* and *The New Testament World*, systematic theologies have remained largely unchanged by this research. In fact, a survey of all of the leading textbooks used in teaching systematic theology across the major theological traditions reveals that although the indexes are filled with references to guilt, the word "shame" appears in the index of only one of these textbooks.[39]

Relevant Western evangelism must move beyond the sole value system of G-I.

A Greater Variety of Value Systems?

Ever since Eugene Nida identified three reactions to sin as guilt-based (G-I), fear-based (F-P), and shame-based (S-H), most have followed suit. The trilogy dominates the past and present literature: 1) G-I: legal language, 2) F-P: control language, and 3) S-H: relational language. But could there be a fourth? Even more?

I added a fourth value system, hygienic language—pollution/purity (P-P). Here's the rationale:

> Werner Mischke addresses purity/pollution (P-P) in *The Global Gospel* as one of the sub-dynamics of the honor/shame value system…, . When considering its dominance in both the Old and New Testaments, and various cultures around the world, I wonder if P-P represents a fourth value system—another possible "first among equals"? One would expect to find this value system in those religions tied to Abraham—Judaism, Christianity, Islam—and other religions, such as Hinduism, Shintoism, and aspects of animism among First Nations tribes. Trauma victims, e.g., those sold into sexual slavery, could also be included.[40]

Interestingly, during the early years of the modern-day orality movement,[41] the definition of orality rarely expanded beyond story, and there was an expectation that when storying, one would only tell stories—no PowerPoint or other aids, no propositions. Oral-preference people just tell stories.

Today, however, those within the movement have greatly enlarged the definition to include song, the arts, symbols, rituals, drama, etc.[42] Even the definitions of orality have changed. And the central theorist, Walter Ong, has been challenged. Those within the honor-shame movement may find themselves on a similar learning curve. The trilogy initially introduced by Nida[43] may need expansion.

Check Your Radar Screen for Shame-Honor

The value system of S-H began to show up on the radar screens of Western cross-cultural workers around 2000. Presently, articles and books continue to roll off the presses. Activities proliferate. For example, in 2014 Andy Crouch, then with *Christianity*

Today, attended an orality consultation convened by the International Orality Network (ION) that focused on honor-shame.[44] Riding with him from the airport to Houston Baptist University, I asked why he was attending this consultation focused strongly on cross-cultural contexts. He responded that he was there to "eavesdrop on this missions conversation." Note this summary with a slight Americanized twist:

> So instead of evolving into a traditional honor-shame culture, large parts of our culture are starting to look something like a postmodern fame-shame culture. Like honor, fame is a public estimation of worth, a powerful currency of status. But fame is bestowed by a broad audience, with only the loosest of bonds to those they acclaim… . Some of the most powerful artifacts of contemporary culture—especially youth culture—are preoccupied with the dynamics of fame and shame.[45]

Edward Welch captures the critical necessity to slow-walk shame through the narrative ark of the Scripture story:

> The Bible, it turns out, is all about shame and its remedy. Why else would it be introduced at the very beginning? … Since shame is so painful, we could be tempted to race to the end of the story and hope to be done with it quickly. But shame rarely responds to quick fixes. Better to walk through the biblical story than run through it. There is much to be learned from shame's long history.[46]

In 2013, the Cook School of Intercultural Studies, Biola University, offered its first graduate course on honor-shame. Distinguished dissertations on the topic have resulted from scholar-practitioners: Patty Toland's "Redeeming and Strengthening Honor and Shame Practices in Church Relations" (2015) and Lynn Thigpen's "Redeeming the Poverty-Shame-Limited Education Cycle through Gracing" (2016).

Discern Value-System Percentages

Most cultures have two or more preferred value systems. For the animistic Ifugao of the Philippines, F-P and S-H dominate. G-I and P-P have little influence on their daily lives. That does not mean that the last two are inferior or unimportant. Rather, the Ifugao value two: F-P and S-H. It also means that my initial evangelism focused on only one of their preferred values (F-P) and one of mine (G-I). Communication noise—the lack of resonance or clarity—naturally resulted.

In sum, what are the assumptions behind identifying a grand narrative of the Scripture story? They include at least the following:

1. History belongs to God.
2. God is the hero of history.
3. History is story-shaped.
4. History is eschatological.
5. Scripture belongs to God.
6. God is the hero of Scripture.
7. Scripture is story-shaped.

8. Scripture is eschatological.
9. Chosen characters advance the storyline.
10. The gospel is embedded in God's total story.
11. We find our story of significance in "(His)Story."
12. God's story provides the hermeneutic to interpret Scripture.
13. God's story exposes heresy.
14. God's story challenges every worldview and theology.
15. God's story provides a framework for authentic local-global theology.
16. God's story offers softness and pliability for various faith traditions.
17. God is defined by what he does.

Whether we are at a buffet or reading the Bible, our unarticulated assumptions prevail in most of our eating and meaning-making practices. It is time to articulate them because it is difficult to leverage what we have not articulated.

Analyzing a Grand Narrative of the Scripture Story

Each value system has its preferred *terms for God* (Satan has counterfeits). The *legal language* of G-I assigns names to God, such as Just, Righteous One, Lawgiver, Judge, Truth, Merciful. The *control language* of F-P assigns him names like King, Master, Victor, Liberator, Almighty, Prince of Peace, Consuming Fire. The *relational language* of S-H prefers Father, Faithful, Wonderful Counselor, Shepherd, Jealous One. The *hygienic language* of P-P favors Purifier, Refiner, Holy, Physician.[47]

Each value system has its preferred *role for Jesus* as well (Satan has counterfeits). The *legal language* of G-I assigns Jesus' role as substitute. The *control language* of F-P allocates Jesus' role as victor. The *relational language* of S-H prefers mediator, while the *hygienic language* of P-P favors purifier.

We must never forget, however, how integrated these value systems are within a culture's daily conversations, music,[48] and perceptions of the Scripture story.[49] All four can be found in 2 Timothy 1:3–13, Hebrews 1:1–8, and 1 Peter 1:21–22. The texts of Bible authors flow smoothly from one value system to another. Overlap is common.

I offer below an example of a grand narrative. It incorporates the four value systems (S-H, G-I, F-P, P-P) while *focusing primarily on shame-honor (S-H)*. This exercise raises two questions: In presenting the gospel, how much emphasis should I place on each of the host culture's four value systems?[50] What are the emphases within my culture?

As mentioned, this example of a grand narrative is based primarily on S-H values:

Father God is Creator-King of the Universe. He alone is God. His most glorious creation is humanity—made in God's image and even given regal responsibility over all the earth. Yes, Father God shares his royal honor and glory with humanity. Together, God the Father and humanity are meant to be co-patrons over the earth for the flourishing of all creation. What beauty, life, and glory is to come for all humanity in relationship with Father God.

But Father God has a terrible enemy—an evil being of immense power and intelligence. Evil Enemy deceives humanity into exchanging God's royal image and responsibility for low and shameful selfishness. Oh, the disloyalty! Oh, how this dishonors Father God, who wants only the very best for humanity!

Tragedy of tragedies! Humanity falls from high regal glory and honor—to death and shame. Evil's curse and evil's shame wash over all humanity. Humanity becomes dirty and ugly—death and pain for everyone. In rejecting Father God's true and honorable ways, humanity becomes haughty, disloyal, polluted, guilty, shameful.

Has Evil Enemy won the battle against Father God and humanity? Will Father God re-establish his rightful noble rule? Will humanity ever recover their honor and glory?

Father God had already conceived a plan before the beginning with God's Spirit and with God's Son, Jesus. In the divine plan, Jesus does the unthinkable: Jesus is King of kings, co-Creator, Holy and Compassionate One. And yet, Jesus humbles himself; he relinquishes his rightful glory. Jesus enters into humanity's relational pollution. Jesus lives among humans, but without sin, without fear, in perfect loyalty and love. He shows us how to truly live. Then Jesus suffers the most shameful death—executed in public, naked, nailed to a cross. Jesus' blood is shed in violent death—in order to kill humanity's violence. Jesus absorbs humanity's sin and shame. Jesus is perfectly loyal as he glorifies Father God; the divine plan to re-establish God's righteous rule over all the earth is now possible. Oh, Jesus! What a Hero, what a Savior!

Father God greatly rewards Jesus' noble, most humble sacrifice. The shame of Jesus' death is vindicated! Father God raises Jesus from death and gives him a name above all names—and the most honorable position at his right hand. Jesus reigns in highest honor with Father God forever and ever!

Now justice, purity, peace, and honor are available to everyone who follows Jesus from every nation and people. His followers demonstrate their obedience, trust, and loyalty as worshiping co-laborers, filling their lives with truth, pureness, power, and honor as they imitate Jesus. Yes, they suffer—but it is a badge of honor reflecting the way of Jesus. They joyfully serve to bring Father's blessing to all the peoples of the earth. And they impatiently await the final restoration of the world. They become more and more like their Hero as they share in his honor, worshiping and modeling their lives to be like King Jesus.

Evil Enemy is defeated! Death and shame are finished! Humanity is re-glorified in union with Jesus! Glory to God forever!

Having a checklist to evaluate one's grand narrative of Scripture will help creative composers to adjust their attempts as they strive toward accuracy and attractiveness.[51] I have therefore created two checklists (see Figures 1 and 2). Who is the protagonist? The antagonist? What is the issue God must deal with first? What issue are people facing? What is the resolution to solve both issues? What choices can people make? What are the consequences of such choices? Is anything of scriptural significance missing from my version of the narrative?

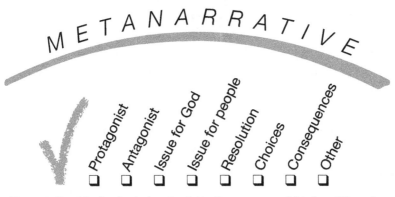

Figure 1: Checklist for Analyzing the Story Components of the Grand Narrative

None of the four value systems ever stands alone. Rather, each is intrinsically tied to other value systems, and to cultural institutions (e.g., economics, politics, social structure, religion, the arts). A second checklist, therefore, is required (see Figure 2).

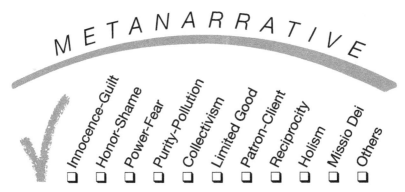

Figure 2: Checklist for Analyzing the Cultural Components of the Grand Narrative

Four Value Systems

The checklist begins with a search for the four value systems—G-I, F-P, S-H, and P-P. As noted above, every culture has all four, but rarely does it give equal emphasis to all four. Most, like the Ifugao, favor two (F-P; S-H). I'm not aware of any that favors all four equally.

Collectivism

Collectivism is strongly tied to relational-based shame and honor. While Westerners tend to place great emphasis on the individual, Scripture awards it to groups—e.g., Jews/Israel, extended families, the church, the elect, the Pharisees, Gentiles, and so forth.

Limited Good

The concept of limited good comes in multiple versions and is as relative today as in Bible times. It is premised on the idea that only so much of a certain good (tangible or intangible) exists, and it cannot be multiplied. If there are only four apples, and someone has three, the rest of us are limited to one. It's a zero-sum game that requires redistribution because "Someone's advantage is someone else's disadvantage."[52] Envy is never far from the concept of limited good. Interestingly, God's offer of grace and mercy is never limited.

Patron-Client

Another inclusion, again tied closely to relational-based shame and honor, is patron-client. Both roles dominate Scripture on the human and spiritual levels. Patron refers to a person or spirit who has the means (networks, advice, money, power to bless or protect) to aid someone in need. On the bottom end of this hierarchy, clients look to the patron to supply their needs, whether short- or long-term. As an African proverb states, "The hand that receives is always under the hand that gives." While either can initiate the relationship, both usually know the social risks involved.

Reciprocity

The bi-directional obligation between patron and client demands reciprocity even in this lopsided friendship. Reciprocity could be defined as "an implicit, non-legal contractual obligation, unenforceable by any authority apart from one's sense of honor and shame."[53] A Chinese proverb captures the patron's perspective: "I shower blessings on those who submit to me and do all I can to subvert those who resist."

When the client is unable to return the gift in kind, there is something that he or she can still offer the patron: public praise. "Honor is the currency of the powerless; it is what clients short on material goods can offer to patrons."[54] A fair return, not an equal return, is expected. Praising your patron in public will often suffice, as it demonstrates the client's allegiance and loyalty.

Word and Works Go Together

The Bible is never content with addressing only soulish or spiritual issues. At creation, souls were given bodies along with a beautiful garden in which to reside. Someday they will receive new bodies and live in a new environment.

We are commanded to multiply the number of those who honor God globally (see Habakkuk 2:14 for end results) and be stewards of the world (Gen 1:28). Whole nations require whole churches. Whole churches require the whole gospel for the whole person and the whole community. The Great Commission and the Great Commandment fit hand in glove.

Missio Dei

Often missed by theologians and, consequently, pastors is the *missio Dei*. The Great Commission didn't originate in the Gospels, but rather early in Genesis. Genesis 3:15 lays the foundation for the good news, as it introduces the antagonist and the necessary warfare that must follow before the Protagonist triumphs in total victory. Abraham begins to grasp God's great concern for the nations as the Lord speaks to him in Genesis 12:1–3. The New Testament gospel finds its roots burrowed deep in the Old Testament. If we are to grasp the *missio Dei*, argue Ashford and Nelson, we must capture its connection to the grand narrative:

In order to build a biblical-theological framework for understanding God's mission, the church's mission, and the church's mission to the nations, one must first understand the unified biblical narrative, including its four major plot movements— creation, fall, redemption, and restoration.[55]

Wrap-Up

Why is it important to view Scripture as a single grand narrative? Because it paints a comprehensive picture of the face of God beyond its individual parts. Whether a linear (Emmaus-road review) or circular clothesline, the clothesline keeps the individual pieces in place even as it reveals the wide range of the wardrobe. While each piece of clothing has value, the cumulative value of all the pieces supersedes that of any one individual piece. *The whole is greater than the parts.* If we are to grasp a bigger, broader, more comprehensive picture of the face of God, we must not only know and value the individual pieces of clothing, but— more importantly—know and value how they together form a comprehensive wardrobe that brings honor to both wearer and Tailor.

Failure to comprehend the Bible as a sacred storybook composed of multiple acts that move mysteriously to completion opens the door to misinterpretation. Our cultures, framed by rival grand narratives, often substitute content, characters, and context. Why is a metanarrative needed? Because "The metanarrative of Scripture fights a fragmented and false understanding of the Sacred Storybook."[56]

All those adhering to rival grand narratives must, and someday will (Phil 2:9–10), submit to the grand narrative of the Scripture story. How well do you know the hermeneutic that interprets the individual events and the grand narrative? Can you articulate it in a few sentences?

The Scripture story centers on relationships. More precisely, it centers on restored relationships designed to reinstate God's rightful honor and universal kingdom among the nations (Rev 21:26–27). Though an ancient story, it remains relevant and true.

Sadly, too much of the gospel—especially segments from the Old Testament that strongly depict God's interaction with humanity through curses and blessings, thereby defining him—has been left scattered on the cutting-room floor. *Far too often, we have made the gospel a mini-narrative, making it ripe for cultural reduction and reinterpretation.* Does your evangelism include an Emmaus-road-review?

The value system of S-H is framed in relationships (spiritual, human, material), a major theme in the grand narrative of the Scripture story. This message speaks with clarity and conviction to tribal peoples in the deepest jungles, to urbanite millennials in the most modern of cities, to international students who study at our universities. Jesus Christ preserves God's honor by being the One by whom God fulfills his promise to bless all the peoples of the earth. Jesus is both the Patron/God who gives his life for salvation and the mediator who bridges the chasm between God-as-Patron and humanity-as-client. The world's peoples, whose inherited and practiced sin deeply dishonors the Patron, are drawn to the unlimited gift of Jesus—salvation: forgiveness of sin, complete acceptance, full inclusion, real community, genuine worth, transcendence.

In return, through the wooing of the Holy Spirit, faith-responders change allegiance, display loyalty, participate in faith communities, and offer God praise collectively and individually. This holistic message from the Creator-Redeemer is especially meaningful to these audiences when communicated through the grand narrative of the Scripture story that includes the value system(s) they appreciate. The clothes hanging on the linear or circular clothesline now define the wide-ranging scope of the wardrobe Owner. The gospel is revealed as good news because the acts in the Scripture story honor its Hero, and its hearers discover themselves and a new community within that unparalleled story.

To gain a more comprehensive picture of the face of God and his story, we need to see him through at least these four cuts of the diamond—G-I; F-P; S-H; P-P. To present a gospel message that hits not only the heads but also the hearts of our audience, we must present the good news through the sweep of Scripture in the percentages of the various value systems that *they* place on its narrative. This will help paint a more precise picture of the face of God, gaining him more honor and devotion.

For Further Reflection

1. Steffen quotes Edward Welch: "The Bible, it turns out, is all about shame and its remedy." How does this claim strike you? How do you read the Bible and its grand narrative in ways that reflect this?

2. Locate the "grand narrative of the Scripture story" that Steffen presents on page 38; read it aloud as if you were teaching it to someone who had never heard this message. In what ways does this differ from your traditional understanding about the overall story of the Bible? How might this impact how you communicate the gospel?

CHAPTER 3 Endnotes

1 Parts of this chapter were originally published in the *Great Commission Research Journal* and are included here with permission.

2 In my training with New Tribes Mission (now Ethnos360), I memorized four New Testament letters.

3 Defining the postmodern age as "incredulity toward metanarratives" in *The Postmodern Condition* (1979), Jean-Francois Lyotard is credited with popularizing the term "metanarrative."

4 Richard Bauckham, *Bible and Mission: Christian Witness in a Postmodern World* (Grand Rapids: Baker, 2003), 87.

5 Christopher Wright asserts, "The Bible presents itself to us fundamentally as a narrative, a historical narrative at one level, but a grand metanarrative at another." Christopher J. H. Wright, *The Mission of God: Unlocking the Bible's Grand Narrative* (Downers Grove, IL: InterVarsity, 2006), 63.

6 David F. Wells, *No Place for Truth, or, Whatever Happened to Evangelical Theology?* (Grand Rapids: Eerdmans, 1993), 224.

7 Philip Yancey, *The Bible Jesus Read: Why the Old Testament Matters* (Grand Rapids: Zondervan, 1999), 21.

8 Two early influential authors who concentrated on the metanarrative of Scripture include W. Graham Scroggie, *The Unfolding Drama of Redemption: The Bible as a Whole* (Three Volumes Complete and Unabridged in One) (Grand Rapids: Zondervan, 1970); and Daniel P. Fuller, *The Unity of the Bible: Unfolding God's Plan for Humanity* (Grand Rapids: Zondervan, 1992).

9 Flannery O'Connor, *Mystery and Manners: Occasional Prose* (New York: Farrar, Straus and Giroux, 1969), 73.

10 T. Desmond Alexander, *From Eden to the New Jerusalem: An Introduction to Biblical Theology* (Grand Rapids: Kregel, 2008), 10.

11 Leland Ryken, *Words of Delight: A Literary Introduction to the Bible* (Grand Rapids: Baker Academic, 2005), 82.

12 Michael W. Goheen, "The Urgency of Reading the Bible as One Story in the Twenty-first Century" (p. 9). Public lecture presented at Regent College, Vancouver, BC, November 2, 2006.

13 Jackson Wu, "Rewriting the Gospel for Oral Cultures: Why Honor and Shame are Essential to the Gospel Story," in *Beyond Literate Western Contexts: Honor & Shame and Assessment of Orality Preference* ed. Samuel E. Chiang and Grant Lovejoy (Hong Kong: Capstone Enterprisers Ltd., 2015), 70.

14 See Steffen, "Pedagogical Conversions: From Propositions to Story and Symbol," *Missiology: An International Review 38, no. 2 (2010):* 153–54; and also Steffen, "Discoveries Made While Reconnecting God's Story to Scripture and Service," *Christian Education Journal Series* 3, 14, no. 1 (2007): 178–79.

15 Wu, "Rewriting the Gospel," 74.

16 Roy E. Gingrich, *Old Testament Survey* (Memphis: Riverside Printing, 2001), 4.

17 J. Daniel Hays contends,

"The prophets are powerful and inspiring. Their criticism of sin and injustice is harsh, scathing, and unyielding. Yet their words to the faithful are gentle and encouraging. Furthermore, in the prophets we are able to engage with God himself, for he is a major character throughout the prophetic material. God speaks and acts. He grieves, hurts, explodes in anger, comforts, loves, rebukes, and restores. God reveals much about himself through the prophets. We see his transcendence—that is, his 'otherness.' He is sovereign over all the world and in total control of history. Isaiah will ask, Who can comprehend God or his ways? Yet we are also shown God's immanence—his presence with us and his 'connectedness' to his people on earth.

"Likewise, the prophets have a lot to say about people. In the prophets we see a story unfold that recounts how the people of Israel (and their neighbors) responded to God and his revelation to them. We see a tragic story of rebellion against God, followed by terrible consequences. Yet at the same time the prophets show us God's great capacity for forgiveness reflected in his constant call for repentance and renewal of the hearts of his wayward people. Although most of the people will reject God's call for repentance, the prophets will also tell us their own personal stories—how they encountered God and then proclaimed his word valiantly and faithfully in dangerous and hostile situations." J. Daniel Hays, *The Message of the Prophets: A Survey of the Prophetic and Apocalyptic Books of the Old Testament* (Grand Rapids: Zondervan, 2010), 22.

18 Alexander, *From Eden*, 10.

19 Personal correspondence with Grant Lovejoy, July 2, 2009.

20 Jennifer Jagerson, "Hermeneutics and the Methods of Oral Bible Storytelling for the Evangelization and Discipleship of Oral Learners," *Great Commission Research Journal* 4, no. 2 (2013): 260.

21 Glenn R. Paauw, *Saving the Bible from Ourselves: Learning to Read & Live the Bible Well* (Downers Grove, IL: InterVarsity, 2016), 13.

22 Bauckham, *Bible and Mission*, 42.

23 Kevin J. Vanhoozer, *The Drama of Doctrine: A Canonical Linguistic Approach to Christian Doctrine* (Louisville: Westminster /John Knox Press, 2005), 204, 206.

24 "Story" also assumes the embeddedness of a cultural context (e.g., political, economic, religious, geographic, etc.).

25 N. T. Wright, *Paul and the Faithfulness of God*, Book 1, Parts I and II (Minneapolis: Fortress, 2013), 517.

26 Duvall and Hays correctly assert, "If we miss God in the story, then we have missed the story." J. S. Duvall and J. D. Hays, *Grasping God's Word: A Hands-on Approach to Reading, Interpreting, and Applying the Bible* (Grand Rapids: Zondervan, 2012), 349.

27 Bruce Bradshaw notes, "According to Jacques Ellul, 'all errors in Christian thought' began when Christianity shifted the center of theology from history to philosophy." *Change across Cultures: A Narrative Approach to Social Transformation* (Grand Rapids: Baker Academic, 2002), 22.

28 Paauw, *Saving the Bible*, 106.

29 Hannes Wiher, *Shame and Guilt: A Key to Cross-Cultural Ministry* (Bonn, Germany: Culture and Science Publ., 2003), 333.

30 Gabriel Fackre, "Narrative Theology: An Overview," in *Interpretation* 37 (1983): 343.

31 In reviving narrative theology (for some in the evangelical world), I'm not including that aspect that denies the historicity of the biblical narrative.

32 Tom Steffen, *Worldview-based Storying: The Integration of Symbol, Story, and Ritual in the Orality Movement* (Richmond: The Rainmaker, 2018), 138.

33 Ruth A. Tucker, *The Biographical Bible: Exploring the Biblical Narrative from Adam and Eve to John of Patmos* (Grand Rapids: Baker, 2013), 2.

34 Steffen, *Worldview-based Storying*, 211.

35 John Goldingay, "Biblical Story and the Way It Shapes Our Story," in *The Journal of the European Pentecostal Theological Association* 17: 5–15 (1997): 6.

36 Rob Bell says it this way: "We have to embrace the Bible as the wild, uncensored, passionate account it is of people experiencing the living God... . We cannot tame it." *Velvet Elvis: Repainting the Christian Faith* (Grand Rapids: Zondervan, 2005), 63.

37 Because of their animistic background, I also included fear-power.

38 The same is true of Western discipleship models.

39 Timothy Tennent, "Anthropology: Human Identity in Shame-Based Cultures of the Far East," in *Theology in the Context of World Christianity* (Grand Rapids: Zondervan, 2007), 91–92.

40 Werner Mischke, *The Global Gospel: Achieving Missional Impact in Our Multicultural World*, (Scottsdale, AZ: Mission ONE, 2015); see chapter 2.9, "Honor/Shame Dynamic #9: Purity," 161–80.

41 Steffen, *Worldview-based Storying*, 102–3.

42 See Michael Matthews, *A Novel Approach: The Significance of Story in the Hermeneutic of Reality* (TellWell, 2017); Steffen, *Worldview-Based Storying*; and Robert Strauss, *Introducing Story-Strategic Methods: Twelve Steps toward Effective Engagement* (Eugene, OR: Wipf & Stock, 2017).

43 Eugene Nida, *Customs and Cultures: Anthropology for Christian Missions* (Pasadena, CA: William Carey Library, 1975).

44 See Chiang and Lovejoy, eds., *Beyond Literate Western Contexts: Honor & Shame and Assessment of Orality Preference*, Capstone Enterprises Ltd. (Hong Kong: International Orality Network, 2015).

45 Andy Crouch, "The Return of Shame," *Christianity Today*, March 10, 2015, 32–41.

46 Edward T. Welch, *Shame Interrupted: How God Lifts the Pain of Worthlessness and Rejection* (Greensboro, NC: New Growth Press, 2012), 113.

47 The Bible does not have these value systems in silos, as I discuss below; these systems sometimes overlap. The name "King" offers an example. In the guilt-innocence system, God as "King" is Ruler and Judge who establishes justice and forgives; in the fear-power system, God as "King" is Master, Victor, Liberator who defeats his enemies and rescues his people; in the shame-honor system, God as "King" is known for his glory and royal majesty—he provides a kingdom in which his people are blessed and flourishing. See Psalm 110:1–7.

48 Can you spot the four value systems in the first stanza of Lauren Daigle's song "How Can It Be?" *I am guilty / Ashamed of what I've done, what I've become / These hands are dirty / I dare not lift them up to the Holy One.* Lauren Daigle (Jason Ingram and Jeff Johnson, songwriters) *How Can It Be?*, "How Can It Be?", Track 2, Centricity Music, 2015. https://genius.com/Lauren-daigle-how-can-it-be-lyrics.

49 In a PowerPoint presentation of the descriptors of Jesus in the Gospels, my student Joel Butler estimated the cumulative breakdown in the Gospels to be: G-I: 2%; F-P: 37%; S-H: 45%; P-P: 16%. Presented in Spokane, WA (Moody Bible Institute), Jan 6, 2017, in my "Honor and Shame in Scripture & Service" class.

50 How dominant is the value system of shame-honor in Scripture in comparison to the West's favorite—guilt-innocence? Timothy Tennent observes: "A survey of all of the leading textbooks used in teaching systematic theology across the major theological traditions reveals that although the indexes are filled with references to guilt, the word 'shame' appears in the index of only one of these textbooks. This omission continues to persist despite the fact that the term guilt and its various derivatives occur 145 times in the Old Testament and 10 times in the New Testament, whereas the term shame and its derivatives occur nearly 300 times in the Old Testament and 45 times in the New Testament" (*Theology in the Context*, 92). Hannes Wiher came up with different statistics from both Testaments. He found that shame and honor had a grand total of 968 while guilt and justice had 1,350 (*Shame and Guilt*, 214–15).

51 James D. G. Dunn shows the strengths of what postmoderns perceive as weaknesses in having a grand narrative, which is applicable for a grand narrative of Scripture: "The problem being that the single grand narrative effectively brackets out a good deal of the data, privileges some of the data as more conducive to the story the historian wants to tell, and orders the selected data into a narrative sequence which validates the view put forward by the modern historian." *The Oral Gospel Tradition* (Grand Rapids: Eerdmans, 2013), 203.

52 George M. Foster, *Tzintzuntzan: Mexican Peasants in a Changing World* (Boston: Little, Brown, 1996), 124.

53 Dictionary of Socio-Rhetorical Terms, http://www.religion.emory.edu/faculty/robbins/SRI/defns/r_defns.cfm . Based upon Vernon K. Robbins, *Exploring the Texture of Texts*, Valley Forge, PA: Trinity Press International, 1996 and Vernon K. Robbins, *The Tapestry of Early Christianity: Rhetoric, Society, and Ideology*, London and New York: Routledge, 1996.

54 Marilyn McCord Adams, *Horrendous Evils and the Goodness of God* (Ithaca, NY: Cornell University Press, 1999), 126.

55 Bruce Riley Ashford and David P. Nelson, "The Story of Mission: The Grand Biblical Narrative," in *Theology and Practice of Mission: God, the Church, and the Nations*, ed. Bruce Riley Ashford (Nashville: B&H Academic, 2011), 6.

56 Steffen, "Discoveries Made While Reconnecting God's Story to Scripture and Service," in *Christian Education Journal* Series 3, 14, no. 1 (2017): 179.

SAVING US FROM ME:
Cultivating Honor and Shame in a Collectivist Church

JACKSON WU

Many dystopian novels have recently emerged in Western culture. *1984* is a classic example. *Hunger Games*, the *Divergent* series, and *The Giver* are a few recent dystopian movies and books. Dystopian stories are extreme versions of a common Western story: the lone individual heroically resists the group. Social power forces conformity and suppresses individuality. From one perspective, the individual is a rebel; from another perspective, he or she simply wants freedom.

But what if we turned this story around? What if, in this alternative story, contemporary Western society is a dystopia—tyrannized not by the state but by the individual? I believe that many of our lives are episodes of this dystopian story.

As a child, I never liked Father's Day—the one day each year that I knew I had to lie. If not, I would be complicit by giving my stepfather a card, which my mother bought on my behalf. Father's Day cards usually express affection for our dads. Or they explain why we have the best father in the world. The problem, however, was that I never thought mine was the world's best dad. I didn't even think he was a "good" dad.

This memory is just one scratch atop countless other bruises. I could tell more stories about my extended family—about suicide, drug addiction, divorce, abandonment, jail, etc. My mom dropped out of school at age fifteen to take care of me. Her family said that she was selfish to bring a child into our chaotic family. They refused to support her. My grandmother told my mother to abort me. In practice, much of our family operated on the principle of "every man for himself."

As a child, I knew I wanted to be different. I did *not* want to be like my family. What I didn't yet know was how much I'd learn about the relationship between honor, shame, and identity—that is, even at that young age I had already internalized important lessons about how our group identity profoundly shapes our sense of honor and shame.

Like anyone else, I wanted to belong to a community. So I focused my efforts on managing my reputation. This was my strategy for being accepted and gaining community. With anger and ambition, I threw myself into girls, sports, and my studies. Unfortunately, my academic success provoked my family. By becoming educated, I became an outsider. They compared themselves to me and felt embarrassed. My mother began to habitually call me "stupid"—to make herself feel better, I suppose.

A few years later, my family responded differently when I earned a scholarship to West Point. When asked why I applied to West Point, I unabashedly said, "I want to be great. And West Point is the best." Yet, once again my mom "stole my glory" by bragging that my achievement was a result of her parenting. She used me as a way of gaining public "face."

Growing up in an individualistic family, I saw plenty of selfish and shameful behavior. They didn't care about the opinions of others. In many respects, my family was shameless. So I wanted to be different, to rise above a banal existence. That was my hope of salvation.

I accepted the standard dystopian story, in which individuality stands above society and brings salvation. Being saved means being an individual who breaks from the community. While this idea is grossly problematic, it reflects the practical thinking of many Christians influenced by Western culture. The Bible tells a very different gospel story of individualism than many Westerners assume; yet, this gospel story is actually no less dystopian.

Whereas typical dystopia is the story of the individual in the community, I want to consider the story of the community that shapes individuals. How does all of this (i.e., dystopia, individualism, etc.) concern honor and shame? Honor and shame are integral to worldview and identity. Where Western individualism pervades the church, it perverts our sense of honor and shame. Therefore, we ask, "How does an individualistic worldview shape our understanding of the church and our approach to ministry?" How do we contribute to a systematic problem that undermines a Christian perspective of honor and shame?

To answer these questions, I will first examine how Western culture subtly influences our view of the gospel and the church. Second, I will consider the relationship between collective identity, honor, and shame. A biblical sense of honor and shame can only grow by fostering collective identity *within* the church. Finally, I will suggest six areas of application.

The Gospel for Individuals: "Be Different"

Western culture implicitly preaches a false gospel. According to this message, we should *"carpe diem,"* or "seize the day." Whether by books, movies, advertising, news media, or public figures, Western culture proclaims our need for salvation—from being average or normal, from authorities that require conformity, from tradition, and especially from "organized religion." Marketers proclaim this false gospel. A sample advertising slogan that targets individualistic Americans involves an Army recruiting commercial in which a Corporal Lovett says, "And I'll be the first to tell you, the might of the US Army doesn't lie in numbers. It lies in me. I am an Army of one."[1]

The felt need to prove our worth is simply another form of legalism. For most people, legalism is not about earning eternal life. At its root, it concerns honor and shame. The mantra is "Gotta do more. Gotta be more."[2] People want acceptance. They want to belong. So they do more to be more.

Fathers want public recognition at work, so they spend countless hours away from family and church. "Gotta do more. Gotta be more." Mothers over-commit themselves (and their kids) to show their capabilities. They fear showing weakness, accepting the lie that they should be able to do everything—and make it look easy. "Gotta do more. Gotta be more." When marriage gets tough, couples divorce, since the relationship suppresses their individuality. The competition for attention on social media is fierce. To stand out, people invest significant time that could be poured into face-to-face relationships. Then they feel the pressure of living up to their public persona. "Gotta do more. Gotta be more."

A Chinese idiom says, "A bird who pokes its head out gets shot." That bird is unique and different. But being different for its own sake is not heroic; it just makes the bird dead. Standing out from the crowd doesn't bring acceptance; it makes us alone.[3]

This individualistic way of thinking creates a conundrum for anyone influenced by Western culture. People have competing desires—as humans, wanting community; but as individuals, competing for honor. Perpetual comparison undermines community. My former pastor often reiterated, "Comparison is the thief of joy. It makes us either proud or discouraged."[4] The idolatry of individuality leads to either fame or shame.[5] Fame is temporary. Shame endures. Inevitably, the truth comes out: You are unique, just like everyone else.

Rod Dreher aptly summarizes the fruit of individualism:

A society that has no strong concept of the Good other than granting individuals within it maximum liberty to live as they prefer to is not a society that has within in it the capacity to govern itself, or to endure. A religion that is only about formless "love" is a religion that worships emotion, and that ends up making an idol of the Self.[6]

When this perspective shapes the church, it stunts our ability to honor Christ and love others. How many Christians influenced by the West unwittingly contribute to this idolatry of self?

Sacrificing the Church to Save Individuals

The Western gospel seeks to save individuals while sacrificing the church. Traditional gospel presentations implicitly foster an individualistic orientation. One Christian website asks, "Why does God love you?" It gives this answer:

> Why does God need you when He has so many billions of others? … So why can we possibly be of such great value that God would die for us? Each of us? What do you have that none other can fulfill? And the answer is: Your "UNIQUENESS." "Unique" is defined as: "Being the only one of its kind. Without an equal or equivalent, unparalleled."[7]

Many Christians repeat this claim: "He loves you so much that if you were the only person living on earth, He would still have sent His Son to die for you on the cross."[8] They think the gospel primarily concerns how an individual person is saved.[9]

What people don't get is this: Focusing on "me" without a "we" is not good news. When my mother was sixteen, she dropped out of school and was forced to leave home because her family would not support her having me; she said she gave up her life for me. When I was a child, my dad said he would die for me. But living with them undermined their words.

I became a Christian at age fifteen, but my conservative, evangelical church merely baptized the individualism of my family and culture. The church preached "Jesus died for me," but acted like a social club, not a family. My church and Christian friends didn't really know me. I was the president of two Christian organizations in school. But no one knew that my home was chaos, that I was sexually active, and that I had fallen into a life-threatening depression. The messages that "God loves you" and that "Jesus died for you" have a hollow ring when churches fail to *be* the church and exist simply as collections of individualist believers.

Of course, I don't deny that God loves individuals. However, popular evangelistic presentations compromise the gospel by settling for what is merely true. In focusing on saving individuals, we marginalize the church. Typical gospel messages concern the "in and out issue of salvation. Because it's about making a decision."[10] This message makes the church and discipleship an optional part of Christian living. No wonder church hopping has run rampant for decades.[11] The fixation on individual salvation in the West makes genuine discipleship more difficult around the world.[12] Because of Western influence, Christians fail to understand that *personal* decisions are not necessarily *private* decisions. However, it is Western thinking, not biblical thinking, that privatizes faith and morality.

The idolatry of self prevents us from being a family and reduces "love" to mere tolerance. Even among Western Christians, people regard offending others as unloving. If two Christians disagree, what often happens? A person simply says, "God told me so" to defend countless decisions and interpretations. The fact that God gives everyone his Spirit justifies a kind of unfettered individualism.

When a church is not a family, being a "good" Christian requires little more than managing one's reputation. Yet maintaining a propped-up reputation creates new problems—the fear of failure, the desire to deceive, and the shame of hypocrisy.

Many churches and Christian organizations are crystal clear about one thing: one's willingness to share the gospel is the mark of maturity. I checked that box early; in fact, my classmates awarded me the title "Most likely to become a preacher." To be considered mature in some evangelical churches, Christians simply share the gospel, attend church more than others, and avoid doing what non-Christians do.

At this point, I'm nervous that some people will agree with me in principle but overlook subtle ways that individualism affects our perspective. Because individualism and collectivism shape our worldview, we might not recognize how they influence our theology and practice.

For illustration, imagine a twelve-piece jigsaw puzzle. Answer the following question quickly: "*Fundamentally,* is the puzzle twelve pieces or just one picture?" What is your immediate instinct? You cannot answer "both," because I asked about the "fundamental" nature of the puzzle. What is fundamental is most basic. If an object is divided beyond its most basic element, it ceases to be whatever it was. If the twelve-piece puzzle *fundamentally* consists of twelve individual pieces, it is not one whole picture. We can't say the picture is a *collection* of individual parts. A collection cannot be most fundamental, since a collection inherently is divisible.

This analogy illustrates how Christians influenced by traditional Western theology typically see the church. Essentially, the church becomes a collection of individual Christians who gather for worship. This is what individualism asserts: *I, the individual, am most basic, not the group.* When Christians see themselves fundamentally as individuals, the church becomes one among many choices when deciding to join a group. Social divisions also creep into the church. Individuals form cliques, small groups, and organizations united by something other than Christ. Practically, economics, politics, ethnicity, citizenship, and neighborhood create boundaries that shape people's lives more consistently and holistically than does their professed faith in Christ. Something must change about how we foster collective identity.

During an extended visit to the United States, I attended a Sunday school class in an affluent suburban church. Every meeting turned into an extended group rant about how Democrats lead America away from God. The people in the class acted like Christian *Americans,* not American *Christians.* The difference is subtle but decisive. The adjective describes the noun, one's primary identity. If US citizens do not fundamentally identify the church as family (even closer than blood), they naturally become Christian *Americans.* The word *Christian* is merely one descriptor among others.

Don't Waste Your Shame

Those with whom we most closely identify both reflect and influence what we deem worthy of honor or shame. One's perspective or standard of honor and shame depends upon one's group identity. This dynamic is evident around us. Trivial examples include school or team spirit. Family pride and patriotism evoke a sense of honor or shame.

Other examples are more tragic. In the 1930s and '40s, Hitler Youth turned in family members who criticized Hitler and the Nazis. These children felt more allegiance to Germany than to their family.[13] During China's cultural revolution, children sent parents to their death. Zhang Hongbing recounts what he told his mother before reporting her to authorities: "I warned her: 'If you go against our dear Chairman Mao I will smash your dog head.' … I felt this wasn't my mother. This wasn't a person. She suddenly became a monster… . She had become a class enemy and opened her bloody mouth."[14]

Put simply, collective identity is the soil where our sense of honor and shame takes root. Apart from social context—that is, belonging to a group—talking about honor and shame bears little fruit.

The Chinese phrase *pào tāng* literally means "to soak in broth or hot water." Idiomatically, it means "to come to nothing." Originally, the expression came from salt traders who feared torrential rains. If water saturated their bags of salt, their treasure and effort would be wasted.

Likewise, without one significant element, our effort to understand and use honor-shame is *pào tāng;* it comes to nothing, like soaking salt in water. What people routinely overlook is this: Honor and shame are significant only within relationships. One's perspective about what deserves honor or shame depends on one's group—that is, collective identity.

To Christians, outsiders do what is shameful. If we are faithful Christians, outsiders will eventually criticize and exclude us. Those honored in one group are shamed by another. Shame is inevitable. We can't spend our lives trying to avoid it. Instead, we choose the type of shame we will bear. Will it be what the world heaps on us? Or will we be ashamed before Christ and the church? To paraphrase John Piper, "Brothers and sisters, don't waste your shame!"

Creating Collectivistic Churches

Whenever biblical writers explicitly discuss the gospel, their consistent message can be summarized thusly: Jesus is King of all nations. Christ's kingship fulfills God's covenant promises to Abraham and David.[15] To believe the gospel is to give ultimate allegiance to Christ. This entails joining his kingdom people—the church—who give no regard to common social distinctions. How does this gospel create a collectivist church? Christ binds people together more than social or cultural background. Love for Christ means seeking to honor what he honors and judging shameful what he regards as shameful. This perspective of honor-shame redefines Christians' collective identify.

The Bible depicts the church in corporate terms—as a temple, body, family, flock, and new *ethnos*. Therefore, faith is personal but never private. Nothing is *more* public than ultimate allegiance. What we regard as sacred shapes every detail of our lives. Stated another way, what we truly honor or dishonor is always expressed in our relationships, actions, speech, and decisions. Having a Christlike sense of honor-shame binds us most intimately to Christ's people—above bloodlines, ethnicity, or country.

Biblical writers highlight an implication that many Christians today regard as absurd or scandalous. God calls Christians to prioritize one another as family, not outsiders.[16] As Gerhard Lohfink notes, "Interpersonal love almost without exception means love for one's brother in the faith, love of Christians for one another."[17] Or, as John Nugent bluntly states, "Scripture teaches us to love fellow believers— not all humans in general. The evidence is so clear and overwhelming that it is hard to believe it is not common knowledge."[18] His point is not that Christians should be unloving toward outsiders; rather, biblical writers unambiguously prioritize love between Christians, not love for nonbelievers. He lists five or six pages of Scripture references to support this point.

For example, in Galatians 6:10, Paul urges the church to prioritize fellow believers. He writes, "So then, as we have opportunity, let us do good to everyone, *and especially to those who are of the household of faith*" (ESV). In fact, the pervasive use of family imagery is meaningless if the church does not define our fundamental identity.[19] In 1 Thessalonians 4:9–12, Paul tells believers to love one another. Concerning outsiders, he says, "Aspire to live quietly, and to mind your own affairs, and to work with your hands, as we instructed you, so that you may walk properly before outsiders and be dependent on no one" (ESV).

In Matthew 12:48–50, Jesus redefines family:

"Who is my mother, and who are my brothers?" And stretching out his hand toward his disciples, he said, "Here are my mother and my brothers! For whoever does the will of my Father in heaven is my brother and sister and mother." (ESV)

Jesus said that people will know we are his disciples if we love one another (John 13:35). Prioritizing those belonging to the church is "an act of solidarity with King Jesus and his kingdom people."[20]

The early church continued to prioritize fellow believers. Modern Christians would likely see this behavior as exclusivist and unloving. Regarding the period following Nero's persecution of the church in AD 64, Alan Kreider writes:

> Churches closed their doors to outsiders. By the end of the second century, most of them … barred outsiders from entering "private" Christian worship services and ordered believers not to talk to outsiders about what went on behind the closed doors… . By the third century, some churches assigned deacons to stand at the doors, monitoring the people as they arrived… . It is not surprising that pagans responded to their exclusion from Christian worship by speculation and gossip… . They knew that worship services were to glorify God and edify the faithful, not to evangelize outsiders.[21]

This background challenges common assumptions about the church's relationship to outsiders. The earliest Christians were far from being "seeker sensitive."

Dreher states, "Instead of being seeker-friendly, we should be finder-friendly, offering those who come to us a new and different way of life."[22] Christians will not fully internalize Christ's standard for honor-shame until we first define our identity *collectively* as fundamentally belonging to God's royal family. I'm not referring to ecclesiology. Rather, I am asking us to examine what we affirm with our current practice.

Christians sometimes warn against focusing too much on the church, lest we become a "bubble." Many people echo William Temple's words, "The Church is the only society that exists for the benefit of those who are not its members."[23] From a biblical perspective, this is a strange way to talk. Do we describe the family as a "bubble"? To those who say we "need to escape from our church bubble," I ask, "Should we escape from our families?"[24]

The Church Contrasts Culture

How then does the church honor Christ in a shameless world? Crouch correctly notes that Christians should engage in "culture making."[25] I would add to his assertion an important follow-up question: "Where do Christians make culture?" I suggest that the answer is *in the church*. When the church has a strong collective identity, it has a culture. If the church is not an alternative culture, it cannot glorify Christ as light in darkness or as a city on a hill.

We honor Christ as a church, a community that contrasts the outside culture. Believers glorify Christ by what they do (not merely by what they don't do). Through godliness, the church shames the world's powers. Although writing to people suffering injustice, Peter says that their conduct should honor Christ so that outsiders "may see your good deeds and glorify God on the day of visitation" (1 Pet 2:12 ESV) and that "those who revile your good behavior in Christ may be put to shame" (1 Pet 3:16 ESV; cf. Matt 5:15–16; Titus 2:7–8).

The early church grasped this strategy. Justin Martyr comments, "He has exhorted us to lead all men, by patience and gentleness, from shame and the love of evil."[26] Such ministry was a community effort. *The Apology of Aristides* testifies:

When one of their poor passes away from the world, and any of them sees him, then he provides for his burial according to his ability; and if they hear that any of their number is imprisoned or oppressed for the name of their Messiah, all of them provide for his needs, and if it is possible that he may be delivered, they deliver him. And if there is among them a man that is poor and needy, and they have not an abundance of necessaries, they fast two or three days that they may supply the needy with their necessary food.[27]

Even an opponent of Christianity, Julian the Apostate, explains the appeal of the early church:

Why do we not observe that it is their [the Christians'] benevolence to strangers, their care for the graves of the dead and the pretended holiness of their lives that have done the most to increase atheism? … [When] the impious Galileans support not only their own poor, but ours as well, all men see that our people lack aid from us.[28]

Does this last statement contradict what I've said about prioritizing the church above outsiders? Not at all. First, family is the primary training ground for learning to love others.[29] We love outsiders only once we've learned to love insiders. Second, as Nugent observes, "To the extent that we display God's kingdom in our life together, God is able to draw people to himself through our witness."[30]

This is God's strategy to bless the world. Nugent explains:

Our life together is, in God's view, the most powerful force he is willing to exert in order to woo all people to himself…. If God's strategy requires a people whose life together reflects his kingdom, then any other strategy is apostasy and any doctrine that competes with it is heresy.[31]

Recall Jesus' prayer in John 17, where he explicitly prays for believers, not the world. He twice asks the Father that we would be one *"so that the world may believe that you have sent me"* (John 17:20–23 ESV). Paradoxically, the best way to love outsiders is to prioritize insiders. Churches and missionaries spend much time thinking of strategies and techniques to reach the world. Countless methods exist for rapidly multiplying churches. In a rush to plant churches, we forget to be the church. Yet the church is our greatest evangelistic tool!

Why are we more prone to minister among outsiders (e.g., social projects, short-term missions, etc.) rather than commit ourselves to invest deeply in our family—namely, the church? McKnight provides a challenging response:

I hate to put it this way, but I must: it is easier to do the former because it feels good, it resolves some social shame for all that we have, it creates a bonded and encapsulated experience, … Not only that, it is good and right and noble and loving and compassionate and just. It is more glamorous to do social activism because building a local church is hard. It involves people who struggle with one another, it involves persuading others of the desires of your heart to help the homeless, it means caring for people where they are and not where you want them to be, it involves daily routines, and it only rarely leads to the highs of "short-term mission" experiences. But local church is what Jesus came to build, so the local church's mission shapes kingdom mission.[32]

We should ask ourselves, "What gets in the way of building churches that honor Christ and put to shame those who oppose the gospel?"

Habits for Cultivating Honor and Shame

How does the church cultivate a biblical sense of honor and shame? Influenced by Western Christendom, many Christians implicitly think laws or rules are the best way to honor Christ and shape culture. Consider the suggestion of a non-Westerner, Confucius, who prioritized shame above law as a tool for shaping morality. He wrote:

> If the people are led by laws, and uniformity among them be sought by punishments, they will try to escape punishment and have no sense of shame. If they are led by virtue, and uniformity sought among them through practice of ritual propriety, they will possess a sense of shame and come to you of their own accord. (*Analects* 2:3)

These words reflect a biblical idea evident in the New Covenant: A right heart is better than a right law.[33] The Spirit is necessary for people to honor or shame what Christ honors or shames. Nevertheless, we can take steps to cultivate a sacred culture. The church can foster habits of thinking and practice that reinforce a biblical sense of honor and shame.[34] To show the practical implications of collectivism, I list several applications. Not all suggestions equally apply to everyone. I organize these into six broad categories.

1. Conversion

We need to fundamentally rethink how to share the gospel. Christians have long preached a gospel contextualized for Western culture. This does not imply preaching a false gospel. But if our view of the gospel neither accounts for the Bible's explicit explanations of the gospel (e.g., God's promise to Abraham) nor *necessitates* the church, we have problems. Do we preach a gospel that logically *requires* the church? Does our message emphasize individual belief in doctrines? Or does it require people to have a new worldview where Christ is king, whose kingdom consists of all nations?

Faith in Christ means giving allegiance to him as king, thus loyalty to fellow believers. As a result, conversion means changing communities. This is precisely why Luther said, "Apart from the church, salvation is impossible."[35] Churches and ministries need to review and retool to correct individualistic evangelism. Otherwise, we implicitly perpetuate an idolatry of self that undermines a biblical sense of honor and shame.

2. Church Identity

We should reevaluate our goals and strategies for planting and growing churches. We do not honor Christ when we merely increase the quantity of individual converts but do not improve the quality of churches.

While trying to love non-Christians, the Church Growth Movement embraced the values of modern culture. Success is measurable, based on speed and size. By contrast, the early church's extraordinary growth contradicts modern sensibilities. While being "exclusivist" by contemporary standards, the church often grew exponentially.

Strong collective identity requires drawing boundaries that define membership; yet doing so is neither unloving nor antithetical to growing churches. What some today call "exclusion" is essential for the church to be defined by its allegiance to Christ.[36] Many church-planting strategies are insufficient or deficient inasmuch as people do not invest in the church's maturity. I refuse to call a church "mature" simply because it propagates itself; even cults do that.

3. Church Leadership

How do we train leaders?[37] Because most collectivist cultures highly respect social hierarchy, leaders can easily abuse their power. Paul illustrates a different way of leading collectivist churches. In 1 Corinthians 3:3–9, he warns against the factionalism that emerges when churches stop seeing their leaders as servants. In 2 Corinthians, Paul defends his apostleship by highlighting his suffering and social shame. Instead of boasting, he says, "I refrain from it, so that no one may think more of me than he sees in me or hears from me" (2 Cor 12:6 ESV). How much contemporary leadership training emphasizes confidence and vision-casting rather than vulnerability and surrendering control?

Church discipline is an uncomfortable but essential aspect of being a collectivist church. The discussion in 1 Corinthians 5–6 depends on three points. First, the church is a single entity, a temple. Second, believers sharply distinguish the church and the world in ways that strip the world, not the church, of authority. Paul gives separate and unambiguous instructions for insiders and outsiders (cf. 5:9–13). Third, our conduct is not a private matter. What we do in the bedroom is the church's business. If these ideas rub us wrong, it is likely because we have absorbed a Western worldview more than we would like to admit. Consequently, we selectively disobey 1 Corinthians 5–6 by labeling it "difficult to understand."

4. Church Priorities

We should reorder economic priorities. How people invest resources reflects and determines their identity. I will mention two potential applications. First, where we choose to live reflects the sort of community with whom we identify. One rightly wonders whether many churches are united more by education, economics, or ethnicity rather than by Christ. Eric Jacobsen described American Christianity:

> For the past two decades … we have been abandoning our strategic locations within city cores and traditional neighborhoods, and we have tried to create for ourselves a new kind of society in the form of suburban megachurches…. Unfortunately, if we were to take a hard look at how Christians in this country have come to view their cities, we would have to conclude that our views have not necessarily been shaped by the Bible, prayer, or meaningful discussions among fellow Christians. It might be more accurate to say that the fear of cities, or the fear of one another, or possibly the love of convenience has been the actual basis of much of our current perceptions about the city.[38]

Second, spending habits either build or break collective identity. In the third century, a pastor sought advice from Cyprian of Carthage about an actor who converted to Christianity. In that context, many felt being a Christian and an actor stood in contradiction (due to the immorality associated with theatre). However, if the convert left his profession, he would have no income and learning new skills took a long time. Cyprian exhorted the church to support the convert financially:

> His needs can be alleviated along with those of others who are supported by the provisions of the Church—on condition, of course, that he can be satisfied with more frugal, and harmless, fare and does not consider that he ought to be bought off by means of a pension, so as to break away from his sins, for he is the one to benefit from such a break, not us…. Accordingly, you should do your utmost to call him away from this depraved and shameful profession to the way of innocence and to the hope of his true life; let him be satisfied with the nourishment provided by the Church, more sparing to be sure but salutary…. But if your church is unable to meet the cost of maintaining those in need, he can transfer himself to us and receive here what is necessary for him in the way of food and clothing.[39]

We can ask ourselves, "Do our local churches similarly prioritize funds to support our members in this way?" Meeting such practical needs requires and reflects mutual identification as family. Churches need higher expectations of their members than is typical in most contemporary churches. What if people downsized their homes and used the money to support single mothers or fund adoptions rather than think that endless political banter in Sunday school classes will change the world?

5. Conviction

The Western church largely accepts cultural convictions about what defines "love" and "success." This must change. Many Christians struggle to see how shaming a person could be loving. Yet Jesus and his followers used shame as a righteous way of turning people to the truth (Luke 13:17; 1 Cor 6:5; 15:34; 1 Pet 3:16). Contemporary views about love cause Christians to confuse love with "tolerance" (as Western culture now defines it).

Christians fall into the same trap as others in the broader culture. As long as people say nice things about Jesus and the church, many Christians are content to think the church is being effective in ministry. The culture's hypersensitivity means offending people is anathema or being unfaithful. However, contemporary Christians compromise when they let outsiders define "love" or dictate what counts as faithfulness.

6. Connection

Since being the church means being family, we need to reconsider what it means to connect with others in significant ways. Television, the Internet, and social media have *un*trained us from having meaningful social interactions. We struggle to maintain conversations of any depth for extended periods. Many of us are unable to love others at this basic level because of how we manage our homes. Families do not eat meals together. Parents allow their families to be exceedingly busy because they value education, sports, and potential scholarships above connection and character.

Family is the primary setting in which we learn how to relate to others. Since families do not eat together and often have competing agendas, it's not surprising that so many Christians rarely host people in their homes. Consistently bringing others into our homes is a simple and easy way to connect with people in personal ways. Proximity is an important ingredient to nurturing close relationships. Where we choose to live and the jobs we take influence our ability to foster a genuinely Christian collective identity. Where we live influences how much time we spend with our church family.

Conclusion: The Glory of Conforming to Christ

The Bible narrates a different kind of dystopian story, where individualism fragments the human family. Throughout history, "Everyone does what is right in his own eyes."[40] The world's fallen cultures are powers of chaos and alienation. Christ saves us *into* the church, who long for freedom from this fallen, dystopian world order.

Individualism without understanding true individuality leads to idolatry. We should not be conformed by the individualism of the world but transformed within the renewed humanity, the church. Biblically speaking, individuality only has value as we fulfill our specific roles within the body of Christ (e.g., Rom 12;

1 Cor 12). Only those conformed to the image of Christ reject worldly shame and find lasting honor.

We will attain a Christian perspective of honor and shame as we embrace the church as our collective identity. We desire more than to rescue lone individuals from the world order. Our ambition is nothing less than to see God achieve his creation purposes through the church, multiplying his image bearers, who are fruitful and fill the earth with his glory.

For Further Reflection

1. In what ways do you prioritize "me" over "we"? Think about this in terms of your faith experience and of reading the Bible. How has this impacted the life of the community in which you reside? Your own faith?

2. Wu suggests we can commit to investing deeply in our church family through "habits for cultivating honor and shame." Identify one of these and consider how you can practice this habit in helpful and transforming ways.

CHAPTER 4 Endnotes

1 See James Dao, "Ads Now Seek Recruits for 'An Army of One,'" *New York Times*, January 10, 2001, https://www.nytimes.com/2001/01/10/us/ads-now-seek-recruits-for-an-army-of-one.html.

2 This line comes from Charlie Dalton's "Poetrusic" in *Dead Poets Society*. Screenplay by Tom Schulman.

3 See Erin A. Vogel, Jason P. Rose, Lindsay R. Roberts, and Katheryn Eckles, "Social Comparison, Social Media, and Self-Esteem," *Psychology of Popular Media Culture* 3, no. 4 (2014): 206–22; Dara Greenwood, "Fame, Facebook, and Twitter: How Attitudes About Fame Predict Frequency and Nature of Social Media Use," *Psychology of Popular Media Culture* 2, no. 4 (2013): 222–36; Wenhong Chen and Kye-Hyoung Lee, "Sharing, Liking, Commenting, and Distressed? The Pathway Between Facebook Interaction and Psychological Distress," *Cyberpsychology, Behavior, and Social Networking* 16, no. 10 (2013): 728–34.

4 Some attribute the first part of the quotation to Theodore Roosevelt.

5 Andy Crouch, "The Return of Shame," *Christianity Today*, March 10, 2015.

6 Rod Dreher, "Weimar America's Long Island Ménage," *The American Conservative*, March 11, 2017. http://theamericanconservative.com/dreher/weimar-america-long-island-menage.

7 "Why Does God Love You?" Bible-truths.com, http://bible-truths.com/WhyGodLovesYou.htm.

8 "A Personal Message," "Walk with the Word" website, http://walkwiththeword.org/Love_Message.html. Examples abound online, in sermons, and in books. For example, Susan Kaye Behm, *The Journey*, (Chicago, IL: Moody Press, 1994), 314.

9 Kevin DeYoung and Greg Gilbert claim that "how" is essential to the gospel. See their *What Is the Mission of the Church? Making Sense of Social Justice, Shalom, and the Great Commission* (Wheaton, IL: Crossway, 2011), 110–11.

10 Scot McKnight, *The King Jesus Gospel: The Original Good News Revisited* (Grand Rapids: Zondervan, 2011), Kindle location 404–5.

11 In 1998, a Barna Research Group study found that "each year, one out of every seven adults changes churches. And one out of every six adults attends a carefully chosen handful of churches on a rotating basis." See "Church Hopping," BeliefNet.com, http://beliefnet.com/faiths/christianity/2000/10/church-hopping.aspx#SOMUc3ZvCOBxBXLW.99.

12 See my article, "Does the 'Plan of Salvation' Make Disciples? Why Honor and Shame Are Essential for Christian Ministry," *Asian Missions Advance* (January 2016): 11–17.

13 Cf. Ted Gottfried, *Children of the Slaughter: Young People of the Holocaust* (Hong Kong: Twenty-First Century Books, 2001), 29–31; Alexa Dvorson, *The Hitler Youth: Marching Toward Madness* (New York: The Rosen Publishing Group, 1999), 30; Susan Campbell Bartoletti, *Hitler Youth: Growing Up in Hitler's Shadow* (New York: Scholastic, 2006), 84.

14 Tania Branigan, "China's Cultural Revolution: Son's Guilt over the Mother He Sent to Her Death," *The Guardian*, March 27, 2013, https://theguardian.com/world/2013/mar/27/china-cultural-revolution-sons-guilt-zhang-hongping.

15 The kingship of Christ has wide-ranging implications for the gospel; these implications are explored in my book, *One Gospel for All Nations* (Pasadena, CA: William Carey Library, 2015); Scot McKnight, *The King Jesus Gospel* (Grand Rapids: Zondervan, 2011); and N. T. Wright, *How God Became King* (New York: HarperOne, 2012).

16 Aside from nearly everything written by Stanley Hauerwas, see Scot McKnight, *Kingdom Conspiracy: Returning to the Radical Mission of the Local Church* (Grand Rapids: Brazos Press, 2014), especially 99–122; Joseph Hellerman, *When the Church Was a Family* (Nashville: B&H, 2009); and Hellerman, "Our Priorities Are Off When Family Is More Important Than Church," *Christianity Today*, August 4, 2016, https://christianitytoday.com/ct/2016/august-web-only/if-our-families-are-more-important-than-our-churches-we-nee.html.

17 Gerhard Lohfink, *Jesus and Community: The Social Dimension of Christian Faith* (Philadelphia: Fortress, 1984), 110.

18 John Nugent, *Endangered Gospel: How Fixing the World Is Killing the Church* (Eugene, OR: Cascade Books, 2016), 90.

19 Cf. Hellerman, *When the Church Was a Family*.

20 McKnight, *Kingdom Conspiracy*, 121.

21 Alan Kreider, *The Patient Ferment of the Early Church: The Improbable Rise of Christianity in the Roman Empire* (Grand Rapids: Baker, 2016), 11.

22 Rod Dreher, *The Benedict Option* (New York: Sentinel, 2017), 121.

23 Cf. Dietrich Bonhoeffer, *Letters and Papers from Prison*, Dietrich Bonhoeffer Works vol, 8; ed. John Degruchy (Minneapolis: Fortress, 2010), 382.

24 From a Western perspective, those questions might not seem strange. Individualism reigns in typical Western families just as it does in the church. People divorce if their spouse doesn't meet their needs. Parents and kids simply coexist in the same home. Parents raise kids to be independent; being "dependent" is treated as shameful.

25 Andy Crouch, *Culture Making* (Downers Grove, IL: InterVarsity, 2010).

26 Justin, *1 Apol* 16:3, trans. Philip Schaff, http://ccel.org/ccel/schaff/anf01.viii.ii.xvi.html.

27 Aristides, *Apol.* 15.8–9, in J. Stevenson, *A New Eusebius*, rev. W. H. C. Frend (London: SPCK, 1987), 53.

28 *The Works of the Emperor Julian*, vol. 3, trans. W. Wright, in Loeb Classical Library (London: W. Heinemann, 1923), 17, 69.

29 Cf. Gregg Ten Elshof, *Confucius for Christians*, 8–28.

30 Nugent, *Endangered Gospel*, 87.

31 Ibid., 101–2.

32 See McKnight, *Kingdom Conspiracy*, 96–97, cf. 121–22.

33 For example, see Jer 31:31–34; Ezek 36:26–27; Mal 2:2.

34 For example, see any book from James K. A. Smith's three-volume series, including *You Are What You Love: The Spiritual Power of Habit* (Grand Rapids: Brazos Press, 2016); *Desiring the Kingdom: Worship, Worldview, and Cultural Formation* (Grand Rapids: Baker, 2016); *Imagining the Kingdom: How Worship Works* (Grand Rapids: Baker, 2013). See also N. T. Wright, *After You Believe: Why Christian Character Matters* (New York: HarperOne, 2012).

35 Martin Luther, *Luther's Works*, vol. 21, ed. J. Pelikan and H. Lehmann (Philadelphia: Fortress, 1955), 127. Charles Colson and Ellen Vaughn elaborate on Luther's comment : "Not that the church provides salvation; God does. But because the "saved" one can't fulfill what it means to be a Christian apart from the church, membership becomes an indispensable mark of salvation." *Being the Body* (Nashville: Thomas Nelson, 2004), 46.

36 McKnight (*Kingdom Conspiracy*, 124) summarizes: "This kingdom story tells the story of a kingdom; kingdom is a people, and that means kingdom mission is about forming the people of God. That is, kingdom mission forms a kingdom people and that kingdom people in the present world is the church. This means kingdom mission is all about forming and enhancing local churches as expressions of the kingdom of God in this world."

37 See my article, "Authority in a Collectivist Church: Identifying Crucial Concerns for a Chinese Ecclesiology," *Global Missiology*, Oct 2011.

38 Eric Jacobsen, *Sidewalks in the Kingdom: New Urbanism and the Christian Faith* (Grand Rapids: Brazos Press, 2003), 16–17.

39 Letter 2.2.2–3 in *The Letters of Cyprian, Vol. 1* (4 vol.; trans. G. W. Clark; New York: Newman Press, 1984), 161. Cf. Hellerman, *When the Church Was a Family*, 100.

40 Deut 12:8; Judg 17:6; 21:25.

THE SHAMING OF JESUS IN JOHN

E. RANDOLPH RICHARDS

Introduction

All four Gospels record the story of Jesus clearing the temple. In the Synoptics, Jesus curses the temple at the very end of his ministry (Matt 21:21–17; Mark 11:15–19; Luke 19:45–48). In John's Gospel, Jesus appears to cleanse the temple at the very beginning of his ministry (John 2:13–22). This difference has long been noted and many explanations have been offered. What has not been noted is that in John's story, Jesus was publicly shamed by his failure to defend why he had the authority to "judge" the temple. Eventually the Judean authorities would conclude that the shaming was *unsuccessful*, while John would argue it was *inappropriate*. Both recognized that a public shaming had occurred. As a modern Western Christian, I am disadvantaged when it comes to seeing this undercurrent in the ministry of Jesus.

As a modern Christian, the deity of Jesus looms large in my vision. My modern Jesus rides above the common currents of humanity and certainly beyond the reach of culture. Yet the Gospels tell us that Jesus and his disciples were identifiable by their accent (Mark 14:70). He was the recipient of cultural prejudice (John 1:46). More significantly, the things that went without being said (often some of the most important aspects of a culture) are clued by statements that seem to my modern Western eyes to be extraneous. John notes that it was years *later* when Jesus' disciples finally understood what Jesus said in his defense, and it was then that they believed his statement (John 2:22).

As a reader, I was supposed to have stumbled over what had just happened. I was supposed to have needed (badly) John's parenthetical defense of Jesus at that point. Yet the entire matter glided past me. My Jesus had needed no defense. His actions were always acceptable. John suggests otherwise.

We will examine how the Judean temple authorities of Jesus' day tried to keep Jesus within the lines. Just like my modern individualist culture, Jesus' Mediterranean *collectivist* culture had its means of enforcing its values. For example, my culture uses guilt. I can still hear my grandmother's voice when I am about to cross a line. In more than merely our legal system, guilt and innocence are tools my individualist culture uses to enforce conformity to its values.

Mediterranean Shaming

Collectivist cultures use their own tools to assist their members in staying within the lines of acceptable behavior. Shaming is one of these. Our English word *shame* can be used to mean something very bad, something sort of bad, or even something good. A man who fails to provide for his family often feels shame. A woman with a child outside of wedlock often feels shame. When, as a child, I did something I should not have, my grandmother would chide me, saying, "Have you no shame?"

Honor *and* Shame, Not Honor *versus* Shame

Three of the most common ways collectivist cultures have of enforcing their culture's values are honor, shame, and boundaries.[1] Two of these are rather self-explanatory. Shame, however, is often misunderstood. It is commonly presented as the antithesis of honor. The New International Version muddles the concept of shame. For example, in the NIV, we read: "The wise inherit honor, but fools get only shame" (Prov 3:35). We are familiar with the concept of antithetic parallelism in Hebrew poetry. Clearly, this proverb is describing opposites. Thus, we are easily led to conclude that the opposite of honor is shame. However, the verse is translated poorly. Note the New American Standard Bible's translation: "The wise will inherit honor, but fools display dishonor." The opposite of honor is dishonor.

The problem isn't merely the NIV. The English language makes a mess of the idea of shame. We can use *shameful* and *shameless* to mean the same thing. What did biblical writers mean by shame? Actually, my grandmother's phrase best captures the ancient (and, somewhat, the modern) Mediterranean sense of shame—to bring negative notice to a person who has transgressed a cultural boundary.

Shame Restores Those Who Transgress the Boundaries

Shame protects the boundaries of a group. As an emotion within a group member, it is supposed to warn that person that he or she is approaching a boundary. This is what my grandmother meant. She was dismayed because my behavior suggested I lacked this sense of shame, that I was shameless, that no sense of shame had warned me not to do what I had done. Shame also, though, functioned to indicate to someone that they had crossed a boundary and encouraged them to move back closer to the "ideal center" and thus back within the boundary.

Shame can be—and, sadly, often is—misused. (Similarly, guilt in my individualist culture is often misused.) Ironically, we often think shame is misused merely by being used. No, shame has a positive and redemptive function. It draws the person back into the group. The prodigal son felt shame over where he was; it drew him back to his father (Luke 15:17–20). Paul used shame to correct the Corinthians (1 Cor 6:5; 15:34). Shame is misused when it offers the person no path back. In the story of Jesus, the temple leadership attempted to use shame to draw Jesus back from a boundary he had crossed. They wanted him to return to acceptable behavior. In fact, they expected him to. Otherwise, he would have been shameless.

Ancient Mediterranean Honor Contests

As noted in modern discussions of ancient Mediterranean culture, honor could be gained or lost in confrontations. These contests had to be public. This was serious adult business.[2] One's place in the assembly or seat at a local banquet was not the prize but rather a physical display of the trophy. One's level of honor (held corporately by the family or group) determined far more serious things, such as what businesses one could join, whom one's children married, which patrons or patronesses would claim you, etc. It indicated your "place" in society. Public questions were not innocent quests for knowledge but rather a challenge for honor. Once someone claimed an honor he[3] did not previously enjoy, others who held that honor were challenged. Honor in the ancient Mediterranean world was a limited good. As with a pie, making one's slice larger inevitably made others' smaller. Thus, honor was jealously guarded and quickly defended.

Honor contests began when someone asserted his right to a particular honor, such as speaking in a synagogue, taking a higher seat at a wedding, teaching in a public place, or sitting in judgment of others. The assertion was a challenge, and the challenged were required to make some sort of response (and no response was considered a response). Since honor was a community (collective) value, the community decided whether or not the challenged person successfully defended his honor.[4] Thus we can see a public process[5] where someone asserted his right to something, together with its inherent honor. Those who were custodians of that right (the ones who held it) demanded proof that this claimant had the right. The claimant then had to demonstrate he had this right, usually by wisdom or power or some indication of being granted the authority. Hence, if he claimed the authority to teach in a synagogue (see, e.g., Luke 6:6; 13:10; 15:1–2), he had to demonstrate it by being able to read from the scroll and expound appropriately. The community, the ultimate keepers of all honor, decided if he had demonstrated the right. If they sat and listened, or better, commented favorably, then the claimant was vindicated. He was then an approved speaker. Scoffing or some other public display of scorn or contempt against his reading or teaching would indicate the public verdict went against him.[6]

John's Temple Clearing as an Honor Contest

Jesus claimed honor by clearing the temple.[7] The right to judge how temple activities were conducted was a claim to very high honor.

Before we discuss Jesus' honor claim, we first need to address a preliminary question. Since temple disruptions were illegal in the Roman Empire, why wasn't Jesus merely arrested? This is a valid question.[8] At the very least, arresting Jesus would require a public trial and perhaps involve the Romans. John's text suggests that Jesus stopped his actions as soon as the authorities arrived, implying that his intention was to claim honor and not for the purpose of actually removing every merchant from the temple. Jesus' language (in John) is that of "cleansing" and not necessarily an immediate threat to the legitimacy of the temple or the authorities. It would not require an arrest "if Jesus' action was very small in scale and basically an acted parable, not an actual cleansing out of any major portion of the temple precincts."[9]

It seems reasonable that the temple authorities initially recognized Jesus' actions as symbolic, as was common by Israelite prophets, and not banditry or an attempt to blaspheme the temple. In fact, they may not have been overly surprised by a prophetic action. As Craig Blomberg notes, "It is quite possible that Caiaphas, the high priest, had only recently introduced this commerce into the temple precincts themselves rather than using the nearby Kidron valley as previously."[10]

Evidence suggests that the market and its animals were moved into the temple precincts that year (or at least recently). While the money changers were a longstanding presence, Victor Eppstein argues that the animals were moved into the temple as part of a squabble among temple leaders.[11] He contends that Caiaphas, the high priest, fell out with the Sanhedrin in AD 30 and withdrew permission for the Sanhedrin to use the Chamber of Hewn Stone. The owners of the traditional animal market (on the Mount of Olives, which was considered an extension of the temple area) gave the Sanhedrin a room to use. In revenge, Caiaphas gave their competitors permission to place their animals in the Court of the Gentiles for the first time in history.[12] Jesus' response may suggest that he reacted the first time he saw it (whether one sees one or two clearings).[13]

The authorities' response was also predictable, even expected. They would question Jesus' right but would also wonder if God had sent a prophet. As Donald Carson states,

> If the authorities had been convinced that Jesus was merely some petty hooligan, or that he was emotionally unstable, there were adequate recourses; that they requested a miraculous sign demonstrated they harbored at least a suspicion that they were dealing with a heaven-sent prophet.[14]

Thus, Jesus' actions could be viewed as a symbolic (prophetic) denunciation of the recent relocation of the market inside the temple. Jesus was claiming (at the very least) the honor of a prophet, likely alluding to Zechariah in his denunciation.[15] His honor claim was challenged, and rightly so. "What sign can you show us for doing this?" (John 2:18 NRSV).[16]

We should be careful not to read the hostility found in the Synoptics into John's story. The tone of their challenge was neutral, perhaps carefully so. Some authorities—at least those who did not approve of Caiaphas' actions—may have been "open" to a prophetic word. Some may even have approved of Jesus' actions. Nevertheless, Jesus would need to prove he had the authority, whether they were rooting for or against him.

Jesus' "Failed" Defense Prompted Shaming

Jesus answered their request for a sign with "Destroy this temple, and in three days I will raise it up" (John 2:19 NRSV). As believers, we might rush to Jesus' defense rather than recognize this for how it appeared at that moment—Jesus failed to provide a persuasive sign. No one was going to destroy Herod's temple to see if Jesus could rebuild it. Everyone recognized it as an unprovable sign (at least the way they interpreted it). The leaders treated Jesus' answer with disdain and contempt. John does not tell us the reaction (verdict) of the crowd. Rather, he rushes to explain why Jesus' response wasn't really a losing answer after all: "But the temple he had spoken of was his body" (John 2:21).

John's immediate correction of the sign should not mislead us. That was *not* how everyone (including Jesus' disciples) interpreted it at the time. No one believed him, including his disciples: "After he was raised from the dead, his disciples recalled what he had said. Then they believed the scripture and the words that Jesus had spoken" (John 2:22). John's point that the disciples *later* believed indicates that *initially* everyone perceived Jesus' response as inadequate.

Shame as the Boundary Keeper

All other honor contests in the Gospels record the verdict of the crowds (e.g., Matt 13:54). In all the other contests, of course, the verdict went to Jesus. In this story, the temple crowd disappeared. Instead, John insists that Jesus' response actually was adequate. John's defense of Jesus is correct, but his appeals to other evidence indicate what the initial verdict was. Jesus lost the honor contest. He was shamed (inappropriately, John argues). At the moment, though, Jesus' failure to perform an acceptable sign showed (in everyone's eyes) that he did not have the authority to clear the temple. Therefore, his behavior transgressed a boundary. Public shaming enforced social conformity. According to Malina and Neyrey,

> People acquire honor by personally aspiring to a certain status and having that status socially validated. On the other hand, people *get shamed* (not *have shame*) when they aspire to a certain status which is denied them by public opinion.[17]

When the community (the witnesses to the act) concluded that the claimant did not prove he had the right, then he was shamed and stripped of the honor to which he had aspired. Since Jesus was shamed, there was no reason, in the eyes of the temple authorities, to pursue the matter further, at least legally.[18] We must recognize the power that shame had to control behavior in the first-century Mediterranean collectivist society. In fact, the authorities might have *preferred* shaming over arrest.[19] Arrests could engender sympathy. Shaming ensured that the public sided with the authorities. If Jesus' actions were seen as shameful by all, then there would be no expectation that Jesus would repeat the behavior. For the temple authorities, the matter was resolved. Jesus' subsequent actions seemed to verify their conclusions.

Shaming Jesus Initially Seemed Successful: Jesus Kept the Boundary

Shaming seemed to have performed its function. Jesus' actions appeared to be the culturally appropriate response to losing the honor contest and then facing a public shaming. He did not "misbehave" again. Jesus visited the temple three more times, and the visit in John 5 is usually argued to be a Passover. If so, which seems likely,[20] then Jesus ignored the market activities during that visit. We might suggest this for theological reasons ("his hour had not yet come"). However, the authorities would interpret it as a successful application of shaming, since "to have shame" is to recognize and keep boundaries. When one is shamed, he is honorable if he has a sense of shame and complies with group expectation.[21]

In the eyes of the authorities, shaming had worked when Jesus acted honorably by not trying to disrupt the temple market again. We read of no additional disruptions by Jesus. The authorities appeared to be the victors. In their minds, Jesus had been shamed (and thus corrected). Case closed.

Nicodemus at Night (John 3)

In this context of a "failed" clearing, a member of the Sanhedrin (John 3:1; 7:50) entered the picture. If the market was relocated inside the temple because of a squabble within the Sanhedrin, then at least some would have initially applauded a prophetic denunciation and would no doubt have been disappointed that Jesus produced no prophetic (miraculous) sign to demonstrate his authority. Nicodemus represented others ("we know," John 3:2), possibly those who opposed the market's new location. Nicodemus noted that Jesus was a teacher *come from God* who did miraculous signs, such as were demanded publicly. He came at night because he wanted a private meeting. His question was not public; it was not an honor contest. Perhaps he and some colleagues were mystified, even frustrated, because Jesus had failed to defend himself with a miraculous sign, which they know he could do ("the signs you are doing," John 3:2). They were unsure if Jesus was *unable at that moment* to perform the sign, and thus worthy of the shaming, or *unwilling at that moment* to perform a sign. In their minds, it seemed much less likely that Jesus was unwilling, since it would result in shaming. Who would submit to that?

This is a valid quandary for Nicodemus. His reasoning might be: If God withheld a miraculous sign, perhaps it was because Jesus had overstepped his bounds, which would mean God didn't mind the market being inside the temple.

Jesus Pushing Against the Boundary

Jesus and the Samaritan woman (John 4). The disciples found Jesus talking to a woman by a well. They knew the stories—biblical heroes often found wives by wells. It would be expected for a rabbi like Jesus to be married and unusual that he wasn't. The disciples wouldn't have questioned the encounter, except the woman was a Samaritan. John tells us they didn't ask his rationale (John 4:27), but it is clear they wanted to.

Here Jesus transgressed another boundary. But, for our topic, he also denigrated the temple again. In his conversation with the woman, as with the temple clearing, Jesus denounced the role of the temple in Jerusalem: "A time is coming when you will worship the Father neither on this mountain nor in Jerusalem" (John 4:21).

The man by the pool (John 5). From the beginning of this story, the authorities were hostile to Jesus. Although he did not claim the honor of temple clearing (staying within that boundary), here he pushed a related boundary. In Sabbath law, the prohibition against work was often illustrated by forbidding the carrying of burdens, especially inside Jerusalem. Note Jeremiah's denunciation: "This is what the LORD says: Be careful not to carry a load on the Sabbath day or bring it through the gates of Jerusalem" (Jer 17:21).

Elsewhere we see that healing on the Sabbath was a bone of contention (e.g., Matt 12:10). Jesus added fuel to the fire in this story by specifically commanding the man to carry his mat: "Then Jesus said to him, 'Get up! Pick up your mat and walk'" (John 5:8). Jesus sandwiched the command to carry the mat in between healing phrases ("Get up ... and walk"), making it impossible to separate the miracle from the command to carry the mat. While man was forbidden to work on the Sabbath, rabbis recognized that God worked on the Sabbath, as seen in births and deaths on the Sabbath.[22] Jesus was claiming divine prerogative and doing it *in Jerusalem.*

Jesus taunted by his brothers. It is not normally noted, but Jesus' brothers' taunts specifically targeted his failure to produce a public sign in the temple. Note their wording:

> When the Jewish Festival of Tabernacles was near, Jesus' brothers said to him, "Leave Galilee and go to Judea, so that your disciples there may see the works you do. No one who wants to become a public figure acts in secret. Since you are doing these things, show yourself to the world." For even his own brothers did not believe in him. (John 7:2–5)

John notes the timing, near a festival—which meant going to Jerusalem and entering the temple—as well as their challenge to perform a miracle and do it in public. This is honor language. They were taunting Jesus about how he was able to do miracles in the Galilean countryside but not in the temple where it really mattered (in their eyes). They also taunted him about whether he would enter the temple again. The taunts are harsh enough that John feels it necessary to explain that his brothers did not yet believe in Jesus (John 7:5).

Jesus publicly spoke in the temple. John 7 notes that both the authorities and the crowds were wondering if Jesus would show his face again in the temple: "Now at the festival the Jewish leaders were watching for Jesus and asking, 'Where is he?' Among the crowds there was widespread whispering about him (John 7:11–12).

Why would they wonder if someone would come to a festival? Everyone was supposed to come. Why wonder if Jesus would come? Because he was shamed previously. Yet Jesus came then and taught publicly in the temple. What he said seriously pushed the boundary of denouncing temple activity. There seems to be some evidence that the Pharisees and Sadducees were disputing over how to implement the water ritual during this festival.[23] Priests drew water from the Pool of Siloam—living water, since it was fed by the Gihon Spring (via Hezekiah's Tunnel). The Sadducees opposed the pouring of the water on the altar. On one occasion the dispute led to the shedding of blood.[24]

The point of the dispute is not important, only that the crowds contested the way the temple authorities were doing it. Jesus then entered the argument:

> On the last and greatest day of the festival, Jesus stood and said in a loud voice, "Let anyone who is thirsty come to me and drink. Whoever believes in me, as Scripture has said, rivers of living water will flow from within them." (John 7:37–38)

From the temple authorities' viewpoint, Jesus was pushing the boundary by indirectly critiquing temple activities.

They attempted to arrest him (John 7:32). Why? The purpose would be "discipline"—i.e., a flogging—as a next step in the public shaming process, since the original boundary was still in place. Jesus had not proven he had the right to "judge" temple activities. Jesus' public teaching in the temple suggested he was claiming this honor, and the authorities needed to demonstrate contrariwise. We can see this in the crowd's confusion (John 7:40–43). They wondered if the authorities' silence represented a reassessment of the original honor contest. The crowd even pondered if it meant that Jesus was the Prophet. Why? Because Jesus' actions in (John's) temple clearing were prophetic actions.

We also note that Nicodemus questioned if Jesus could be condemned without a hearing first (John 7:51). Nicodemus didn't mean an assessment of Jesus' teachings but of his prophetic status, perhaps even a reassessment of the original incident in the temple. By then Jesus was known as a miracle worker (John 7:31; 11:47). A clue that Nicodemus wanted a hearing over whether Jesus was a prophet (and thus, able to judge the temple activities) is seen in the authorities' reply: "A prophet does not come out of Galilee" (John 7:52). Their comment is often interpreted as referring to "the Prophet," the Messiah (John 7:40), but their reference is anarthrous.[25] While prophets could and did speak against temple actions, the authorities concluded that Jesus' temple actions were rightly condemned without further hearing because he was from Galilee and thus not a prophet (John 7:51–52). The original boundary was still in place, and Jesus' shaming needed reinforcement by a public flogging. In John 7, the opportunity was lost by timid guards (John 7:46).

Shaming Jesus proved unsuccessful: Jesus broke the boundary (a second temple clearing). It is quite unpopular in modern scholarship, even among evangelicals, to suggest that Jesus cleared the temple twice: "Few would suggest [Jesus] did it twice" (Ben Witherington); "improbable" (Kingsley Barrett, Ramsey Michaels); "historically implausible" (Craig Keener); "an historiographic monstrosity" (Gerald Borchert). The possibility of two clearings is not even mentioned by F. F. Bruce or A. M. Hunter. As Craig Blomberg notes, one is discouraged from even raising the question: "It does seem odd how reluctant some are today to consider the possibility of two separate events."[26] Elsewhere I have argued for two clearings.[27]

Jesus didn't defend the second clearing. Mark's and Luke's accounts are silent about the authorities' reaction, except that they plotted to kill him (Mark 11:18; Luke 19:45–47). Matthew tells us they were indignant, demanding he denounce the messianic claims (Matt 21:15–16). In all three Synoptic accounts, it was his popularity that prevented the Judean leadership from arresting Jesus. The crowds believed that Jesus, like John the Baptizer, was a prophet. The authorities believed otherwise.[28] Disrupting the temple again, in the same way, did not cause them to demand a sign. They didn't acknowledge his claim to the honor (and authority) to judge the temple. In their minds, he was shamed and should not have tried again. Crossing this boundary demonstrated to the Judean leadership that Jesus was *shameless.* He didn't comply with the limits of the initial shaming.

Jesus failed as Messiah (in the eyes of the crowd). Jesus was given the honor of Messiah in the Triumphal Entry. He was greeted as the Son of David (Matt 21:9,15; cf. John 19:12). His unwillingness to lead the revolt against Rome led the crowd to reject him as Messiah. After all, they had committed treason against Rome by lining the roads proclaiming Jesus as king.

The Verdict on Jesus

The Crowd Concluded Jesus Was Shameless

By being arrested, Jesus demonstrated (in the crowd's eyes) he was not the Messiah and not a prophet. Thus, he had no authority to clear the temple. He did it a second time, which made him shameless. It is noteworthy how this reappears in the taunts at the crucifixion. The Synoptics' accounts of the temple clearing do not record Jesus' statement, "Destroy this temple, and in three days I will raise it up" (John 2:19 NRSV). Yet the false witnesses testified against Jesus, "We heard him say, 'I will destroy this temple that is made with hands, and in three days I will build another, not made with hands'" (Mark 14:58 NRSV; cf. Matt 26:61).[29] Those passing by the crucified Jesus taunted him, "Aha! You who would destroy the temple and build it in three days, save yourself" (Mark 15:29–30 NRSV; cf. Matt 27:40).[30]

What we need to notice is that these statements were used as a taunt, to ridicule and to shame. Jesus' temple saying was connected to shaming.[31] While, technically, Jesus' claim was as yet unproven, the public clearly had reached a verdict—it was a "shameful saying" and suitable for taunting a "loser."

The taunt had staying power. Morris concludes, "It is clear that the charge was persistent and repeated."[32] When Stephen was charged in Acts 6, Luke notes:

> They set up false witnesses who said, "This man never stops saying things against this holy place and the law; for we have heard him say that this Jesus of Nazareth will destroy this place and will change the customs that Moses handed on to us." (Acts 6:13–14 NRSV)

Two to three years after Jesus' death, the saying was still being repeated by *opponents*. All Synoptic allusions to the Johannine saying are *negative* and on the lips of opponents. This saying, I propose, had such a persistent life among opponents because it shamed Jesus (in their opinion). The saying is cited (at the very least in Mark 15:29 and Matthew 27:40) as seeming to imply failure by Jesus. It is significant that the taunt is *not* that Jesus was anti-temple, but that he had already failed once and was failing again.

John's Defense of Jesus

John feels it is necessary to explain. Jesus had actually successfully defended his actions in the first clearing; thus, the shaming wasn't appropriate. This fits with an established motif in John's Gospel of explaining unresolved issues. In his story of the temple clearing, John is silent on the crowd's verdict. Instead, John contends that Jesus won. First, he notes that they misunderstood the proof Jesus provided (John 2:22). Second, John adds that many believed on his name because Jesus was doing miraculous signs (2:23), which is what the authorities had requested.

John's defense of Jesus is correct, but his statements also indicate the initial verdict. Jesus had been shamed—inappropriately, John argues—because Jesus would provide the sign he offered. By providing the sign, Jesus proved he had the authority to clear the temple.

Conclusion

As a prophet and miracle worker, Jesus had the right to cross that boundary, to stand in judgment of temple activities. If we maintain two temple clearings, the first one in John, where Jesus cleansed the temple, and a second in the Synoptics, where Jesus, like Jeremiah (Jer 26:6), cursed the temple, then an interesting image develops. The text from Malachi cited consistently for John the Baptizer notes that after the messenger comes, then YHWH appears at the temple: "'I will send my messenger, who will prepare the way before me. Then suddenly the Lord you are seeking will come to his temple; the messenger of the covenant, who you desire, will come,' says the LORD Almighty" (Mal 3:1).

In the days of Solomon, God immediately appeared at the first temple upon its dedication (2 Chr 7:1–3). It appears God chose not to appear immediately upon the dedication of the second temple (Ezra 6:16–18).[33] In John's Gospel, YHWH finally did appear. When he did, he judged the temple, cleansing it (in John's clearing) and then cursing it the second time (in the Synoptic clearing).

Once cursed, the temple was empty and capable of being destroyed (by the Romans). Soon, both the Samaritan and the Judean temple would lie in ruins, but, according to Jesus, it wouldn't matter: "Yet a time is coming and has now come when the true worshipers will worship the Father in the Spirit and in truth, for they are the kind of worshipers the Father seeks. God is spirit, and his worshipers must worship in the Spirit and in truth" (John 4:23–24).

For Further Reflection

1. Regarding honor-shame dynamics in the Gospels, Richards says, "As a modern Western Christian, I am disadvantaged when it comes to seeing this undercurrent in the ministry of Jesus." Consider the various honor-shame dynamics Richards discusses. Apply an honor-shame lens to two or more significant events in Jesus' life. How does this shed new light on those events/stories?

2. Where do you see public shaming and honor contests in your family, community, or nation? How does the gospel speak to these attitudes and behaviors?

CHAPTER 5 Endnotes

1 For a full discussion, see my forthcoming work, Richards and James, *What Went Without Being Said: Cultural Values in the Biblical World* (Downers Grove, IL: InterVarsity).

2 Scholars have called these "the game of challenge-riposte"; see, among others, David A. deSilva, *Honor, Patronage, Kinship & Purity: Unlocking New Testament Culture* (Downers Grove, IL: InterVarsity, 2000), 29; Bruce Malina, *The New Testament World*, 3rd. rev. ed. (Louisville: Westminster/John Knox Press, 2001), 33–36; and Bruce Malina and Jerome Neyrey, "Honor and Shame in Luke-Acts," in *The Social World of Luke-Acts: Models for Interpretation*, 25–66, ed. J. Neyrey (Peabody, MA: Hendrickson, 1991), 30.

3 The masculine pronouns "he" and "his" are used intentionally here and below. Honor contests were conducted in public, and "males were thought to belong to the public world and females to the private world." See Jerome Neyrey, *Honor and Shame in the Gospel of Matthew* (Louisville, KY: Westminster, 1998), 29–30; 212–15.

4 DeSilva, *Honor*, 29.

5 Although the process isn't disputed, modern Western descriptions vary, such as 1) Honor Claimed, 2) Honor Challenged, 3) Riposte, 4) Public Verdict. Sometimes the honor claim itself is called the challenge. See, e.g., Malina, *New Testament World*, 34–36; and Malina and Neyrey, "Honor and Shame," 30. Malina blends the riposte and public verdict together (33).

6 For example, the tribes scorned Saul's anointing, thus rejecting Samuel's claim that Saul had the honor of being king (2 Sam 16:5–14).

7 See also my article, "An Honor/Shame Argument for Two Temple Clearings," *Trinity Journal* 29 (2008): 19–43.

8 Raymond Brown argues that Jesus would have been arrested, as we see in the Synoptics. He argues for one temple clearing and that the account in John was relocated from Passion Week, where Jesus was arrested; see *John*, Anchor Bible, vol. 29, 2 vols. (New York: Doubleday, 1966), 1:117ff.

9 Ben Witherington III, *John's Wisdom: A Commentary on the Fourth Gospel* (Louisville: Westminster/John Knox Press, 1995), 378, n. 5. Craig Keener argues that the size of the temple and the size and loudness of the crowds make it reasonable that "a small scale act by a single person need not have drawn the attention of the Roman guards," especially if it quickly turned into a discussion between Jesus and the authorities. See Keener, *The Gospel of John*, 2 vols. (Peabody, MA: Hendrickson, 2003), 1:520.

10 Craig Blomberg, *The Historical Reliability of John's Gospel: Issues and Commentary* (Downers Grove, IL: InterVarsity, 2001), 91.

11 Victor Eppstein, "The Historicity of the Gospel Account of the Cleansing of the Temple," *ZNW* 55 (1964): 42–58, esp. 56–57.

12 Not all agree; see, e.g., E. Haenchen, *John 1*, Hermeneia (Philadelphia: Fortress, 1980), 183.

13 Witherington argues that it is best not to press Eppstein's dating and just to argue that the market's move had been "recent"; *John's Wisdom*, 87.

14 Donald Carson, *The Gospel According to John*, PNTC (Grand Rapids: Eerdmans, 1991), 181.

15 Jesus joins that of other prophetic voices, critiquing worship corrupted by greed (1QpHab IX, 3–7; CD-A VI, 15–16; MT Jer 8:10; Mic 3:11); see the discussion in Albert L. A. Hogeterp, *Paul and God's Temple: A Historical Interpretation of Cultic Imagery in the Corinthian Correspondence*, BTS (Leuven, Belgium: Peeters, 2006), 126.

16 It is possible that Jesus' *supporters* from among the authorities were the ones to demand a miraculous sign, since they knew he was capable of them (John 3:2).

17 Malina and Neyrey, "Honor and Shame," 45; emphasis theirs.

18 R. V. G. Tasker argues that Jesus' assault on the temple was countered with an assault on Jesus' character: "He casts out spirits by Beelzebub" (Mark 3:22); see Tasker, *The Gospel According to St. John,* TNTC (Grand Rapids: Eerdmans, 1972), 61.

19 Caiaphas may have been glad to have a resolution that avoided a public discussion of why the merchants were in the temple.

20 Jesus visits Jerusalem thrice more in John (5:1; 7:10; 10:22) before Passion Week. Andreas Köstenberger argues that if the unnamed feast in 5:1 is not a Passover, then Jesus cleansed the temple on his next visit for a Passover; see Köstenberger, *Encountering John,* EBS 2nd ed. (Grand Rapids: Baker Academic, 2013), 76–78. This does not change my point, however, because we would then argue that Jesus avoided attending Passover, and the authorities would assume for "shame" reasons.

21 See the excellent discussion of the subtleties of "shame," "having shame," "being shamed," and "shameless" in Malina and Neyrey, "Honor and Shame," 41–46.

22 Rabbis argued that while man is prohibited to work on the Sabbath, God is exempt, because "a man is permitted to carry on the Sabbath in his own courtyard" and the whole world is God's courtyard (Isa 6:3). Likewise, a man is permitted to carry a distance equal to his height and God fills the heavens and so God can carry as far as he wants. See *Exodus Rabbah* 30:9 and Rodney A. Whitacre, *John,* InterVarsity Press NTC (Downers Grove, IL: InterVarsity, 1999), 125.

23 For example, T. Sukka 3.17; see Gerhard Kittel and Gerhard Friedrich, eds., *The Theological Dictionary of the New Testament,* ed. and trans. W. Bromiley, 10 vols. (Grand Rapids: Eerdmans, 1964–76), s.v. "Σαδδουκαιος" by R. Meyer, esp. 7:51.

24 See, e.g., Alfred Edersheim, *Jesus the Messiah: An Abridged Edition of the Life and Times of Jesus the Messiah* (London: Longmans, Green & Co., 1890), 59.

25 There is a definite article (*the* prophet) in John 7:40, but no article in 7:52.

26 Craig Blomberg, *The Historical Reliability of John's Gospel: Issues and Commentary* (Downers Grove, IL: InterVarsity, 2001), 90.

27 Richards, "An Honor-Shame Argument for Two Temple Clearings" *Trinity Journal,* 29.1 (Spring 2008), 19–44; see also Carson, *John,* 177; Blomberg, 90; Leon Morris, *The Gospel According to John,* NICNT, rev. ed. (Grand Rapids: Eerdmans, 1995), 167–69; and Darrell Bock, *Luke,* vol. 2: 9:51–24:53, BECNT (Grand Rapids: Baker, 1996), 1577.

28 One could argue that Jesus' subsequent signs should have prompted a reevaluation of the first clearing (and perhaps some leaders did), but the majority held that the matter had been decided.

29 The slight variation (Jesus: "Destroy …" vs. witnesses: "I am able to destroy …") is often explained by suggesting Jesus' comment does not technically constitute blasphemy. It was the witnesses who modified it to make it blasphemy. It is possible the witnesses themselves modified Jesus' original statement, but the second citation in the Synoptics suggests otherwise.

30 There is no reason for the crowd to choose to alter Jesus' statement. It was sufficient ridicule merely to say, "You who would build the temple in three days, save yourself." It seems reasonable that there was a rumor that Jesus had claimed to plan to destroy the temple and rebuild it.

31 It is notable that every account of the saying is in the context of shaming.

32 Morris, *John,* 174, citing Stephen (Acts 6:14, cf. Acts 7:48; 17:24) and possibly echoed in the charge against Paul (Acts 21:28).

33 The biblical text records no miraculous signs of God's arrival (Ezra 6:16–18). The early extra-biblical source is likewise silent (1 Macc 4:54–56). Later Jewish legends ascribe the miraculous multiplication of oil, suggesting God's favor.

EMPOWERING PERSONAL HEALING:
Through the "Medical Substitutionary Atonement"

MAKO A. NAGASAWA

A Milestone Retreat

I was speaking to more than one hundred college undergrads at a weekend retreat. More than ten of the students identified themselves as not Christian. The topic was "Images of God in a Broken World." On the walls hung pictures of children from around the world in various forms of distress and suffering. In light of all this suffering, many wonder, *Is God at least partly evil?* On a communal level, and sometimes on an individual one, the reality of profound suffering shames us. Perhaps rightfully so.

Yet I wanted to urge these students to give their lives to a God who was and is good—*100 percent good.* Only a God who is 100 percent good could figure out a way to defeat and undo the evil within each of us in a loving way, without becoming unloving or evil himself.

How did God do that?

He came as Jesus of Nazareth to acquire the same human nature we have. He lived a life of human faithfulness to the Father, by the Spirit. Throughout his life, Jesus resisted every temptation to be self-centered. At every moment, with every breath, he received his Father's love; he loved his Father in return; he poured out the Father's love to others. He glorified, or revealed, the Father (John 1:14,17; 17:4). On the cross, with more pressure on him than ever before, he broke through the corruption of sin—the same corruption that kills us. He killed it. He defeated every shred of selfishness and fear. Then, in his resurrection, God raised his cleansed, healed, and God-soaked new humanity. By his Spirit, he shares himself with us, cleanses us, and heals us.

During the retreat, I told various stories to illustrate this message. Being a big fan of Tolkien's *The Lord of the Rings,* I told the story of Frodo. Heroes typically go on a quest to gain something. Frodo, however, went to lose something. When he chose to carry the One Ring to be undone in the fires of the volcano in which it was forged, Frodo fought a long and arduous battle. The Ring wasn't just a neutral object. The Ring drew dark forces to him. It tried to make him more self-centered. The Ring caused delusions of grandeur and paranoia. It tempted him to use its power over other people. Frodo resisted. But in the end, Frodo was not able to cast the Ring into the volcano. Even though he stood at the very edge, the alluring and addictive power of the Ring was too great. Frodo took the Ring off its chain and slipped it onto his finger, to identify himself with it.

The moment the Son of God entered Mary's womb as a human baby is like the moment Frodo took hold of the Ring of Power. He began a long battle. Jesus' human nature was not a neutral object, like clothing. It was corrupted by the same sinfulness we all have in our humanity, because we all inherit the sin problem Adam and Eve passed down to us. As a man, Jesus had to fight the human orientation toward sin every step of the way, every moment of his life. Unlike Frodo sharing the burden of the Ring with his friend Sam, Jesus' burden of bearing humanity's nature could not be shared with anyone. Jesus couldn't "put it down"; it was part of him.

What was that struggle like for Jesus? C. S. Lewis wrote, "Only those who try to resist temptation know how strong it is. After all, you find out the strength of the German army by fighting against it, not by giving in."[251]

If you surrender, you don't know how strong your enemy is because you haven't defeated your enemy.

In the same way, we don't understand how to fight our own sinfulness and selfishness. Why? Because we give in. We give up. We cave in to temptation. But Jesus never did. Jesus is the only human being who knows how strong sin actually is, because he's the only one who ever fought it, always beat it, and never gave in.

Frodo didn't throw the Ring into the fire. Likewise, we don't destroy our own selfishness in the holy fire of God's other-centeredness. But Jesus—as humanity's representative but without ever giving in to sin—took the corruption of sin lodged in humanity all the way to its destruction. That moment of destruction was the full judgment of God at the cross when Jesus plunged into death. Jesus carried out the judgment of his Father (John 5:27), with his Father (John 16:32), against the corruption of sin within his human nature, condemning it (Rom 8:3).

Jesus' victory revealed what he had been doing all along: undoing the corruption and disorder of sin. When Jesus was raised in his resurrection, he had a God-drenched, God-soaked new humanity. That's what he had been fighting for the whole time. And now Jesus shares himself with us by placing his Spirit in us, that he might be victorious over the human evil in us and through us.

In Jesus, we see a God who is 100 percent good. He personally restored humanity's image in his own human nature, so he could restore it in us by his Spirit. Which means a loving God found a loving way to love the evil out of us—every single one of us. God's way of undoing evil is drawing people to Jesus. And that makes God fully and completely *good*.

I asked the retreat participants to stand up and face the picture of the suffering child or children that impacted them the most. For the sake of those children and others like them, I asked the college students to make a wholehearted decision for Jesus: *Draw on Jesus' love and strength to fight the selfishness and evil within you. Participate in who Jesus is and in what he did for us—for our sake, and for the sake of others. And participate in his mission to the whole world.*

I was explicit: *Please know that when you commit to Jesus, you are committing to let him heal and develop you, and to evangelism and Christian social justice, because that's how you share in Jesus' healing of others.*

It was a high-bar call to faith. I had never made it all so explicit.

That evening, five of the non-Christians gave their lives to Jesus. For many others, the retreat was a personal milestone. For the student leaders I was mentoring, the retreat was a milestone in how they understood Jesus and ministry. Jesus fully addressed Christians and non-Christians alike.

Years later, those five people who came to Christ were still walking in faith. One of them said,

> This emphasis on Jesus as God's new humanity has made Jesus so much more relatable.... I never really understood how Jesus undid all the sins and evil within the nature of human beings. In many ways, Jesus' death had made me feel guilty, because I found that I was so unworthy to have Jesus suffer on behalf of my sins. However, understanding how Jesus conquered sin through healing humanity during his life and finally conquering the evil of death, I now see his act on the cross as a moment of triumph.

Two Problems Jesus Solves, and Which is Most Fundamental

The way I presented Jesus at the retreat differs from other approaches to the gospel. I emphasized Jesus' entire human life: from conception to adulthood to death to resurrection. I portrayed Jesus as an active, victorious champion, overcoming—

through the cross and resurrection—the pathology of human nature. Jesus was not a passive victim, enduring something terrible thrust upon him.

I invited the students to see that *God is wholly good.*

I refer to this presentation of the life and work of Christ as "medical substitutionary atonement."[2] It cures the pathology of human evil and its source in each one of us—the objective cause of our deepest sin and shame.

Other presentations of Jesus place him in the foreground against a different background, solving a different problem. At the crux of various gospel presentations is the question: From what does Jesus save us?

Saved from Satan's Influence

Jesus saves and delivers us from Satan and his demons. And the reason we are vulnerable to them is because of the emptiness and sinfulness inside us. Jesus said that demons seek to inhabit us as if we were an empty house (Matt 12:25–29). Paul said the devil gains a foothold in us through anger (Eph 4:26–27). The demonic is an undeniable force in the whole world.

But Jesus has reclaimed authority over the whole world from the devil (Matt 28:16–20; 1 John 3:8). He carries out that authority by teaching us to be his followers and bringing us under his kingly authority. Jesus replaces the emptiness with his own Spirit and heals the sinful pathology in us that made us vulnerable in the first place.

Saved from the Wrath of God

The Apostle Paul states assuredly that "we shall be saved from the wrath of God through [Christ]" (Rom 5:9 NASB). But the wrath of God that Paul speaks of involves God allowing us to experience the consequences of our own sinful choices (Rom 1:24, 26, 28). When we resist God, our hearts and bodies (Rom 1:24–25), our desires (Rom 1:26–27), and our minds (Rom 1:28) become more corrupt, troubling, and relationally toxic (Rom 1:29–32) because something happens to our very humanity (Eph 4:17–19).

For example, neuroscience tells us that viewing pornography actually shapes our brain circuitry; we find it a little harder to make healthy choices the next time.[3] Examples abound. Those consequences point us back to God (Jer 2:19). Therefore, Paul says "we shall be saved" from this experience "by His life" (Rom 5:10 NASB).

Saved by Jesus' Life

In hero stories, the heroes typically must undo the tragic consequences they inherit. They must relive a familiar story, while making the faithful choices that everyone else fails to make.

Jesus inherited the human heart in the Jewish covenant story. God called Israel to internalize his commandments so deeply into their humanity that (in Jewish idiom) they were to circumcise their own hearts (Deut 10:16; Jer 4:4; 17:1–10; Rom 2:26–29; Col 2:12). That is, they were to cooperate with God's Spirit to cut away from within themselves that which never should have been lodged there in the first place. But no Israelite could (Rom 7:14–25).

Therefore, Jesus retold Israel's story through his own life.

- Jesus was faithful in every choice—whereas God's people before him had failed.[4]
- Like Israel, Jesus went through water and wilderness; whereas they had succumbed, he conquered every temptation (Matt 3:13–4:11).
- Jesus came to a mountain to receive and give God's commandments; whereas God's people had resisted, he fully cooperated (Matt 5:1ff.)

What Jesus would do in us by his Spirit, he did first in himself. And what Jesus did in himself, he pictured in his work serving others: He healed people of disease, death, and the demonic. Matthew, seeing the symbolism, recalls how the Suffering Servant of Isaiah would bring us "healing" on the most fundamental level, by first sharing in our "wound" (Isa 53:4–5; cf. Matt 8:17).[5]

By partnering with the Spirit of God, Jesus resisted the pathology of humanity that resists God: "the flesh." The flesh is human nature—corrupted and decayed (Rom 7:14–25; John 3:6). And Jesus' life was filled with the glory of the Father, like God's shining pillar of light and fire of old. At his death, Jesus crucified "the old self" (Rom 6:6), the human nature that inherited the ancient Adamic flaw (Rom 5:12–21). Jesus died to reconcile human nature to God (Rom 5:9). Through his human faithfulness, he overcame all human resistance to God.

In this view of Christ's life, atonement, and resurrection (called "recapitulation"[6]), Jesus brought forth humanity's new "heart"—an idiom for new human nature as a whole, which God had promised (Deut 30:6; Ps 51:9–10; Jer 31:31–34; Ezek 11:18; 36:26–36; Heb 8:7–12). This heart is no longer an enemy of God in the slightest (Rom 5:10), but a heart at peace with God (Rom 5:1).

By receiving the Spirit of God (Rom 5:5; 7:6; 8:5–11), we, as Christ-followers, participate in who God truly meant us to be. God always wanted to restore his magnificent work of art—*all creation*—but he starts with human beings. Jesus is the "new Adam" (Rom 5:15–21; 1 Cor 15:21–28). Truly we are saved by Jesus' *life,* by his death *and* resurrection, for "if Christ has not been raised, your faith is worthless; you are still in your sins" (1 Cor 15:17 NASB).

Jesus does indeed save us *by his life* from the demonic and the wrath of God. He does so by saving us from the corruption of sin and evil within us. Jesus' answer to our sin and shame is his glory-soaked humanity (Rom 5:5; Col 1:27; 2 Cor 3–5).

Early Christians Proclaimed the Problem and Solution

Irenaeus of Lyons (AD 130–202) was mentored by Polycarp, bishop of Smyrna. Polycarp was mentored by the apostle John. John lived out his last years in Asia Minor, a region where people had already been evangelized and mentored by the Apostle Paul and others.

In AD 177, Irenaeus became bishop of Lyons in Roman Gaul. He had the knowledge and standing to rebuke and correct Victor, then bishop of Rome. And he wrote a massive treatise against the gnostic heresies (*Against Heresies*), which was widely received.

Irenaeus also authored a book, now lost, called *That God Is Not the Author of Evil.*[7] The title suggests that he was concerned to present God as 100 percent good.

In *Against Heresies,* Irenaeus contends that Adam and Eve corrupted their own human nature. They took into themselves the power and desire to define good and evil; they refused to let that rest with God. Irenaeus argues that God's response was *not retaliatory,* even though it made life much more challenging for humans. Rather, God's response was *preventative:*

> Wherefore also He drove him out of Paradise, and removed him far from the tree of life, not because He envied him the tree of life, as some venture to assert, but because He pitied him, [and did not desire] that he should continue a sinner forever, nor that the sin which surrounded him should be immortal, and evil interminable and irremediable. But He set a bound to his [state of] sin, by interposing death, and thus causing sin to cease, putting an end to it by the dissolution of the flesh, which should take place in the earth, so that man, ceasing at length to live to sin, and dying to it, might begin to live to God.[8]

Rather than allow corrupted human beings to immortalize their sin forever by eating from the tree of life, God exiled them from the garden, and withdrew that special bit of heaven on earth. From God's perspective, at that point death and our vulnerability to nature was better than immortalized sin. Why? *Because God could undo death through Jesus Christ.* Moreover, God wanted to give humans the chance to participate in the undoing of that damage within themselves, and "live to God." We may observe this view in the writings of other early Christian leaders as well.[9]

Irenaeus said this concerning the work of Jesus in saving us from our *sinfulness:*

> Man, who had sin in himself ... was liable to death. [So] it behooved Him who was to destroy sin, and redeem man under the power of death, that He should Himself be made that very same thing which he was, that is, *man;* who had been drawn by sin into bondage, but was held by death, so that sin should be destroyed by man, and man should go forth from death.... Thus, then, was the Word of God made man.... God recapitulated in Himself the ancient formation of man, *that He might kill sin,* deprive death of its power, and vivify man; and therefore His works are true.[10]

Irenaeus was nurtured in a strong and thriving Christian community over the course of many years. He became one of its most trusted leaders.[11] Could he have gotten wrong such important theological truths?

Athanasius of Alexandria (AD 298–373) was another towering figure. Called "the fountain of Christian theology," he was the bishop of Alexandria, Egypt, from AD 328 to his death in AD 373; a courageous defender of the doctrine of the Trinity from the Nicene Creed of AD 325; and the first to recognize the twenty-seven-book New Testament as we receive it today.[12]

Sometime early in his life Athanasius wrote a two-volume work, which is both evangelistic and pastoral. In this work he laid out his theological understandings, from which he never departed. He introduces Part One, *Against the Heathen,* by calling Christian faith "the healing of creation." He introduces Part Two, *On the Incarnation,* by saying he is narrating "the renewal of creation." Those summary statements are refreshing and helpful, framing Jesus as God's new humanity.

To help his readers understand the Christian view of the world, Athanasius describes other beliefs by contrast in the first part of *Against the Heathen.* He faults them for being inconsistent or presenting a deity that was partly evil. This, again, inspires me as a powerful way to present Jesus.

Athanasius says this about the human problem and God's solution in Christ:

> Had it been a case of a trespass only, and not of a subsequent corruption, repentance would have been well enough; but when once transgression had begun men came under the power of the corruption proper to their nature and were bereft of the grace which belonged to them as creatures in the Image of God. No, repentance could not meet the case... . Thus, taking a body like our own ... this He did that He might turn again to incorruption men who had turned to corruption, and make them alive through death by the appropriation of His body and by the grace of His resurrection. Thus He would make death to disappear from them as utterly as straw from fire.[13]

This passage is significant because Athanasius does two things: First, he asks us to imagine Adam and Eve making a small mistake or committing a small offense against God, each other, or their future children—a raised voice, an inappropriate gesture, an unthankful or wasteful attitude, a fearful self-defense, etc. And he says that if they had done this, "repentance would have been well enough," because God would have easily forgiven them that. In some circles, people believe that any small offense against God calls forth infinite, unlimited anger from him. We may be startled to find Athanasius casually dismissing it as beneath God.

Second, Athanasius shows that he regards "the trespass" as an intrusion into human nature, and a turning away from God's image of glory in us which left us "bereft." That is where the disorder and corruption occurred.[14] God, as the loving Creator, had to resolve that problem—that our sin and shame is located in us, not in God's attitude toward us.

Jesus and Personal Healing

If Jesus is the solution to the problem of human evil in the form of personal brokenness, then Jesus is our deepest healing.

I know a deeply traumatized woman who has been transformed by love—love for her child. In order to be a stable mother, she entered a drug treatment program and overcame her addiction. She went to anger management classes and grew in patience. She sought regular counseling instead of living a fiercely private life. And somewhere along this long journey, she opened herself up to Jesus.

This woman recognized that Jesus "learned obedience from the things which he suffered" (Heb 5:8 NASB). She fell in love with Jesus not because he was born already perfect, but because he overcame something that coursed through his human body. But for the sake of us who needed God's love, he was faithful to his Father, and "having been made perfect" (Heb 5:9 NASB) through his human struggle to be perfectly faithful (Heb 12:1–2), he "became … the source of eternal salvation" (Heb 5:9 NASB) from sin. Jesus became not just her inspiration, but her source of holy love and strength. He was the one who sympathized most with her (Heb 4:14–16), not through distant pity but through a deep personal experience that included her and by going so far beyond it.

Because of love, this woman grew as a person. She had met the person of Jesus Christ—love himself.

Jesus and Economic Discipleship

If Jesus is the solution to the problem of human evil, then evangelism and Christian social justice go hand in hand with our personal healing.

My friend Gary VanderPol and I coauthored a small-group curriculum on Christian economic discipleship called *Lazarus at the Gate* (which I've referred to as *Global Poverty Impact* for college students). In it we encourage people to recognize giving money as not simply a command which we either keep or do not keep, but a spiritual gift (Rom 12:8), like teaching, evangelism, pastoring, etc. In other words, *giving* is a muscle that needs to be exercised, honed, and strengthened by regular workouts.

Our first group gave $40,000 after meeting once a month for twelve months. We shared our budgets with each other. We shared best practices on saving. We challenged one another to take the next step during this curriculum. *Cut your hair at home. See fewer movies in the theater. Don't buy that car.* We saved money together. We researched organizations serving people in poverty and vulnerability around the world. We debated about where to give the money we saved. Then we wrote the checks. We loved it.

Gary and I released the curriculum to the Boston Faith and Justice Network. The BFJN later told me that they counted various church groups giving about $750,000 toward the poor around the globe.

We rely on Jesus for emotional strength. One woman realized she went over budget regularly because she was insecure about her friendships and therefore often picked up the tab for coffee and meals. She realized that Jesus wanted to heal her wounded self-esteem and to build true vulnerability to help her deepen her friendships.

A community activist realized he needed to surrender his anger to Jesus when a very wealthy man said his next step was cutting back on wine. The *workout paradigm of developing giving as a spiritual gift* helped him. After all, if he saw an obese man in the gym, just beginning an exercise program, he wouldn't criticize him. He'd try to encourage him as much as possible. This activist recognized that part of his heart looked back over his shoulder with longing and regret since he'd taken a lower-paying job and lived on a tighter budget. He didn't fully believe Jesus' words that giving is a good thing in itself—a participation in Jesus' own generosity and love (2 Cor 8:9). Money matters affected the way he related to others. Jesus wanted to cleanse him of self-centeredness, like a personal trainer wants to free an obese person from unhealthy habits.

How readily we envy and judge people for how much more money they make or spend than we do. It's easy to feel proud and/or embarrassed when we make, or give, more than others. Giving those attitudes and emotions to Jesus is a spiritual discipline. We need to affirm our identity in him, first and foremost. We give him our feelings of discomfort, jealousy, or pain.

The deeper we push into our finances—or rather, let Jesus push into them—the more we need him. Jesus battled all the temptations regarding comfort, wealth, privilege, security, and ease. He conquered them all. He prioritized the love of the Father. We need him to keep doing that in us.

I ran many groups for college students. I asked the Christian students to invite their non-Christian friends to be part of the experience. People who didn't yet know Jesus were open to the small-group experience because they agreed with the end goal. One such young man found it intriguing that Christians cared about putting their money where their mouths were, to care for vulnerable people in the developing world. He cared a bit too—enough to try exercising his giving muscle. The Christian students, being of more humble financial backgrounds, gave up coffee, junk food, or late-night snacks for a while. Each one contributed about $100 over the course of six to seven weeks. The non-Christian student gave up some alcohol, and contributed $300!

Conclusion

God made humanity in his image (Gen 1:27), "crowned with glory and honor" (Ps 8:5). God invests dignity in every person—thus leveling the playing field. God's image in us challenges every oppressive socially constructed hierarchy.[15] Jesus crowns us with new honor: We are temples for his Spirit, so we, in turn, must honor his claim on ourselves and others.[16]

On this firm foundation, we approach ourselves and all others with grace. We can do this regardless of the degree of another's shame/guilt or honor, failure or success, outsider or insider status, family background, citizenship, educational credentials, or other measure of moral or social capital (Rom 3:22–23).

We are compelled unwittingly by the vestiges of our God-given glory. We yearn for love, goodness, justice, meaning, beauty, order. Those yearnings can lead us to embrace the gospel of the very good God, for he alone anchors and personifies those qualities in Jesus Christ. Only Jesus' death, resurrection, and eternal life offer healing from sin—personally and corporately—for a new humanity.

Of course, part of us resists God and diminishes the light of his glory in us. If you think it's easy to be as other-centered and as dedicated to the Father as Jesus, it's because you haven't really tried. But Jesus helps us overcome our resistance. We meet Jesus, and we know we are meant to be like him and be with him. Jesus does not increase our shame. He defeats it. And through his life he shares with us his glory.

Only a God who is 100 percent good will reveal himself in such a loving, powerful, compelling way.

For Further Reflection

1. In what concrete ways does Nagasawa's perspective on atonement address the human condition and connect with scriptural truths?

2. How does "medical substitutionary atonement" cure the pathology of human evil and its source in each of us? How does this aspect of the gospel address the cause of our deepest sin and shame?

CHAPTER 6 Endnotes

1 C. S. Lewis, *Mere Christianity* (C. S. Lewis Signature Classics) (HarperOne: Kindle edition), 142.

2 I use the phrase "medical substitution" to contrast with "penal substitution." "Penal substitution" refers to the theory that Jesus substituted himself for us by absorbing the penalty that God would ordinarily inflict on us. The framework for this theory is legal and penal; the framework for "medical substitution" is medical and restorative. "Medical substitution" refers to Jesus substituting himself for us as God's fully cooperative human patient, because God wants our partnership in repairing the fallen humanity we bear. God is fundamentally for our good and is working with us, not positioned against us.

> The term "medical" also reflects the Sinai covenant, which God framed as a "spiritual health regimen" for Israel in a medical frame. "Circumcise your hearts" (Deut 10:16) is a surgical analogy and serves as an umbrella summary for how an Israelite was supposed to cleanse and heal his/her human nature by internalizing God's commandments. Israel was God's focus group to diagnose and document the problem with human nature, in partnership with him. Ultimately, Israel could not heal sin's corruption in human nature, and the health regimen of God as Doctor was too demanding for them. So Jesus became the "substitute" (with a "medical" or "therapeutic" purpose) to restore human nature (Deut 30:6; Ps 51:9–10; Jer 31:31–34; Ezek 11:18; 36:26–36). Historically, this theory and emphasis has gone by other names, for example, Irenaeus's *recapitulation theory;* Athanasius's *real exchange;* T. F. Torrance's *total substitution.*

3 Michael D. Lemonick, "How We Get Addicted," *Time*, July 5, 2007; William M. Struthers, *Wired for Intimacy: How Pornography Hijacks the Male Brain* (Downers Grove, IL: InterVarsity, 2009); Gary Wilson, *Your Brain on Porn: Internet Pornography and the Emerging Science of Addiction* (Kent, England: Commonwealth Publishing, 2014); Samuel D. James, "See No Evil," *First Things*, April 27, 2016; John Schwartz, "Learning to Learn: You, Too, Can Rewire Your Brain," *New York Times*, August 4, 2017; Janelle Nanos, "Stop Answering Your Phone," *Boston Globe*, January 6, 2018.

4 Fleming Rutledge, *The Crucifixion: Understanding the Death of Jesus Christ* (Grand Rapids: Eerdmans, 2015); chapter 12 has an excellent treatment of "recapitulation" as Jesus retelling Adam's and Israel's story while undoing sin. See also T. F. Torrance, *Incarnation: The Person and Life of Christ*, edited by Robert Walker (Downers Grove, IL: InterVarsity, 2008); chapter 2 discusses the incarnation, the meaning of "flesh," and Jesus as the embodiment and recapitulation of Israel. In *The Trinitarian Faith* (London: T&T Clark, 1983), 168, Torrance writes, "When we ask what the precise nature of this vicarious activity of Christ was, we find Nicene theologians regularly falling back upon familiar biblical and liturgical terms like ransom, sacrifice, propitiation, expiation, reconciliation to describe it, but always with a deep sense of awe before the inexpressible mystery of atonement through the blood of Christ. They used these terms, however … to refer, to not any external transaction between God and mankind carried out by Christ, but to what took place within the union of divine and human natures in the incarnate Son of God." Roman Catholic scholar Thomas Weinandy gives a concise survey of patristic evidence in *In the Likeness of Sinful Flesh: An Essay on the Humanity of Christ* (Edinburgh: T&T Clark, 1993).

5 Interestingly, the Greek Septuagint (LXX) translation of Isaiah 53:10 reads: "And the Lord desired to purify/cleanse him from his wound." The "wound" must either be death or the corrupted human nature lying behind it. In *Jesus and the Suffering Servant: Isaiah 53 and Christian Origins* (Norcross, GA: Trinity Press, 1998), William Bellinger Jr. and William Farmer (editors) discuss the differences between the LXX and the Hebrew Masoretic Text (MT), which reads, "It was the Lord's will to crush him and cause him to suffer." NRSV acknowledges in a footnote the uncertainty in Isaiah 53:10. It is significant that in Romans 11:26 Paul follows the LXX of Isaiah 59:20. The Redeemer will, according to this manuscript family, come to "turn transgression from Jacob." Paul does not quote from the MT, which refers to the Redeemer who will come to "those who turn from transgression in Jacob." That is a subtle but significant theological difference. Paul deliberately chooses to quote exclusively from the LXX version of Isaiah throughout Romans 9–11, a section where he considers Isaianic material in dense frequency. Paul quotes from LXX Isaiah whenever he quotes Isaiah.

From these indications, I believe Paul would have also preferred the LXX variant of Isaiah 53:10. Furthermore, some early church theologians preferred the LXX version of Isaiah 53:10. It is cited by Clement of Rome, *Epistle to the Corinthians*, chapter 16. Justin Martyr cited it in two places: *First Apology*, chapter 51, and *Dialogue with Trypho*, chapter 13. Augustine quoted it in *Harmony of the Gospels*, book 1, paragraph 47. John Chrysostom cited it in *Homilies on First Corinthians*, Homily 38, regarding 1 Cor 15:4. Irenaeus of Lyons, *Demonstration of the Apostolic Preaching* 68–69, quotes from LXX Isaiah 52:13–53:7. The great third-century biblical commentator Origen of Alexandria also preferred to quote LXX Isaiah (*Commentary on the Gospel of John*, book 6, paragraph 35 quotes LXX Isaiah 53:7; *Commentary on the Gospel of Matthew*, book 12, chapters 29–32 quotes LXX Isaiah 53:2–4). Origen's preference for LXX Isaiah is suggestive, since he wrote the monumental *Hexapla*, a twenty-eight-year project where he did word-for-word comparisons of six versions of the Hebrew Bible, including one Hebrew version, the Greek LXX, and other Greek translations.

6   See Rutledge, *The Crucifixion*, 536–70.

7   Church historian Eusebius of Caesarea attests to the book in *Ecclesiastical History* 5.20.4–8.

8   Irenaeus of Lyons, *Against Heresies* 3.23.6

9   Methodius of Olympus (d. AD 311), wrote in *From the Discourse on the Resurrection* 1.4–5: "In order, then, that man might not be an undying or ever-living evil, as would have been the case if sin were dominant within him, as it had sprung up in an immortal body, and was provided with immortal sustenance, God for this cause pronounced him mortal, and clothed him with mortality… . For while the body still lives, before it has passed through death, sin must also live with it, as it has its roots concealed within us even though it be externally checked by the wounds inflicted by corrections and warnings… . For the present we restrain its sprouts, such as evil imaginations, '[l]est any root of bitterness springing up trouble' us, not suffering its leaves to unclose and open into shoots; while the Word, like an axe, cuts at its roots which grow below. But hereafter the very thought of evil will disappear." In *On the Incarnation* 8.1, Athanasius of Alexandria (AD 298–373) wrote, "For the Word, perceiving that no otherwise could the corruption of men be undone save by death as a necessary condition… ." Gregory of Nazianzus (AD 329–390) wrote in *Oration 45*: "Yet here too he makes a gain, namely death and the cutting off of sin, in order that evil may not be immortal. Thus, his punishment is changed into a mercy, for it is in mercy, I am persuaded, that God inflicts punishment."

10 Irenaeus of Lyons, *Against Heresies* 3.18.7. Irenaeus also wrote a training manual called *Demonstration of the Apostolic Preaching*, in which he says in chapter 31, "And because all are implicated in the first-formation of Adam, we were bound to death through the disobedience, it was fitting, therefore, by means of the obedience of the One, who on our account became man, to be loosed from death. Since death reigned over the flesh, it was necessary that, abolished through flesh, it release man from its oppression. So 'the Word became flesh,' that by means of the flesh which sin had mastered and seized and dominated, by this, it might be abolished and no longer be in us. And for this reason our Lord received that same embodiment (*sarkosis*, 'enfleshment') as the first-formed, that he might fight for the fathers and vanquish in Adam that which had struck us in Adam."

11 In the judgment of patristics scholar Johannes Quasten, *Patrology Volume I: The Beginnings of Patristic Literature: From the Apostles Creed to Irenaeus* (Louisville, KY: Westminster: Christian Classics Inc., 6th ed., 1992), 291, Irenaeus' second-century contemporaries Hippolytus of Rome and Tertullian of Carthage seem to quote liberally from Irenaeus' writings, although we cannot be sure that they simply inherited material in common. Eusebius of Caesarea, *Ecclesiastical History* 5.28.5, named Irenaeus as one of two writers whose theology was eminently reliable: "Who does not know the books of Irenaeus and Melito which proclaim Christ as God and Man?" Khaled Anatolios, "The Influence of Irenaeus on Athanasius," *Studia Patristica* 36 (2001): 463–76, considers the question of Athanasius' reliance on Irenaeus. Augustine quoted from Irenaeus, *Against Heresies* 4.2.7 and 5.19.1, in his writings against Pelagius and Julian of Eclanum (*Contra Julian* 1.3.5), and mentions Irenaeus by name (1.7.32). He might also have quoted *Against Heresies* 4.30.1 in his *Christian Doctrine* 2.40.60.

12 Athanasius is celebrated as one of the four greatest teachers of the Eastern Church, along with Basil of Caesarea (330–79), Gregory of Nazianzus (330–90), and John Chrysostom (347–407). Gregory of Nazianzus, *Oration* 21.6, delivers a tribute to Athanasius by saying that while the Alexandrian knew classical literature and philosophy, yet "From meditating on every book of the Old and New Testament, with a depth such as none else has applied even to one of them, he grew rich in contemplation, rich in splendor of life, combining them in wondrous sort by that golden bond which few can weave; using life as the guide of contemplation, contemplation as the seal of life." See Catholic scholar Thomas G. Weinandy, *Athanasius: A Theological Introduction* (Burlington, VT: Ashgate Publishing Company, 2007); the Greek Catholic scholar Khaled Anatolios, *Athanasius: The Coherence of His Thought* (New York: Routledge, 1998); Orthodox scholars Georges Florovsky, "St. Athanasius' Concept of Creation" (publisher and date unknown); and George Dion Dragas, *Saint Athanasius of Alexandria: Original Research and New Perspectives* (Rollinsford, NH: Orthodox Research Institute, 2005); Protestant scholars Thomas F. Torrance, *Divine Meaning: Studies in Patristic Hermeneutics* (Edinburgh: T&T Clark, 1995), chapters. 7–8 and *The Trinitarian Faith* (Edinburgh: T&T Clark, 1995); Peter J. Leithart, *Athanasius* (Grand Rapids: Baker, 2011); and Matthew Baker and Todd Speidell, eds., *T. F. Torrance and Eastern Orthodoxy: Theology in Reconciliation* (Eugene, OR: Wipf & Stock, 2015), chapter 4.

13 Athanasius of Alexandria, *On the Incarnation* 2.8–9.

14 See Rik Van Nieuwenhove, "Bearing the Marks of Christ's Passion," in *The Theology of Thomas Aquinas* ed. Nieuwenhove and Joseph Wawrykow (Notre Dame: University of Notre Dame, 2005), 296. He summarizes his analysis of Aquinas on atonement by saying, "Aquinas describes sin in terms of a sickness of soul whereby the sinner loses her proper focus in life; our incorporation in Christ through faith and charity radically transforms us, heals the soul, and allows us to begin to share in the trinitarian life." He asserts that the "disease" metaphor for sin and the "medicinal" metaphors for Christ are preeminent in Aquinas (282–84).

15 Gregory of Nyssa, in his *Fourth Homily on Ecclesiastes*, argued against slavery on the grounds that a master cannot interfere with another person's wealth, a principle that God intended from creation.

16 Paul states that "you were bought at a price" in 1 Cor 6:20, and then repeats the phrase in 1 Cor 7:23, applying it to the Greco-Roman *doulos* expression of slavery. In his *Homily on 1 Corinthians 7*, John Chrysostom recognized that Paul placed limits on the authority of any relationship because of Jesus' assertion of his lordship over us.

ABUSE AND SHAME:
How the Cross Transforms Shame

STEVE TRACY

Introduction

Our Congolese host had arranged for our team of trauma counselors to drive to a village several miles in the bush to visit a ministry to sexually abused women. This was in 2007, not long after the Second Congo War had ended. Staggering numbers of women were being raped in this province, particularly by soldiers and militia. Christian ministries like this one were overwhelmed by the needs.

Shortly after we entered the dilapidated building, a dozen women arrived and began sharing their stories. We were utterly unprepared for what we saw and heard. Woman after woman told us of being captured and sexually assaulted by soldiers, often at gunpoint. The most haunting story came from a woman who recounted being seized by a small band of militia as she was on her way to the *shamba* (garden). All night she was raped, beaten, and tortured. She literally crawled back to her home early in the morning and collapsed unconscious just outside the entrance to her hut. When her husband found her, he declared that she had brought shame on him, the family, and the village. So he threw her out.[1]

Nearly all the other women reported similar experiences. Many were cast out of their churches and driven from their villages. One woman reported that when she would go to fetch water, the other women in her village would come up behind her, curse her, and bite her on the back. Again, she had brought shame on the community.

We were traumatized just listening to their stories. As Westerners from a highly individualistic culture as opposed to an honor-shame and collectivistic culture, we had no way to understand such seemingly irrational and cruel responses to sexual victimization. Our intuitive response was simply to (1) condemn the culture, and (2) redouble our efforts to educate victims and communities regarding sexual assault, seeking to remove victims' shame through cognitive reframing ("Rape wasn't the victim's fault," "It isn't the victims' shame to carry," etc.) This educational strategy was met with limited success.

After ministering in East Africa for the past eleven years and studying the dynamics of honor-shame cultures, I am now beginning to appreciate the beauty of honor-shame cultures, understand what these abused women experienced from their communities, and offer suggestions for transforming sexual-abuse shame.

Cultural and Biblical Understandings of Abuse and Shame

In reality, the culture we experienced in the Congo was much closer to the cultures of the biblical world than our Caucasian American culture. In fact, some 80 percent of modern cultures can be described as "honor-shame," particularly those found in Africa, Asia, Latin America, and the Middle East. A basic definition of honor is "a claim to worth that is publicly acknowledged."[2] In other words, honor is the value and respect individuals in a community give to another person. There are two primary types of honor: *ascribed* (particularly through one's parents, ancestors, or tribe) and *achieved* (gained through actions considered worthy of honor). The Apostle Paul alludes to his possession of both types of honor prior to his conversion. He had ascribed honor by being a Jew of the tribe of Benjamin and achieved honor through his scrupulous observance of the law (Phil 3:5–6).

Shame is the opposite of honor, meaning "to be denied or to be diminished in honor"[3]—in other words, to be devalued and demeaned by others. While the experience of shame is universal among humans, shame and its antithesis, honor, play a particularly pervasive, critical role in some cultures, thus making these "honor-shame" cultures.[4] No two honor-shame cultures are identical. For instance, how shameful versus honorable behavior is defined and responded to varies greatly from culture to culture. But honor-shame cultures do share certain general traits, which distinguish them from non-honor-shame cultures.[5]

In particular, compared to most Western cultures, honor-shame cultures prioritize shame and honor over guilt or innocence, and social well-being and harmony over individual fulfillment and expression. Recognizing these characteristics helps to explain the seemingly cruel and irrational responses experienced by Congolese women raped at gunpoint. The community was not focused on the raped women's legal/moral innocence or even on the raped women's individual personal needs (as we were); they were primarily looking at the shame their sexual abuse had created for the community and on the resultant needs of the collective group. Clearly, if one is going to minister effectively to sexually abused women, cultural context must shape ministry strategy.

In terms of a biblical theology of shame, note that shame and honor appear prominently in Scripture. The English word *shame* and related terms (*dishonor, reproach, humiliation,* etc.) appear approximately three hundred times in the Old Testament. In the New Testament, Paul most fully develops the concept of shame, using sixteen different Greek terms for shame and eight different words for honor. Shame and honor were exceedingly important to the biblical writers, an obvious fact which until recently escaped the notice of many Western biblical scholars.

Since all humans experience shame, one of the most powerful of all emotions, it is essential to understand, appreciate, and appropriate the honor-shame promises in Scripture. God promises to remove his children's shame, turning it into praise and honor (Zeph 3:11,19; cf. Joel 2:26–27). Those who wait on Yahweh will not be put to shame (Isa 49:23). Believers who faithfully endure trials and persecution will receive divine honor and glory (2 Cor 4:15; 1 Pet 1:7; 5:4). The pursuit of honor is encouraged—it is offered as a reward to those who patiently pursue truth and godliness (Rom 2:6–10).

Interestingly, shame and honor are often addressed in Scripture in the context of abuse, particularly physical and verbal abuse. For instance, the psalmist laments that God had allowed the Israelites' abusive enemies to shame, taunt, and scorn them, making them "a laughingstock among the peoples" (Ps 44:13–15 ESV). Dangerous abusers brought shame and dishonor upon the psalmist, which had broken his heart and left him in despair (Ps 69:19–20). Slanderous, murderous enemies cursed and wagged their heads to shame the psalmist, making him an object of scorn to others (Ps 109:25–29, 31). Being shamed by their abusive enemies caused even the psalmists' neighbors to reject and dishonor them (Ps 31:11 and 89:41).

Note that since shame has such destructive power, God promises to shame abusers and not his own people (Ps 37:19; cf. Isa 41:11; 45:17). Also note that the most frequent context for shame in the Psalms involves the psalmists asking God to shame their abusers.[6] Finally, we should note that sexual abuse and the resultant shame are addressed much more robustly in Scripture than most evangelicals realize.[7] Biblical texts which shed important light on sexual abuse and shame include Genesis 34,[8] Deuteronomy 22:25–29, Judges 5:30, Judges 19, 2 Samuel 11,[9] 2 Samuel 13.

Early Church Fathers' Understanding of Sexual Abuse and Shame

The New Testament is set in a thoroughly shame-honor world. From the time a Roman citizen got up in the morning until he went to bed at night, virtually all of his or her actions were shaped by what would maximize honor and minimize shame.[10] And sexual behavior, particularly a woman's, was a particularly powerful matrix for the cultivation of shame. This was predicated on the patriarchal nature of Roman and Jewish society. Sexual standards, and thus what would be considered shameful, were quite different for men and women. For instance, a husband could prosecute his wife for infidelity, whereas a wife could not bring similar charges against her husband. Furthermore, a married woman would be legally guilty of adultery if she had sexual relations with anyone other than her husband, whereas a husband was only guilty if the other woman was married.[11] This gender-based shame disparity is quite relevant to sexual assault since rape was viewed primarily as a violation against the victim's husband.

Most significant for this study is the story of Lucretia's rape and subsequent suicide in 510 BC. This iconic story was among the most well-known Roman legends, since it purportedly led to the birth of the Roman Republic. King Tarquinius' son raped Lucretia at knife point when her husband was out of town. Afterwards she committed suicide because of the dishonor she bore.[12] In the ancient Roman world, Lucretia was viewed as the ultimate model of chastity and virtue.[13] Ironically, this pagan story was cited by several of the early church fathers to justify a Christian woman committing suicide to prevent the dishonor and moral defilement resulting from rape. For instance, Jerome commends Lucretia, who "would not survive her violated chastity, but blotted out the stain upon her person with her own blood."[14]

The church fathers' view of the impact of rape reflects their honor-shame orientation. Eusebius, who positively recounts the example of a Christian mother who persuaded her two daughters to join her in drowning themselves to prevent soldiers from raping them, argues that they were justified in killing themselves to prevent "the threat of fornication."[15] In other words, the experience of being forcibly violated intrinsically made one guilty of terrible sexual sin. What is ironic is that while the pagan Romans did not generally consider suicide immoral, Christians did except in the case of rape, indicating the great dishonor and moral corruption they believed sexual assault created for the victim.

The view that raped women are somehow guilty and morally polluted continues to prevail in many modern honor-shame cultures. For instance, I asked some of our ministry partners in Uganda and the Democratic Republic of the Congo (DRC) to conduct surveys of raped women, caregivers, and pastors regarding how raped women are viewed by others and whether rape brings shame on the woman, her family, and the community. The answers were quite homogeneous. The most common beliefs were that raped women (1) are often to blame for being assaulted; (2) are dirty and shameful; and (3) bring shame on their families and communities.[16] Here is a representative sampling of the responses:

> "There is usually a feeling that the rape victim is somehow tainted, that the body is a part of the crime. Thus, feelings of shame become almost unavoidable."

"Raped women bring shame to their husband, their family, and their village. The rapist leaves his 'dirt' on his victim, and not only on her but also on all those who approach her and those who live with her. That's why people avoid the raped one."

"The shame of a raped one is so great no one is fit to express it."

"The raped woman is looked at as a *mukumbira* (one who smells). She is accursed, miserable, and no longer has value or worth."

"She feels dirty. She finds that she cannot serve the holy God—she is dirty, impious. Why sing in a choir? How can she lead a devotion time?"

Augustine, one of the most influential theologians in the history of the Christian church, gave a valuable corrective to the views espoused by other early church fathers and contemporaries similar to those surveyed in East Africa. In his magnum opus, *The City of God*, Augustine responded to the widespread rape of consecrated Christian virgins when Rome was sacked in AD 410. He argued in considerable detail that the sin, guilt, and shame belonged only to the rapists and not to the women. He acknowledged that rape can inflict pain and a sense of shame, but asserted that it cannot take away one's virtue. He stated that shame can "invade a thoroughly pure spirit from which modesty [sexual purity] has not departed."[17] Furthermore, he argued that a godly woman who is raped remained pure and honorable in God's eyes. The guilt and shame belong solely to the rapist: "When a woman is violated while her soul admits no consent to the iniquity but remains inviolably chaste, the sin is not hers, but his who violates her." "The sanctity of the soul remains even when the body is violated."[18] In other words, rape in itself cannot remove a woman's virtue or honor.

Given the fact that in many contemporary honor-shame cultures raped women are believed to be dishonorable, Augustine's three major assertions are beneficial in modern honor-shame cultures: (1) The rapist alone is guilty of sin; the victim bears no blame; (2) The rape victim may feel shame, but doesn't have legitimate shame; and (3) In God's view, raped Christian women are as pure and honorable as they were before being raped.

Unfortunately, after providing a salutary discussion of rape and the impropriety of actual or potential victims committing suicide, Augustine goes on to speculate regarding why God allowed the consecrated virgins to be raped. He admonishes the rape victims directly: "Faithfully interrogate your own souls" to discern whether you have become "unduly puffed up" over your own chastity due to a desire for human honor so that God needed to take away your source of sinful pride.[19] Then, anticipating that many of the rape victims would respond by asserting that they did not take pride in their chastity or desire human praise, he says they must not complain that God gave the barbarians permission to "so grossly" dishonor them since they may well have had a subconscious character defect that would have ultimately betrayed them had they not been subjected to the "humiliation" [shame] of being raped.[20] In other words, Augustine suggests that these women were at least partially responsible for being raped and that ultimately they were raped for their own good.[21] Historically, blaming the victim and minimizing the pain and evil of rape are two of the most common and destructive responses to sexual assault given by Christian leaders.

The Role of the Cross in Transforming and Removing Abuse Shame

The atonement of Christ is one of the richest, most complex doctrines in Scripture. It is the very foundation of the Christian faith. A robust understanding with personal application of this doctrine is essential for the transformation of shame. Evangelicals have fixated almost exclusively on the penal nature of Christ's death—the satisfaction of God's righteousness and the appeasement of his wrath. This is often referred to as the "objective" nature of the atonement, in that it was designed to achieve something in God, something outside of humans. The penal view thus places the focus on how human guilt can be removed by virtue of what happened to God through Christ's death.

While Scripture certainly teaches that Jesus' atonement was penal (Isa 53:5–6; 1 John 4:10) and effected change in God, biblically this is merely one of many results of the atonement. The New Testament writers also recognized and highlighted the "subjective" nature of Christ's atonement (i.e., the way it impacts humans). This is a significant point, particularly for honor-shame cultures. As Timothy Tennent notes, Western theology books are filled with references to Christ's death removing guilt, but virtually silent regarding his death removing shame and conferring honor. Tennent then puts this into biblical perspective by way of emphasis:

> This omission [explaining that Christ's death removes our shame] continues in spite of the fact that the term *guilt* and its various derivatives occur 145 times in the Old Testament and 10 times in the New Testament, whereas the term *shame* and its derivatives occur nearly 300 times in the Old Testament and 45 times in the New Testament.[22]

To understand how the cross can transform and remove abuse shame, we must begin with the nature of crucifixion in the ancient world. For the Romans, loss of honor was a fate worse than death. So it is understandable that they used crucifixion as the preferred form of execution for the dregs of society—slaves and enemies of the state.[23] It was a diabolical method for creating not only prolonged pain and death, but utter, permanent shame. Jerome Neyrey argues that crucifixion "at every step entailed a progressive humiliation of the victim and loss of honor."[24] He then lists numerous ways crucifixion shames the victim: It was the punishment of those considered the most shameful; it followed "status degrading" public trials; it included torture while nude which often maimed the body and caused the victims to soil themselves with urine and/or excrement; it included carrying the cursed cross; it involved the confiscation of one's clothes and public execution while nude; it stripped the victim of all power through pinning their hands and feet to the cross; it was a form of crude public entertainment and public ridicule; it often denied victims an honorable burial—their bodies were left to rot on the cross or to be devoured by scavenger animals and birds.

Truly, crucifixion was the ultimate experience of shame and disgrace. For this reason, it is quite understandable that in spite of the fact that crucifixion was a daily occurrence in the Roman Empire, it was considered such a disgusting and obscene topic that ancient writers were loath to discuss it. Cicero said, "The very word 'cross' should be far removed not only from the person of a Roman citizen but from his thoughts, his eyes, and his ears."[25] In other words, crucifixion was too shameful to even speak about.

This helps us understand why the message of Christianity was so offensive to the pagans. It glorified that which was utterly shameful. In fact, the earliest extant picture of crucifixion comes from the second century AD. It was found on the wall of a school for imperial pages in Rome. The picture is of a rough cross on which is a man with the head of a donkey.[26] To the left of the cross stands a man with one arm raised in worship. Underneath are the words "Alexamenos worships [his] God." To the Romans, worshiping a crucified man named Jesus was as foolish and shameful as worshiping a donkey and calling it God.

Ironically and quite strategically, the New Testament writers acknowledge and reframe the worldly foolishness of the cross. That which is most shameful to the world is in fact most honorable and powerful (1 Cor 1:18). The shameful cross is the very means by which human shame is removed and honor is bestowed. Jesus became a curse for us so that we could be honored with the blessing of Abraham (Gal 3:13). Jesus was despised so that we could be made whole (Isa 53:3, 5). Jesus was rejected, mocked, and spit on by sinners so that we could be welcomed, honored, and embraced by God (Matt 27:30–31; Rom 8:16–17; Eph 2:16–19). As Bruce Longenecker notes, "The transmutation of the cross from being an object of disgrace into a symbol of honor and glory (by way of its association with the resurrection) lies at the heart of virtually every text of the New Testament."[27]

The New Testament forcefully reframes the humiliation and shame of Jesus' crucifixion into honor, victory, and glory through his resurrection and ascension (Phil 2:5–11; Col 2:12–15). And this transformation is applied to the followers of the crucified Jesus because they are united with him in his death and resurrection (Rom 6:5–11). They are now sons and daughters of God, members of the royal family, and joint heirs with Jesus (Rom 8:17; Gal 4:4–6; 1 Pet 2:9). Jesus' followers enjoy his glory (John 17:22).

Thus, the crucified Jesus is the believer's only true boast and source of honor (Phil 3:1–10; Gal 6:14). Paul, in Philippians 3:8, makes this point most dramatically.

After noting the great ascribed and achieved honor he possessed as a Pharisee, Paul says he has gladly given all that up for the sake of gaining Christ and sharing in the sufferings of Jesus. In fact, compared to the honor of being linked to Jesus, he considered his former glory to be nothing more than excrement (*skoubalon*)—that which is most shameful! Hence, Paul's life ambition was to "share his sufferings, becoming like him in his [shameful] death" (Phil 3:10 ESV).

The transformation of shame into honor is very relevant for abuse victims. When unbelievers abused and shamed the early Christians for their faith, the Christians reframed that shame as honor. For instance, when the apostles were beaten for proclaiming Jesus, they left the Jewish council "rejoicing that they were counted worthy to suffer dishonor for the name [of Jesus]" (Acts 5:41 ESV; cf. 1 Pet 4:12–13).

This transformation is very challenging to sexual abuse victims, however, due to the heightened shame of sexual violation and due to the motivations of rapists. Few raped Christians in the ancient or modern world are raped because of their Christian faith. Rather, they are most often assaulted for other reasons such as male lust, misogyny, and tribal hatred. Therefore, we must clarify how rape victims can experience the transformation of their shame. Two principles which flow out of the previous discussion are most helpful.

First, Jesus experientially relates to abuse victims. He experienced all major types of abuse, including public sexual shame. Thus, the abuse victim can and should look to Jesus for compassion and help. This is precisely what the writer of Hebrews urged his readers to do:

> Since then we have a great high priest who has passed through the heavens, Jesus, the Son of God, let us hold fast our confession. For we do not have a high priest who is unable to sympathize with our weaknesses, but one who in every respect has been tempted as we are, yet without sin. Let us then with confidence draw near to the throne of grace, that we may receive mercy and find grace to help in time of need. (Heb 4:14–16 ESV; cf. Heb 2:17)

Second, regardless of the source of shame, Scripture is patently clear regarding how God views his children. Because of their union with Christ, believers are unconditionally loved, valued, and accepted by God. No human or demonic abuser can separate them from his love; no one can legitimately shame a child of God; no matter what has been done to a believer, God views them as precious and honorable (Rom 8:31–39).

Practical Ministry Suggestions

We can now draw out three specific action steps for helping sexual abuse survivors overcome their shame.

1. Redefine Sexual Purity

This is where Augustine's comments to the raped Christian virgins is most helpful. Abuse victims, their families, and their spiritual leaders need to be educated regarding the nature of sexual purity. They particularly need to understand that a raped woman remains pure and honorable in God's eyes because the guilt and shame belong solely to the rapist. Rape cannot remove a woman's virtue or honor. This kind of sexual purity teaching, particularly through the ministry of an African pastor/theologian who shares an honor-shame worldview and has dealt with mass abuse trauma, can be very powerful.

Augustine's comments can be further strengthened by noting that Scripture repeatedly speaks of abusers, including sexual abusers, shaming their victims (2 Sam 13:12–17; Ps 69:19–21). But the shame and "moral pollution" is the abuser's, not the victim's (Deut 22:25–26). Thus, we see in Psalm 4 that while abusers deceitfully try to turn victims' honor into shame (v. 2), God honors his children who are victimized; he "sets them apart" (lifts them up) and listens to them (v. 3 ESV; cf. Ps 69:19, 33). While abusers treat their prey as impure and shameful, God loves, delights in, and "does not despise" abuse victims (Ps 57:3–4; 69:33). In fact, God comforting and honoring abuse victims shames their abusers (Ps 71:20–21, 24; 86:17).

We must, however, go one step further. Augustine helpfully addressed "objective shame"—i.e., shame before God based on real guilt. But this does not go far enough because it is still focused solely on objective moral purity. This is probably why Augustine only addressed the rapes of holy virgins. He had absolutely no pastoral guidance or comfort to give to the countless non-virgin Christian women who were raped. Even the raped virgins he addressed received little practical guidance regarding removal of shame. This is where the subjective nature of Christ's atonement is most critical. Christ died not only to effect a change in God (satisfaction of his righteous anger at sin), but to effect a change in us—namely, our experience of shame, both from sin we have committed and from sin committed against us.[28]

Shame can be properly defined as "the fear, pain, or state of being regarded unworthy of acceptance in social relationship."[29] Christ's life and death allow us to experience the removal of shame through reentry into relationship. As we have seen, subjective shame is often experienced in terms of ritual or moral impurity which separates individuals from the community. The New Testament repeatedly shows Jesus cleansing impurity and removing shame so that people experience reconciliation with God and other people.[30] For instance, Jesus cleansed the impurity of a leper, removing his shame and social alienation (Luke 5:12–14; cf. Lev 13–14). He healed a woman who had been impure for twelve years due to chronic bleeding, thus allowing her to fully reenter her community (Luke 8:43–48; cf. Lev 15:19–30). Jesus healed and restored a naked, demon-possessed man who lived in the tombs experiencing overwhelming impurity, shame, and social isolation (Luke 8:27–35; cf. Lev 15:19–30).

These purity cleansings foreshadow the greater cleansing produced by the atonement of Christ. He died to wash and cleanse us (Titus 3:5; Heb 1:3). This purification allows believers to experience a cleansed conscience (Heb 10:22), new intimacy with God, and intimacy with "unclean" outsiders (Acts 10:11–28). Ultimately, believers' experience of honor instead of shame comes from their new identity with Christ and other believers (Rom 12:10; 2 Thess 2:14; 2 Tim 2:10).[31]

In 2016 my wife and I had the privilege of conducting several trauma-ministry trainings in the Congo. During some of the small-group interaction, we discovered that in one of the groups three of the five participants, all pastors, had daughters who had been raped. None of these men knew this about each other, and yet all had responded in virtually identical ways—they had shamed their daughters and forbidden them from partaking in communion because they were no longer "pure." But because of the teaching they had just received on the nature of sexual abuse, they made immediate personal application. Each humbly shared that they were sorry they had treated their daughters this way and would immediately go home, apologize, and rectify their previous blaming, shaming responses. They had come to realize through education on the nature of rape and sexual purity that their abused daughters were not to blame and were not "dirty." And thankfully, their daughters experienced the removal of shame.

2. Expand the Atonement of Christ—Jesus and the Father Were Shamed to Remove our Shame

Helping abuse survivors *experience* the subjective aspects of Christ's atonement is essential for helping them heal. So in our African trauma conferences, we teach extensively on the nature of ancient crucifixion and how the cross removes shame. We place particular attention on the New Testament emphasis on Jesus suffering abuse shame (including the shame of public nakedness) and hence being able to experientially relate to and have compassion for abuse victims' shame. Hence, we commissioned a professional artist to paint a realistic picture of Jesus hanging on the cross to use for the cover of our training book, *By His Wounds*.[32] Expanding abuse victims' understanding of the atonement must, however, be more than a cognitive educational process; personal application is essential. In our Africa trauma conferences, we incorporate several exercises from *By His Wounds* to help abuse victims overcome their shame. These include:

(1) Expressive art exercises, reflections, and prayers centered on the crucifixion of Christ. These include having attenders (a) draw a picture of Jesus on the cross looking at abuse victims; (b) write down some of the shame they experienced through their abuse and symbolically nail the shame list to a wooden cross; (c) draw a picture of the presence of God in heaven above Jesus on the cross

and reflect on what God experienced watching his Son suffer on the cross;[33] (d) write a prayer to Christ about their shame after reflecting on the cross picture.

(2) Public reading of "The Father's Love Letter."[34] This is a list of forty-five biblical statements and applicable Bible verses regarding how God sees his children, written as a love letter from God. We find great benefit in having conference attendees turn to the love letter in their book and take turns reading aloud, progressing around the room one statement at a time. This multi-sensory, corporate exercise can help abuse survivors begin to hear and feel how God lovingly views them. This has been one of the most transformative exercises we use in our trainings.

(3) A final Christocentric shame tool we utilize is a reflection exercise. The participants receive a beautiful picture of Jesus hugging a child. We explain that the picture images Jesus' eternal love for each of his children. The attenders reflect on the details of the picture for several minutes and then write their thoughts and/or a prayer from their reflections. In one conference, we gave each participant a copy of this picture at the end of the day. We asked them to do the reflection at home and to be prepared to discuss their experiences the next day. One of the first people to share was a young man in his mid-twenties. He explained that he should never have been born and grew up hearing he was nothing but a shameful bastard. He had always considered himself to be nothing more than a bastard child. (Given his age and self-description, it is likely he was conceived through rape during the 1994 genocide.) Furthermore, he said he had been suicidal and did not believe he should continue to live. However, in doing this reflection he came to realize for the first time that he had worth because Jesus truly loved and embraced him. The fact that he shared his shameful birth status with a room full of fellow Rwandans evidenced the shame-relieving power of this simple exercise.

3. Give Sexual Abuse Victims Honor in the Christian Community

We have seen that the early Christians dealt with the extreme shame heaped on them by their unbelieving community members by honoring each other in the Christian community. Members of Christian congregations are to function as an "alternative 'court of reputation' that grants esteem to one another on the basis of our worth in Christ."[35] Scripture expressly says believers are to honor everyone, particularly fellow believers (1 Pet 2:17). In fact, honoring each other in the Christian community is to be such a priority that we are commanded to "outdo one another in showing honor" (Rom 12:10 ESV). The many "one another" commands in the New Testament help to flesh out what honoring (valuing) one another looks like in concrete terms.[36]

This honor command has particular relevance to sexual abuse survivors since they have experienced some of the greatest levels of dishonor. Jesus is the perfect model for such honoring, for he repeatedly and extravagantly honored the sexually shamed, often shaming their accusers in the process (Luke 7:36–50; 15:1–32; John 4:1–42; 8:1–11). As Georges and Baker note, "Overcoming shame requires a remaking or transformation of the self. One's identity must change, and this happens only as their relationship to the group changes. That usually means a person of a higher status must publicly restore honor to the shamed."[37]

We have witnessed amazing examples of African believers honoring sexual abuse victims. Mama Abia, the founder and director of CEPIMA, a Congolese ministry with five residential centers for the mentally ill, is one of the most beautiful. Most of the CEPIMA patients have suffered severe abuse, often sexual. In a culture where sexual abuse as well as mental illness are exceedingly shameful, Mama Abia and her staff have created an environment of love, compassion, and acceptance. We have visited her facilities numerous times and always marvel at the incredible respect and gentleness she and her staff give to their patients, regardless of what they have done or how they are acting. We have repeatedly witnessed miraculous healing of shame as these abuse victims experience being consistently treated with great honor.

Conclusion

Shame from sexual assault is overwhelmingly destructive for victims and their families, particularly those in honor-shame cultures. Yet we are not left without hope. The message of the cross of Christ, experienced in loving community, is the most powerful antidote for removing and transforming sexual abuse victims' shame. May God give us his grace and power to see and treat abuse survivors as he does!

For Further Reflection

1. Consider Tracy's "educational strategy" to address the victims of sexual-abuse shame and his "practical ministry suggestions" from the perspective of honor-shame. What relates to your own observations or experience? Why?

2. Stigma is powerful. In your own context, what marks people as socially disfigured, defiled, or irrevocably shamed? How does the gospel speak to these individuals? How does your own local church demonstrate this aspect of the gospel?

CHAPTER 7 Endnotes

1 The similarities between this story and the one recorded in Judges 19:1–29 regarding the gang rape of the Levite's concubine are tragically ironic.

2 John J. Pilch and Bruce J. Malina, eds., *Biblical Social Values and Their Meaning: A Handbook* (Peabody, MA: Hendrickson, 1993), s.v. "Honor/shame."

3 Ibid.

4 Timothy C. Tennent, *Theology in the Context of World Christianity: How the Global Church Is Influencing the Way We Think About and Discuss Theology* (Grand Rapids: Zondervan, 2007), 80.

5 See Jayson Georges and Mark Baker, *Ministering in Honor-Shame Cultures* (Downers Grove, IL: InterVarsity, 2016), 35–46; and Werner Mischke, *The Global Gospel: Achieving Missional Impact in Our Multicultural World* (Scottsdale, AZ: Mission ONE, 2015), 41.

6 For instance, Ps 31:17; 35:4, 26; 40:14–15; 53:5; 57:1–3; 70:2–3; 71:13; 83:16–18; 86:17; 109:29; 129:5. For a concise discussion of abuse victims asking God to shame the abuser see my book, *Mending the Soul: Understanding and Healing Abuse* (Grand Rapids: Zondervan, 2005), 89.

7 One of the best concise surveys of sexual abuse in the Old Testament is Richard M. Davidson, "Sexual Abuse in the Old Testament: An Overview of Laws, Narratives, and Oracles," in *The Long Journey Home: Understanding and Ministering to the Sexually Abused*, ed. Andrew Schmutzer (Eugene, OR: Wipf and Stock, 2011), 136–54.

8 Historically scholars have debated whether Dinah was actually raped or whether the text suggests she bore some responsibility. For arguments in favor of this being a clear case of forcible rape, see Susanne Scholz, "Was It Rape in Genesis 34? Biblical Scholarship as a Reflection of Cultural Assumptions" in *Escaping Eden: New Feminist Perspectives on the Bible*, ed. Harold Washington et al. (Sheffield, England: Sheffield Academic Press, 1998), 183–98.

9 Richard Davidson makes an excellent case for this being an example of "power rape" by David, the sovereign Hebrew monarch. He gives eighteen different arguments to support this thesis in *Flame of Yahweh: Sexuality in the Old Testament* (Peabody, MA: Hendrickson, 2007), 523–32.

10 David deSilva, *Honor, Patronage, Kinship & Purity: Unlocking New Testament Culture* (Downers Grove, IL: InterVarsity, 2000), 23–24.

11 Jane Gardner, *Women in Roman Law and Society* (Indianapolis: Indiana University Press, 1986), 127.

12 In Livy's classic account of this event, Lucretia states that while she was guiltless, her honor had been lost (and, by inference, her husband's honor) and thus "while I acquit myself of the sin, I do not absolve myself of the punishment," Livy, *History of Rome 1*, trans. B. O. Foster, Loeb Classical Library 114 (Cambridge, MA: Harvard University Press, 1919), 196–211.

13 For instance, Ovid recounts this story, emphasizing Lucretia's chastity and virtue by noting that when she was falling down after stabbing herself "even in dying she took care to sink down decently," Ovid, *Fasti*, trans. J. G. Frazer and rev. G. P. Goold, Loeb Classical Library 253 (Cambridge, MA: Harvard University Press, 1931), 114. Since her rape brought her great dishonor and shame, her elevation to such a stature likely was a result of her committing suicide.

14 Jerome, *Against Jovinianus* 1.46. Joan Stivala argues that the example of Lucretia was actually more influential for the early church fathers than for the pagan Romans; "Death before Dishonour! Suicide of Christian Victims of Rape," *Eras* 13 (2011): 1–17.

15 Eusebius, *The Church History* 8.12; cf. 8.14. Other early church fathers who justified (or even admonished) suicide to prevent rape include Jerome, Commentary on Jonah 1.12.390–391, *Against Iouinianum* 1.43; and Ambrose, *Concerning Virginity* 3.7.32–34.

16 See also J. T. Kelly et al., "Experiences of Female Survivors of Sexual Violence in Eastern Democratic Republic of the Congo: A Mixed-Methods Study," *Conflict and Health* 5 (2011): 1–8; and J. T. Kelly et al., "'If Your Husband Doesn't Humiliate You Other People Won't': Gendered Attitudes towards Sexual Violence in Eastern Democratic Republic of the Congo," *Global Public Health* 7 (2012): 285–98.

17 Augustine, *City of God*, 1.16.

18 Ibid., 1.19; 1.18. Similarly, in 1.28 Augustine states that "purity both of the body and the soul … cannot be forcibly taken from an unwilling person."

19 Ibid., 1.28.

20 Ibid., 1.28

21 For a thorough critical evaluation of Augustine's treatment of rape in *City of God*, see Mary Pellauer, "Augustine on Rape: One Chapter in Theological Tradition," in *Violence against Women and Children: A Christian Theological Sourcebook*, ed. Carol Adams and Marie Fortune (New York: Continuum, 1995), 207–41.

22 Tennent, *Theology*, 92. Tennent draws from Bruce Nichols, "The Role of Guilt and Shame in a Theology of Cross-Cultural Mission," *Evangelical Review of Theology* 25 (2001): 231–41.

23 One slave owner upon being challenged that she was about to crucify an innocent slave retorted, "You idiot! Is a slave a person?" In other words, crucifixion is always fitting for those who are subhuman. Juvenal, *Satires*, trans. and ed. Susanna Morton Braund, Loeb Classical Library 91 (Cambridge, MA: Harvard University Press, 2004), 252–55.

24 Jerome Neyrey, "Despising the Shame of the Cross," *Semeia* 68 (1996): 113.

25 Cicero, *Pro Rabirio Perduellionis*, trans. H. G. Hodge, Loeb Classical Library 198 (Cambridge, MA: Harvard University Press, 1927), 466–67.

26 Everett Ferguson, *Backgrounds of Early Christianity, 2nd ed.* (Grand Rapids: Eerdmans, 1993), 559–61.

27 Bruce Longenecker, *The Cross Before Constantine: The Early Life of a Christian Symbol* (Minneapolis: Fortress, 2015), 44.

28 Soong-Chan Rah helpfully distinguishes abuse sin as "the unjust act of the oppressors" and *han* (a rich Korean word) as "the passive [shameful] experience of their victims." He notes that Western "concepts of sin lead us to feel guilty when we do something bad, but we often do not have the language of shame when we are sinned against." *Prophetic Lament: A Call for Justice in Troubled Times* (Downers Grove, IL: InterVarsity, 2015), 57. *Han* is particularly relevant to subjective shame.

29 Jackson Wu, "Have Theologians No Sense of Shame? How the Bible Reconciles Objective and Subjective Shame," *Themelios* 43 (2018): 206.

30 For a detailed discussion of honor-shame and purity, see Mischke, *The Global Gospel*, 161–80.

31 Wu ("No Sense of Shame?" 214) catalogs six ways God solves the problem of shame, all of which are objective except for one: "because we have a new identity, we no longer feel ashamed."

32 Steven and Celestia Tracy, *By His Wounds: Trauma Healing for Africa* (Phoenix: Mending the Soul Ministries, 2014).

33 This exercise is particularly important for husbands in honor-shame cultures whose wives or children were abused. In patriarchal honor-shame cultures these husbands/fathers experience a great sense of impotence and resultant shame. As one study done among Congolese rape survivors and their spouses revealed, "A husband's failure to protect his wife is perceived as a humiliation, and blaming the woman become[s] the best way for the man to recover his dignity," Nissou Ines Dossa, et al., "Social Consequences of Conflict-Related Rape: The Case of Survivors in the Eastern Democratic Republic of the Congo," *Journal of Peace Psychology* 20 (2014): 244.

34 To read "The Father's Love Letter" in its entirety, visit https://www.fathersloveletter.com/copyright.html.

35 DeSilva, *Honor, Patronage, Kinship & Purity*, 318.

36 For instance, believers are to "love one another with brotherly affection" (Rom 12:10 ESV); "Welcome one another as Christ has welcomed [us] (Rom 15:7 ESV); "Be kind to one another, tenderhearted, forgiving one another" (Eph 4:32 ESV); "Encourage one another and build one another up" (1 Thess 5:11 ESV); "Keep loving one another earnestly," "Show hospitality to one another without grumbling," and use spiritual gifts to "serve one another" (1 Pet 4:8–10 ESV).

37 Georges and Baker, *Ministering in Honor-Shame Cultures*, 38.

HONOR-SHAME IN VARIOUS MISSION CONTEXTS

THE DARK SIDE OF ORALITY

Lynn Thigpen

At Harvard's 2007 commencement, Bill Gates made this profound statement: "Humanity's greatest advances are not in its discoveries—but in how those discoveries are applied to reduce inequity."[304]

For those of us who read books like this one, a great inequity lies hidden before our eyes. I write with urgency, with a plea that some who read this chapter will begin to understand the situation, and this information will stir them to address the situation.

For more than a decade and a half, I have worked with "oral learners" in Southeast Asia. Who are these "oral learners"? In Cambodia, they are mostly adults with few opportunities to study, whether as a result of war or due to poverty-driven circumstances. These non-readers are *adults with limited formal education*. In my research and teaching, I call them ALFE (pronounced "al-phee") for short.[2]

Although I have been involved in storytelling and the training of storytellers among my ALFE friends for some time, I found myself at a loss to completely grasp how they learn. So I decided, over the last few years, to dive more deeply into the hidden recesses of how ALFE learn best. In the beginning I thought I was embarking on a cognitive journey, a sort of fact-finding mission. However, I encountered more emotions than I imagined. The true issues contradicted my surface impressions. And the villain? The villain of the story shocked me.

The Predicament and Prevalence

As I talked at length with adult after adult having six years or less of formal schooling, I came to understand their arduous plight because they graciously introduced me to their world. The first day of interviews etched memories in my mind. I journeyed to a familiar place and listened to familiar people, but their deepest educational woes and the many obstacles they had conquered lay buried in the deep recesses of their hearts and unknown to my ears.

Shame on me. That day I finally felt the pain of being uneducated in a place where schools exist. I heard the pangs of poverty and the sting of people giving up their right to an education because their family needed them to work.

One young mother told me she attended school and tried to read, but simply could not "get it." She could not learn to read no matter how hard she tried. During our interview, her younger sister sat by her side and did something quite common in many Asian cultures. Younger Sister decided to shame Older Sister into better performance, chiding: "I don't know why she can't get it. I don't know why she doesn't just try harder. I think she's stupid."

Her words reverberated in that public space—a clear and cutting message. I knew that kind of thing happened all the time, but I had never been present to feel the sting. Being heavily schooled in Western self-esteem, I could not bear the weight of her hurtful words. Younger Sister lathered on words of shame. By the time she finished, her toxic talk drowned us, giving little hope of survival. Meanwhile, Older Sister sat licking her wounds and drinking the poison. I would not have imagined my dissertation research unfolding in such an emotional way.

I looked at that precious young mother and realized she was not stupid at all. Thankfully, the thought dawned on me that Big Sister might have a learning disability—dyslexia. So, while sitting on a wooden bench in a village on the Mekong, I held her hand and explained another learning style, one belonging to millions, one that is just a little different. I knew no word for it in the Khmer language, no one word for issues like mixing up letters; but I explained the concept and told her not to worry. People with dyslexia are not stupid. She wept. I wept. Big Sister proclaimed, "I have goosebumps. I am so happy to hear this news!" This, too, was not the way I imagined research going—interviews dripping with emotion.

Not everyone experienced the same situation. Some adults did not study because their tender lives intersected with war. Others had limited education because working to support their families became more essential than learning. While one friend was a top student in elementary school, her parents forced her to drop out in order to work. Feelings of deep regret and unfairness weaved through her shared memories.

Why do I share these stories? Because millions of people just like these surround us. Don't let published statistics mislead you. In Cambodia, like most parts of the world, illiteracy is high. In fact, most of the women I know at the village level hardly attended school. The older ones endured war; the younger, poverty and lack—circumstances beyond their control.

Is the situation in Cambodia out of the norm, or is it widespread? The International Orality Network estimates that four billion people over the age of fifteen, and thus two-thirds of the world's population, are oral communicators—people who cannot or prefer not to read.[3] Read that sentence again. Four billion people is a huge portion of the world population—a majority, in fact.

On the flip side, how many of us are literate? Highly proficient readers—those who have studied at advanced levels—number a tiny minority across the globe. A study conducted in the United States and listing six levels of literacy, from level zero to level five, found that only 2 percent of the US adult population functioned at the highest level of literacy—that is, the uppermost level of being able to read, learn, analyze, and engage in activities like inductive Bible study.[4] Let that statistic sink in—*only 2 percent!* We hand people books when the majority of the world would rather not open one.

Please do not misunderstand. Reading is a precious and valuable skill. I encourage it. I love to curl up with a good book, and some of my friends with limited formal education have gone on to learn to read and write. Some, however, have not and/or could not.

These statistics represent the situation surrounding literacy. What about associated poverty? Not every non-reader comes from a background of poverty, but most of the ALFE with whom I had discussions lived in desperate situations. We usually think about poverty in terms of numbers, about people making less than one US dollar per day. More recently, the Oxford Poverty and Human Development Initiative "developed a new international measure for poverty, the Multidimensional Poverty Index or MPI."[5] This indicator examines education, health, and standard of living. Interestingly, the MPI considers years of schooling. If no family member completes five years of schooling, the index labels the family deprived; if no one completes at least one year of schooling, the MPI considers them destitute.[6]

The Real Problem

Poverty, however, represents so much more than even these indicators (income, education, health, etc.) would suggest. Researchers lament the "missing dimensions" of poverty, "dimensions that are of value to poor people, but for which we have scant or no data."[7] What might those elements be, and why should we care?

In the 1990s, the World Bank surveyed over sixty thousand of the financially poor throughout the developing world and how they described poverty. The poor did not focus on their material need; rather, they alluded to social and psychological aspects of poverty. The study highlights that, by nature, poverty is innately social and psychological.[8]

In a similar study, *Voices of the Poor,* researchers found that "employment, dignity, and hope are valued as much as livelihoods, education, and health."[9]

This predicament staggers the imagination. But what is the real problem? Many of the people I interviewed lived each day caught in a cycle of lack—a cycle from which they knew no escape. Lacking material resources and living in poverty due to a multitude of factors, many experienced the unfortunate situation of being forced to drop out of school or having never been given the opportunity to attend in the first place. Some still lived in the grip of poverty, but some escaped. While they existed in situations of limited education, they all had something else in common. In primary oral societies or tribal settings with no written languages or reading material, lack of formal schooling does not walk hand in hand with shame. There, no one fails to learn.[10] However, in societies having the expectation of their offspring receiving an education, like everyone else, lack of formal schooling and/or lack of reading ability can be a source of great shame.

In the lives of my friends, the condition of lack (poverty) caused a subsequent lack of formal education, resulting in a lack of honor or dignity in the face of the community. Researchers Chase and Bantebya-Kyomuhendo call this the "poverty-shame nexus"[11]—that is, a lack of material goods, formal education, opportunity, understanding, and honor, but no such lack of shame. During the interviews, another young mother explained her situation this way:

> Sometimes I feel small talking to people who get to go to school and sometimes people look at me and tell me that I am stupid. Sometimes I get angry with my kids because they do not want to study, and they procrastinate. I have to yell at them so that they do their homework because I don't want them to be stupid like me.

Surrounded by a group-oriented culture, these ALFE heard the call to live up to societal norms, a call to flee shame of every sort. Living in that environment while failing to fulfill social expectations invites cajoling and shaming. It is permissible to shame someone who doesn't live up to social norms and accepted ideals—as in the story about the sisters.

All of us have experienced psychological shame and embarrassment, but these adults were drowning in the toxic and debilitating variety of shame.[12] One writer explained it this way: "The Chinese sign for shame is composed of the sign for 'ear' and the sign for 'heart,' which means: I hear with my ears and I feel in my heart what the others speak about me."[13] *Hearing and feeling. Limited education. Unlimited shame.* No one talks about this much in orality circles.

Shame lurks at the very core of poverty.[14] I never imagined this emotion to be a part of an oral learner's life, let alone at the forefront. I told many Bible stories, but never really addressed this integral life concern. Unfortunately, this kind of toxic shame also leads to the regrettable addition of "pretense, withdrawal, self-loathing, 'othering,' despair, depression, thoughts of suicide, and generally to reductions in personal efficacy," all of which beg to be addressed.[15]

Add to poverty and limited education a learning disability and we see potential for the "conundrum of failure" that Kathleen Tanner mentions.[16] Many adult dyslexics who have struggled with learning to read feel intensely this spiral of failure and subsequent emotions like "feeling incomprehensibly flawed."[17] Combining a conundrum of failure with a cycle of lack creates a storm of epic personal proportions. People just want to be able "to go about without shame."[18] You might not meet them or know of their plight, but there are multitudes surrounding us and living in the overwhelming downpour of emotional precipitation.

I met a very young father I will call Samnang, which means *lucky* in the Cambodian language. He was lucky in work, but not in other areas. He had an excellent job in agriculture with a nongovernmental organization. However, like so many others, he entered the doors of school only to greet failure in full force. He explained the inability to "get" reading and pronounced his diagnosis as *"ree-un aht jole,"* meaning the learning would not enter his mind.[19] I realized he likely had some undiagnosed learning disability as well. So we had another very familiar talk about dyslexia. However, what he said next about his church experience grips me to this day.

Samnang confided, "When I go to church and see the hymns and songs on the screen and watch people read from the Bible, I just want to die. I want to kill myself because I cannot read like other people can."

Such shame—*and in the church.* As people of the Book, how can we deal with this hidden emotional turmoil in the souls of those in our pews? Our Master suffered some of the worst humiliation so we as his followers might enjoy honor and connection with him. How can we allow such a situation to exist?

This discussion leads me to the villain in this story. Who is at fault? Is it the ALFE? Certainly not. In our respective cultures, we are socialized to understand what is honorable and what is shameful. Why do these learners feel shame? Despite their strengths, they feel shame because they lack schooling or because they lack literacy. Modern Western education applauds learner-centered strategies, but what about being learner-centered with non-readers? That idea does not even make the list. Most programs seem to shout, "We'll teach you to read!" Why? What if adults just want to learn something else?

Herein lies the inequity I introduced in the first paragraph of this chapter. Have you discovered the culprit? We do not provide learning in ways ALFE prefer. We shove books at them instead of providing learning in the ways they prefer. Shame on us!

Arlene Fingeret, who studied illiteracy decades ago, alleged: "'Literacy' represents an ideal state. The sorting process occurs in the dominant class, and the criteria, therefore, represent dominant-class norms."[20] Reading is a valuable skill, opening new vistas. But could we not provide learning opportunities for people before they can read? Admittedly, this idea challenges traditional practices. Couldn't adults be given opportunities to shine in their own special ways before or until they learn to read?

These issues result from a literate majority "calling the shots," the results of overlooking ALFE and non-readers, elevating one way of learning above all others. Why do we do this? In a world full of tolerance, why do we still think this way? Consider this quote: "Emphasizing success at school as a criterion for success in life can be debilitating for those whose interest and aptitudes lie elsewhere, and who are stigmatized as failures on account of their school performance."[21] We do not provide learning in the ways ALFE prefer.[22] We emphasize reading instead of figuring out how to adapt to their learning style. We should be the ones feeling shame.

The Prescription and the Place

As I have stated in my dissertation, serious dignity issues exist for ALFE.[23] This leads me on a quest for antidotes for this poisonous situation. Formal schooling and literacy studies cannot be the only solution. The problem—the loss of face and the pain—started in school. Those working in development advise, "The body of Christ needs to move away from dependency-creating strategies toward dignity-enhancing strategies."[24] This situation pleads for dignity. One United Nations official concurred, stating that the international community "would be more effective were it to focus on the dignity of individuals, communities, and nations."[25]

What does someone who feels disgrace need? An old concept running through an ancient text can provide an antidote. The idea has only recently been embraced by anthropology. ALFE steeped in toxic shame, living in the dark side of orality, do not need shaming; they need the opposite. They need grace, meaning "to confer honour or dignity upon, to do honour or credit."[26] Henry Cloud calls this Greek concept of grace (*charis*) "unbroken, uninterrupted, unearned, accepting relationship," a potent prescription indeed—if you can find it.[27]

The poverty-shame nexus results in disconnection. People steeped in shame withdraw. The remedy for this problem? Connection, relationship, welcome, the body of Christ, and gracing. "If shame can interfere with a student's feeling of community … community may also be the best remedy."[28] ALFE need settings that promote self-efficacy, honor, dignity, and validation—settings in which they are not shamed, in which they do not lose face or fail.

According to Hannes Wiher, "Love banishes shame."[29] God's love seemed to gush from my heart to those I interviewed. I felt God's presence to heal hurts, to rescue, and to help these adults continue learning the way they prefer. Donna Hicks, a conflict resolution specialist, believes we do not instinctively know how to foster such dignity.[30] But our Master knows. A significant part of Hicks' therapeutic work involves inviting parties to experience personal stories, full of need and emotion—just as I did. She says, "When people suffer injury to their sense of worth, the antidote is time with people who know how to treat them in a dignified way."[31] A listening ear and space to tell one's story is vital in showering ALFE with grace. We can all offer this kind of empathic kindness in sharing the gospel.

Instead of the schoolroom, the prime space for this kind of redemptive gracing is the faith community where people can connect with a Savior and followers well-acquainted with shame, with the grand story of the King's great love. No other place on earth can offer this kind of potent antidote for the poison ALFE have ingested. What has happened to grace and dignity for these shamed—grace for the non-reader? I pray our sanctuaries will become welcoming places for ALFE, places like those in the early church, not places where they feel dread and shame.

Presenting the Gospel to These Shamed

Remember the story of Big Sister? I didn't know it then, but the gospel actually came to Big Sister's village through her testimony. Sadly, although Big Sister had a parental role for birthing the church among her people, she later fell away from the faith. But through our encounter with Big Sister, our Father covered her shame. He restored her honor. In recovering her dignity, she returned home to her faith and church family. Watching her be baptized brought the community and me much joy. Although she still cannot read, she receives a hearty welcome among the family of God.

At the beginning of this chapter, I cited Bill Gates' strong admonition. He followed that statement with this: "Reducing inequity is the highest human achievement."[32] The highest achievement? Perhaps. Whether reducing inequity ranks number one on the charts of human achievement or not, I do believe something must be done to obliterate this particular one. Unfairness abounds—in situations that foster limited education, in people being shamed because of this lack, in their feeling unwelcome at church, and in their experiencing obstacles that continually impede learning—especially learning about their faith.

What can we do about these inequities? As we have seen, the gospel of grace can reverse the toxic effects of this poison. What can bring healing? Encounters with the living Christ who bore our shame. Connection and embrace in the body of Christ. Love, affirmation, and dignity.

Acts 4:13 (NASB) says, "Now as they observed the confidence of Peter and John and understood that they were uneducated and untrained men, they were amazed, and began to recognize them as having been with Jesus." Limited formal education does not limit God using people. We can be like our Master and walk with ALFE, connect with them, and teach them. Peter, the successful Pentecost preacher, made his living as a fisherman. Priscilla and Aquila made tents, Tabitha made dresses. God used many ordinary working folks to turn the world upside down. Most educated Pharisees, on the other hand, did not fulfill kingdom purposes to the same extent.

Presenting the gospel to non-readers, making them feel welcome in the midst of our book-loving communities—that entails new strategies, ones that express kindness and acceptance to our ALFE friends.

For Further Reflection

1. Reflect on Thigpen's predicament and her assessment, "Shame on me." Have you had similar shame-on-me moments? What might help us become more aware of shame dynamics among people we serve—particularly as they relate to limited literacy, or educational and financial lack?

2. Thigpen says, "Shame lurks at the very core of poverty." What examples can you describe that show this is true? How does a gospel more attuned to honor and shame help restore dignity to those who live in various types of poverty?

CHAPTER 8 Endnotes

1 Bill Gates, "Remarks of Bill Gates, Harvard Commencement," *Harvard Gazette,* June 7, 2007, http://news.harvard.edu/gazette/story/2007/06/remarks-of-bill-gates-harvard-commencement-2007.

2 This name is an adaptation of the term *SLIFE* (Students with Limited or Interrupted Formal Education) introduced by Andrea DeCapua and Helaine W. Marshall. I needed to adapt the term because the participants in my study were not students or English-language learners.

3 International Orality Network and Lausanne Committee for World Evangelization, *Making Disciples of Oral Learners* (Lima, NY: Elim Publishing, 2005), 3.

4 Madeline Goodman, R. Finnegan, L. Mohadjer, T. Krenzke, J. Hogan, E. Owen, and S. Provasnik, *Literacy, Numeracy, and Problem Solving in Technology-Rich Environments among U.S. Adults: Results from the Program for the International Assessment of Adult Competencies 2012* (Washington, DC: National Center for Education Statistics Institute of Education Sciences, U.S. Department of Education, 2013), 3.

5 Sabina Alkire and M. Santos, "Multidimensional Poverty Index," *OPHI,* University of Oxford (2010): 1, http://www.ophi.org.uk.

6 Sabina Alkire and G. Robles, "Multidimensional Poverty Index, Winter 2016: Brief Methodological Notes and Results," *OPHI Briefing* 44, University of Oxford (2016): 6, http://www.ophi.org.uk.

7 Sabina Alkire, "The Missing Dimensions of Poverty Data," *OPHI Working Paper No. 00,* University of Oxford (2007): Abstract, http://www.ophi.org.uk.

8   Peter Greer, "'Stop Helping Us': A Call to Compassionately Move Beyond Charity," in *For the Least of These: A Biblical Answer to Poverty,* ed. A. Bradley and A. Lindsley (Grand Rapids: Zondervan, 2014), 232.

9   *Participate, People's Experiences of Living in Poverty: Early Findings for High Level Panel Deliberations* (Monrovia, Liberia: Institute of Development Studies and Beyond, 2013), 5.

10 Carla P. Childs and P. Greenfield, "Informal Modes of Learning and Teaching: The Case of Zinacanteco Weaving," in *Studies in Cross-Cultural Psychology Vol. 2,* ed. N. Warren (London: Academic, 1980), 285.

11 Elaine Chase and G. Bantebya-Kyomuhendo, "Poverty and Shame," in *Poverty and Shame: Global Experiences,* ed. E. Chase and G. Bantebya-Kyomuhendo (Oxford Scholarship Online, 2014), 299.

12 Susan A. Adams, "Using Transactional Analysis and Mental Imagery to Help Shame-Based Identity Adults Make Peace with Their Past, *Adultspan Journal* 7, no. 1 (2008): 2.

13 Hannes Wiher, *Shame and Guilt: A Key to Cross-Cultural Ministry* (Bonn: Verlag für Kultur und Wissenschaft, 2003), 120.

14 Robert Walker, G. B. Kyomuhendo, E. Chase, S. Choudhry, E. K. Gubrium, J. Y. Nicola, I. Lodemel, L. Mathew, A. Mwiine, S. Pellissery, and Y. Ming, "Poverty in Global Perspective: Is Shame a Common Denominator?" *Journal of Social Policy* 42, no. 2 (2013): 215.

15 Ibid., 216.

16 Kathleen Tanner, "Adult Dyslexia and the 'Conundrum of Failure,'" *Disability & Society* 24, no. 6 (2009): 785.

17 Myrna Orenstein, "Picking Up the Clues: Understanding Undiagnosed Learning Disabilities, Shame, and Imprisoned Intelligence," *Journal of College Student Psychotherapy* 15, no. 2 (2000): 36, doi:10.1300/J035v15n02_05. https://www.tandfonline.com/doi/abs/10.1300/J035v15n02_05.

18 Amartya Sen, "Capability and Well-being," in *The Quality of Life,* ed. A. K. Sen and M. Nussbaum (Oxford: Clarendon Press, 1993), 36.

19 This Khmer phrase រៀនអត់ចូល is very colloquial.

20 Arlene Fingeret, "The Illiterate Underclass: Demythologizing an American Stigma" (PhD diss., Syracuse University, 1982), 83, UMI No. 8301638.

21 Jo Boyden and M. Bourdillon, "Reflections: Inequality, School, and Social Change," in *Growing Up in Poverty: Findings from Young Lives,* ed. M. Bourdillon and J. Boyden (New York: Palgrave Macmillan, 2014), 273.

22 If you want to learn more about how ALFE prefer to learn, consult my website, http://lynnthigpen.wixsite.com/connectedlearning.

23 "Society is ill-prepared to restore the dignity of ALFE once they have left formal schooling." L. Lynn Thigpen, "Connected learning: A grounded theory study of how Cambodian adults with limited formal education learn" (PhD diss., Cook School of Inter-cultural Studies, Biola University, 2016), 168, ProQuest No. 10245810.

24 Brian Fikkert and Russel Mask, *From Dependency to Dignity* (Grand Rapids: Zondervan, 2015), 20.

25 Jason Borges, "'Dignified': An Exegetical Soteriology of Divine Honour," *Scottish Journal of Theology* 66, no. 01 (2013): 75, doi: 10.1017/S0036930612000312. https://www.cambridge.org/core/journals/scottish-journal-of-theology/article/dignified-an-exegetical-soteriology-of-divine-honour/0CA928233013D834A293012C036B5CAD.

26 Julian Pitt-Rivers, "The Place of Grace in Anthropology," *HAU: Journal of Ethnographic Theory* 1 (2011): 445.

27 Henry Cloud, *Changes That Heal: How to Understand Your Past to Ensure a Healthier Future* (Grand Rapids: Zondervan, 1992), 22.

28 Diane E. Johnson, "Considering Shame and Its Implications for Student Learning," *College Student Journal* 46, no. 1 (2012): 13.

29 Wiher, *Shame and Guilt*, 159.

30 Donna Hicks, *Dignity: Its Essential Role in Resolving Conflict* (New Haven, CT: Yale University Press, 2011), 18.

31 Ibid., 197.

32 Gates, Remarks.

MUST HONOR CLASH WITH HUMILITY?
Transformed Honor within the Emerging Church in Muslim Societies

ARLEY LOEWEN

Introduction

A vibrant church is emerging from Muslim societies of the Middle East and South Central Asia. This began in the 1980s among Iranians, but it has spread to other nations, as David Garrison highlights in his *Winds in the House of Islam*, with over seventy significant movements to Christ from Muslim societies in recent decades.

While we rejoice at the growth of God's community of faith, at the same time we see traditional ways entrenched in believers who come from societies where honor is the highest virtue. Group splits and territorial struggles abound among first-generation believers. The culture of warlords, drug lords, and other power lords raises its ugly head as pastoral ministry becomes a path for power, leading to "pastor-lords," in direct contrast to Peter's words to church leaders in the first century regarding "not lording it over those entrusted to you" (1 Pet 5:3).

Of course, this is nothing new.

In *Embracing Shared Ministry*, Joseph Hellerman highlights power and status struggles in North American church culture.[1] The South Korean church has been fraught with recent scandals as successful leaders "fall from honor." *Operation World* describes churches in one African nation in this way:

> One-man ministries, dictatorial leadership, empire-building and unwillingness to entrust responsibility to the upcoming younger

believers are common weaknesses… . Expatriate ministries, seeking high-profile campaigns … foster further division.[2]

Where is Jesus in all of this? Indeed, the radical mindset of humility, as exemplified by our Messiah, was revolutionary in the Greco-Roman society of the first century. It is just as revolutionary today.

This chapter addresses a call for Christlike humility for emerging church ministers in honor-shame societies. Christ does not reject honor in his kingdom; rather, he calls us to embrace him as our new source of honor and to embody a cruciform other-centric culture in which believers embrace the mind of Jesus and esteem one another.[3]

We Need Honor

Although Western culture has disdained honor cultures and favored an individualized "right and wrong" approach to relationships within the church, honor is a basic God-given need for humans.

At creation, God crowned humans with glory and honor (Ps 8:5). We carry his image (Gen 1:26) with a mandate to represent God's face to the rest of creation. But in the Fall, the first humans sought to take God's place. As a result, they experienced shame (Gen 3:5–7). They fell short before God and one another. Ever since, people have tried to regain honor, but it invariably ends up as false or counterfeit honor. Humans worship and serve themselves rather than the Creator (Rom 1:25).

We boast about how good we are. We gossip about how bad others are, tearing down their honor so we can have more. We shame others or boast about group superiority and manufacture honor to make up for group weakness. We dismiss it as pride or conceit, which Scripture condemns.

God honored Abraham with a promise to make his name great and a mandate to bless the world (Gen 12:1–3). God took Israel from their shameful disposition as slaves and "enabled [them] to walk with heads held high" (Lev 26:13).

God ultimately honored humankind by entering our world as the Messiah. Jesus cared for the leper, the shameful woman, and the outcast "sheep without a shepherd"—restoring them back to community and dignity. God fulfilled the Messianic text: "In the past he humbled the land of Zebulun … but in the future he will honor Galilee of the nations" (Isa 9:1).

Jesus offered his own life to carry our shame and restore dignity to every human being. We become Jesus' brothers and sisters, bearing a new name. God restores sinful, shameful people to honor.

The gospel moves us from a worldly type of honor competition—to "outdo[ing] one another in showing honor" (Rom 12:10 ESV). Boasting is cancelled (Rom 3:27). Grace births humility, freeing us to cheerfully overcome selfish ambition and esteem others (Phil 2:3–4). This is part of God's salvation story.

Yet the ancient struggle for honor remains deeply imbedded in humans. It is ironic that people will pursue dishonorable and even immoral practices to maintain a good reputation.[4] People want honor without seeking to be honorable.

Here's the question: How can we move toward a new, transformed honor in our families, churches, and organizations? Is it possible to gain honor in an honorable way?

Finding and Enjoying New Status

The ancient Romans developed a highly stratified society. Everyone knew their place or position in relation to everyone else in the social group. This was vital. If these distinctions were unclear, then there would be confusion about whom to respect, whom to look upon with less respect, whom to be respected by. Invariably those with higher status had more power to promote themselves and their families. As a result, this class stratification easily became fixed.[5]

Those who live today in shame-based groups struggle keenly with their position in comparison to others around them. They need to know their position in the group—who is on top and how the rest of the group relates to one another.

Humans naturally want to have good status so that they can enjoy more value, respect, and honor from others. *The higher my status* (rank, position, standing, station), *the greater my worth. I matter to myself and to others. The lower my status, the lesser my worth. If I do not matter to others, I will receive less respect from others and have less influence.*

A New Status—Belonging to Jesus

When a person becomes a follower of the Messiah, what happens to his or her status? Believers from Muslim communities often experience deep shame from their family and social group when they move their allegiance to Christ. It is essential that they understand their status as Christians. It is vital that believers learn they have gained a new source of honor in Christ and can experience a renewed honor socially through the body of Christ, the church.

Scripture clearly asserts that believers have many privileges as followers of Jesus. We are embraced by the love of God (Rom 5:5). God lifts up our heads (Ps 3:3). We are adopted as children of the heavenly Father (Rom 8:14–15) and become members of the royal family of God (1 Pet 2:9). We can call this *objective honor;* it is the honor of the redeemed members of the family of God, whether we know it or not.[6]

But that often is not enough. We also need honor or recognition from our new social group (the church). This is *subjective honor*—part of human *experience.* This honor need can be met when believers "give honor" in a spiritually healthy manner to other believers.

However, this honor need is often met through unhealthy, even sinful, ways. A Christian leader views leadership position as pastor, director, or manager as a means to gain more status and privilege. This easily leads to suspicion, arguments, and even corruption—clearly not the intended result for the honor given to God's people.

Young believers in the early churches at Rome, Philippi, and elsewhere in Asia Minor understood well the competition for status and honor in religious or political associations. For Jews, greater status sometimes came through keeping the Mosaic law. Such competition for honor was replicated in all levels of society, in various associations and social gatherings.

As young believers in the early church began to follow King Jesus and gather together, what would this new association look like? Would young believers compete for rank and privilege in their new group as they did in their former associations?

If a young man whose father was or had been a respected Roman general joined a Messiah group, would he carry special respect because of his ascribed honor—his high status as a general's son? Would those who had little status previously continue to be "nobodies" in the new group? Would they experience the counter-cultural, elevated honor status that the Apostle Paul intended when he wrote, "There is neither Jew nor Gentile, neither slave nor free, nor is there male and female, for you are all one in Christ Jesus. If you belong to Christ, then you are Abraham's seed, and heirs according to the promise" (Gal 3:28–29).

Paul had *ascribed honor*—being both of Hebrew stock and a Roman citizen. Prior to encountering the risen Christ, he also relished his *achieved honor* and good standing by having faultlessly followed the Jewish law. But because of the supreme relational honor of knowing Christ, he rejected both, considering these titles of honor meaningless (Phil 3:4–8).

As a follower of Jesus, Paul genuinely experienced a new honor status in the Messiah, which, relatively speaking, made all other honors to be as "rubbish." True value and honor lay in belonging to the Messiah and the Messiah group, and following the Messiah way. Paul claimed that all "nobodies" in Roman, Greek, or Judaic societies enjoy an elevated status in the Messiah (1 Cor 1:18–31). They have become real "somebodies."

Can this new elevated honor status of believers become a visceral experience so that Christ-followers can shed the default behaviors of honor competition, boasting, gossip, and rivalry in their new Messiah groups?

A New Status Symbol—Serving Like Jesus

Shaikh Saadi, the fourteenth-century Persian poet wrote:

It is the person himself that gives dignity to a human, not these lovely clothes that are a sign of a human.[7]

People with higher status often use symbols to display their position and to impress upon others in their group that they are worthy of respect. Titles like *Doctor* or *Professor* (or *Pastor* or *Engineer* in some cultures) can carry exceptional respect. Wearing certain types of jewelry or driving an SUV, for example, also communicates honor status.

The ancient Romans relished such symbols. They displayed their achievements and status through statues and public inscriptions that boasted of their feats.

As Jesus proclaimed the kingdom and invited disciples to join his group, many expected they would gain honor through this new Messiah movement. Once Jesus set up his rule, each one of them would receive special privilege and position. The disciples argued among themselves about who had more status (Mark 9:34).

Jesus did not tell the disciples to reject honor and greatness. Rather, he told them, essentially: *In my kingdom, the way to achieve status and have more respect is by caring for other people* (Mark 9:35; 10:43).

This is Jesus' greatness—his "serving status." It is the new way of humility, esteeming others ahead of oneself. This is how God's kingdom works and reflects our position with Jesus.

Can we enjoy a natural delight in the recognition of serving one another, regardless of who the "other" is and how we are recognized?

Lessening the Distance through Caring

In leadership workshops in Central Asia, I often ask the class to compare an *authoritarian (power, position) leader* with a *people (relational) leader*. Normally everyone in the group will say that they appreciate a people leader—someone who likes being with their staff, drinks tea with them, and relates as a friend. But then someone in the class will blurt out, "But it won't take long before we will have ripped such a leader into shreds," or "If the director is too friendly, he loses respect."

In one leadership workshop at a college, the professors invited me to first meet the director. They led me up a broad stairway, down the hall, into a receiving room, and then into a large office with couches and chairs. At the far end of this great room was an immense desk with a leather armchair. Rising from behind the desk was a smallish man in a white suit—the president of the college. He greeted me cordially, but I soon wondered, "Does he even know that we're having a leadership seminar today?"

This president had honor. He carried respect because of his title: President. But he seemed distant from those he was leading.

Culture experts call this "high power distance"; the leader remains separate from the people he or she leads.[8] This distance is both physical and psychological, expressed by behavior and attitude. Because the director is "higher up," the staff "looks up to" (respects) the director—and the director "looks down on" (has less respect for) the staff.

In a leadership class in Afghanistan, we gathered these answers:

- Distance gives a director a sense of significance. He is busy with major issues, and relating to petty issues is demeaning.
- Distance shelters a director from criticism. He can hide or cover up his shortcomings and failures if he mingles less with staff and clients.
- Distance helps a director keep secrets. He need not be accountable or open with others. This breeds suspicion and more easily leads to corruption.

Here is the question for leaders, including pastors and teachers: *What distance do we maintain in relation to those we lead?* Westerners like to talk about equality, but should power be distributed equally? If all were to become equal, would we then settle for bland egalitarianism and sameness?

We teach servant leadership, with Jesus presented as Servant of all. We emphasize horizontal, "on-the-floor" management, where managers connect with those they lead.

But if honor depends on position, titles, and status, and if directors naturally give orders "from the top," how should we understand servant leadership? Is this actually feasible? Do we need to reject top-down patterns or adopt horizontal, egalitarian ways in order to serve others? How can "position leaders" also be "people leaders" without losing their authority and honor?

Caring Leadership

Paul urged the believers in Philippi to follow the mindset of their Master by being genuinely interested in others, to esteem and honor them:

> Do nothing out of selfish ambition or vain conceit. Rather, in humility value others above yourselves, not looking to your own interests but each of you to the interests of the others. In your relationships with one another, have the same mindset as Christ Jesus. (Phil 2:3–5)

This is how we serve like Jesus—by showing *interest* in others. Paul describes the young leader, Timothy, in this way. He cared for Christ because he cared for others. "I have no one else like [Timothy], who will show genuine concern for your welfare. For everyone looks out for their own interests, not those of Jesus Christ" (Phil 2:20–21).

Genuinely showing interest in others was far from the minds of the Roman elite. One Roman satirist wrote, "[The elite] not only have never shared with us, but never deign even to notice ordinary people."[9] Humility, in the sense of considering others, was no virtue in Roman ethics.

Is it not feasible that authoritarian pastors can genuinely *care* for their church and yet carry respect and maintain their own honor?

If we understand that every person has God-given worth, we will *care* for those we relate to. In so doing, rather than losing honor, do we not gain honor? When a pastor moves "downward" in order to sit with their flock, listen to their stories, and seek to understand their issues, the pastor will not lose respect but experience more.

When we esteem others and care for their welfare, we become people of transformed honor.

Releasing Control through Exampling

People honor their leaders by respecting them (1 Tim 5:17), but more so by *following* them. Effective leaders ensure that people follow them and remain loyal. How should pastors express authority to their flock?

Every culture has its own understanding of how authority and power relate to leadership. People from egalitarian cultures normally prefer a "friendly father," whereas people from "high-position" cultures often prefer a "ruling father." Which is the better model?

In the "patron-client" relationship, common in traditional societies even today, a patron functions like a father, with means and authority. The patron protects and provides for his followers. The more followers a patron has, the more honor the patron has.

When clients find a good patron, they will repay him with honor, loyalty, and obedience. As they receive the patron's benefits, they in turn boast and spread the patron's fame, which further increases the patron's honor.

The patron needs to project a measure of control to ensure that clients remain faithful. The constant question is: *How much control?*

As one who cares for the sheep and ensures their protection (Acts 20:28), a pastor is indeed called to be the congregation's patron. Many pastors selflessly sacrifice their time and energy for the sake of the flock.

But if a pastor's honor depends on a loyal following, how should the pastor relate to individual members who have contrary ideas or ideals? What if the patron/pastor is not able to provide the support requested? What if someone finds better support elsewhere? What if the members aren't as loyal as the pastor expects?

Pastors easily become territorial in order to keep their flock under their domain. Leaders become *directive* in the name of giving guidance, and they easily manipulate clients in order to garner needed respect and praise.

The relationship between a pastor and a young church often sours because the members feel that their pastor tries to rule them and actually does not care for them.

Jesus: Another Model of Patron

Jesus rebuked the religious leaders of his day for their efforts to be fathers (patrons?):

Do not call anyone on earth "father," for you have one Father... . The greatest among you will be your servant. For those who exalt themselves will be humbled, and those who humble themselves will be exalted. (Matt 23:9–12)

When Jesus' disciples argued over who was more honorable among them, he rebuked them:

The kings of the Gentiles lord it over them; and those who exercise authority over them call themselves Benefactors. But you are not to be like that. Instead, the greatest among you should be like the youngest, and the one who rules like the one who serves. (Luke 22:25–26)

Worldly leaders normally control people by force (threats and military power) and by benefits (money, patronage, and gifts in kind). A benefactor does good to others; a pastor should care for his people. Yet Jesus says that God's servant-leaders are not to be like such benefactors.

The pastor's true honor comes not from controlling the flock, but in proactively serving and modeling the Christian life. The Apostle Peter writes that a basic characteristic for leaders is *humility*. Patrons/pastors care for their flock by presenting themselves as humble examples.

Be shepherds of God's flock that is under your care, watching over them—not because you must, but because you are willing, as God wants you to be; not pursuing dishonest gain, but eager to serve; *not lording it over* those entrusted to you, but being examples to the flock... . All of you, clothe yourselves with humility toward one another, because, "God opposes the proud but shows favor to the humble." *Humble yourselves*, therefore, under God's mighty hand, that he may lift you up in due time. (1 Pet 5:2–6; emphasis mine)

Rejoicing in the Success of Others

Good Christian teachers know that they must train others in skills, character, and Bible knowledge, so that God's kingdom will grow. Such teachers seek to empower their students, but problems often develop.

When a teacher notices that a student or colleague performs better or grows stronger in their capacities, the teacher grows concerned: *What if that person becomes more successful than me? What if my colleague will get more credit than me?* Without realizing it, the teacher allows a spirit of envy to take root in his or her heart. And so the teacher withholds some information and retards that student's or colleague's process.

For example, when someone else receives recognition or honor, we may easily feel hurt. The ancient Greeks described envy as an emotional or even physical pain when a person sees someone else's good fortune. The Koreans have a saying: "When my cousin buys land, I get a stomachache." James says that envy leads to "disorder and every evil practice" (Jas 3:16).

We may express our envy over another person's success in various ways:

- *Ignoring the person.* Since it is so hard to appreciate another's success, we might decide not to notice that person, as if "out of sight, out of mind" will lessen our pain.
- *Boasting of our own (real or fabricated) successes.* Because we want others to notice us, we elevate ourselves, trying to make a self-name by bragging about our accomplishments.
- *Dishonoring others with gossip and slander.* The logic goes: If others are lowered, then I will rise higher.
- *Competing.* Healthy competition energizes us to improve and work harder. Excessive competition, however, easily breeds "disorder and every evil practice."
- *Abandoning trust.* We suspect hardworking colleagues of trying to make a show of themselves or of having a hidden agenda. Suspicion causes friendships to die.

Envy robs us of joy and diminishes delight in others. Indeed, it is our pain over another's gain.

Here are some practical steps to defeating this spirit of envy:

- *Self-awareness:* When we recognize this pain in our hearts, we can address the feeling and make a covenant with ourselves not to allow this spirit to ruin our peace and destroy our relationships with others.
- *God's gifts:* As we recognize and practice the gifts God has given us, we develop a healthy confidence, doing the things we are capable of doing as well as possible, instead of coveting others' abilities and successes.
- *Win-Win:* When we measure another person's success against our own, our vision shrinks inward. When we see the bigger picture of God's kingdom, we focus beyond ourselves rather than on the person who achieves success (who receives honor).
- *This is your honor:* A great music teacher is one whose students outdo them in their musical accomplishments. Parents wish for their children to achieve greater success than them. A great leader delights in helping others flourish; their success becomes the leader's honor and success. A Persian poem says, "When others flourish, I flourish; I enjoy the joy of others." This is like Paul's instruction in Romans 12:15: "Rejoice with those who rejoice."
- *Sow and reap:* Keeping information to ourselves—excluding others from growth opportunities and taking the credit ourselves—results in stagnation both for ourselves and for those with whom we serve. If instead we generously share information and give others the credit, we build up our brothers and sisters. We reap a harvest, and joy with it.

God draws people to himself, but he also gives himself to the world. Jesus modeled this by expending himself for others and then saying to his disciples, "As the Father has sent me [to others], I am sending you [to others]" (John 20:21). We too are sent to others. This shows people what God is like. The power of the Spirit within us must propel us outward to serve and bless others. If we only receive grace, the flow of grace will stop.

When the Messiah saw the crowds, he was moved with compassion and served the people (Matt 9:36). In what I consider the greatest story in the Gospels, when the young, shameful son was still far off, his father saw him, was filled with compassion, and ran to him (Luke 15:20). This is God's story. God sees our condition and is moved with compassion. We overcome the eye of envy when we see others, and we are moved with compassion for them.

Jesus taught his disciples to store up treasures in heaven by being generous and rich toward God. This requires a healthy eye.

> The eye is the lamp of the body. If your eyes are healthy, your whole body will be full of light. But if your eyes are unhealthy, your whole body will be full of darkness. If then the light within you is darkness, how great is that darkness! (Matt 6:22–23)

A person with healthy eyes is generous and excited about blessing others. Then his or her entire being overflows with light and health. But if we have a "bad eye," a stingy, envious outlook, we experience misery and anguish—darkness indeed!

Stories That Illustrate the Struggle for Honor and Status

Who Gets the Credit?

I was sitting in a board meeting for a successful, cutting-edge, evangelistic media ministry serving a Central Asian nation. A young IT expert was also in attendance. He was a relatively new Christian and just becoming familiar with ministry. He was deeply bothered when he heard that Christian leaders from his nation were not working in harmony. The emerging church was experiencing unprecedented growth despite insurmountable odds from a repressive government. But with all this spiritual victory, why were the leaders not ministering together?

A key church leader from their nation was also on this board. The young IT expert asked him, "Why aren't our church leaders united?"

The leader did not answer. The IT expert probed further, "Is money the problem?"

Hesitant at first, the church leader responded, "No, it's not money."

"Then what is it?"

The leader dropped his head in shame. "I think it's about who gets the credit. That's what it is."

The underlying concern was receiving public honor.

Another person added, "Once you have credit, you will have easier access to funds as well."

And the cycle of struggling for honor continues.

In what ways can Christian leaders enjoy their need to receive attention (credit) from others without falling into a spirit of competition?

Overbearing Patrons

Allan pastored a successful church comprised of Middle Eastern immigrants in a large Western city. A group of believers in a neighboring city started gathering and invited Allan to teach there. They soon formed a daughter church led by Mariam, an experienced believer. She and a few others worked hard to help establish this young group. Soon after Akbar and Najia arrived as refugees from abroad, they began attending this daughter church and demonstrated passionate faith and evangelistic fervor. Through their ministry, other Middle Easterners came to faith.

Appreciating Akbar and Najia's zeal, Allan asked them to teach in the daughter church without informing Mariam. As a result, Mariam felt severely slighted and left the church.

Because Akbar and Najia received honor in this young church, they quickly took on more responsibilities. However, Allan, even from a distance, retained control as the senior patron, and relationships began to fracture. Akbar and Najia soon "felt the Lord telling them" to start their own church, which prospered. As new people joined this fellowship, Akbar and Najia initially esteemed them with great honor, but when parishioners missed a few Sundays, this leadership couple rebuked or ignored them. They also exhorted their members to remain loyal to their group and not to attend Allan's daughter church. Because of Akbar and Najia's power and patronizing leadership, many young believers have felt slighted and abused and have left the church.

How can a pastor enjoy the honor and respect of leading a congregation without being controlling?

Finding Status in Jesus

Mani had come to faith in Jesus and was growing in his new life. He enjoyed his college studies, but struggled with a lack of confidence. Being small in stature he sensed others looking down on him. He shared his insecurity with his online Christian tutor, who had also come to faith from a Muslim background. The two had established a friendship but had never met face to face. When the tutor learned that Mani was only 130 centimeters (four feet, three inches) tall, he laughed. "Guess what, Mani? I am smaller than you, but because the one I believe in and follow is above everyone else, no one can look down on me."

The tutor, also young in faith, had experienced a new status and confidence in Jesus.

How important is it for a follower of Jesus to experience subjective honor and recognition (or status) from their social group?

Releasing Control

After leading a small faith-based media team for many years, Basir had reached retirement age. Because of health issues and pressure from family due to his Christian faith, he was ready to retire. However, Basir cared about the ministry and wanted it to continue. He committed himself to building a new team, and continued his work for two more years. After consulting with others, he selected a young couple and threw himself into helping them grow in faith and media skills so they could replace him. He spent time with them, advised them, and began to organize and transfer his resources to them.

Two years later, when the larger media team convened, he could have stepped forward to showcase what he had produced. Instead, he withdrew, saying, "Now it is time for the younger couple to present the report. It is my joy to see them take over this team."

Why do many ministers find it difficult to hand over their ministries when they reach senior age? Which is more honorable—to see one's ministry continue through others, or to continue one's ministry as long as possible?

Conclusion

When we experience the new honor status of belonging to the Messiah, we no longer need to compete for honor. We carry a new name and see the world and people around us differently.

We are able to honor others as God has honored us in the Messiah. True honor does not come as we "rise to the top," but as we care for others.

Our experience of honor need not be based on whether, or to what degree, people follow us. Rather, our honor can be found in the privilege of serving others, participating in the humility and mind of Christ (Phil 2:3–7). We may appreciate the credit given to us; yet because we experience an honor surplus in knowing Christ, we can freely rejoice in the success of others. Our experiential honor in Christ erodes the impulse for rivalry in the church.

As the Christlike cruciform message and life penetrate us, our relationships are transformed and we genuinely care for others' welfare, esteeming them above ourselves.

For Further Reflection

1. Loewen suggests that Western Christianity has had an ambivalent relationship with the notion of honor. How do his various points counter any approach that rejects honor as unbiblical?

2. Loewen suggests that Jesus, as well as some biblical authors, flip or subvert the dominant cultural honor codes and reframe these in a new way. How does Jesus' new honor code address the problem of envy between Christian leaders?

CHAPTER 9 Endnotes

1 Joseph Hellerman, *Embracing Shared Ministry: Power and Status in the Early Church and Why It Matters Today* (Grand Rapids: Kregel, 2013).

2 Jayson Mandryk, *Operation World* (Downers Grove, IL: InterVarsity, 2010), 645.

3 This chapter is adapted from my booklet, *Rethinking Shame and Honor*, published by Micah Network (2017) and written for emerging leaders in honor-shame contexts.

4 Kwame Appiah, *The Honor Code: How Moral Revolutions Happen* (New York: W. W. Norton, 2010).

5 Hellerman, *Embracing Shared Ministry*, 30–50.

6 For a thorough discussion of honor and shame—objective and subjective—in the Bible, see Jackson Wu, "Have Theologians No Sense of Shame? How the Bible Reconciles Objective and Subjective Shame," *Themelios* 43, no. 2 (2018): 205–19, http://themelios.thegospelcoalition.org/article/have-theologians-no-sense-of-shame.

7 Shaikh Saadi, تیمدآ ناشن ، تس ابیز سابل نیمه نه ،تیمدآ ناج هب ، تسا فیرش یمدآ نت Collection of Ghazals, Ghazal 18, https://ganjoor.net/saadi/mavaez/ghazal2/sh18.

8 See the discussion of "power distance" in Geert Hofstede, *Cultures and Organizations: Software of the Mind: Inter-cultural Cooperation and Its Importance for Survival* (New York: McGraw-Hill, 2005), 39–72.

9 Quoted in Hellerman, *Embracing Shared Ministry*, 38.

Rob,

Thank you for being
God's grace to me.

May
these words bring shalom!

Philip Gulley

SHARING GOD'S LOVE IN AN URBAN, PLURALISTIC CONTEXT

STEVE HONG

"We must be able to value and love people as they are, whether or not we agree with their views or choices. Above all we are interested in their good and the goods that will contribute to their flourishing. If we only gather and discuss our views with those who agree with us on primary matters, then tolerance is never an issue. Tolerance is only in play in the midst of discord." —Dallas Willard[1]

One Evening, 250 People, and a Taste of Heaven

Through the years, God has given me the rich blessing of friendship with people in San Francisco from diverse backgrounds, races, worldviews, and sexual orientations. Part of the reason I deliberately moved my family to this city was to learn how to love as Jesus would, to give others a taste of the kingdom in a way that would produce a desire to know the King. In pluralistic San Francisco, "Each person is free to believe what he or she prefers."[2] This city would stretch me beyond my previous experiences, teaching me how to love those who have very different views from mine.

Since I cannot love those whom I do not know, I sought to get to know the city's musicians, cyclists, tech people, atheists, gays, Buddhists, Jews, and politicians through shared activity and lots of coffee.

These connections have led to hundreds of spiritual conversations, invitations to work together, and even to blog together.[3] Many have become friends.

I wanted to honor, value, and appreciate these friends for how they had opened their homes, businesses, music, stories, and hearts to me. In 2017, I decided to use the occasion of my upcoming fiftieth birthday to invite my friends to a party as a way to honor them. By faith, I rented a hall with a capacity of 250 people. By the morning of the event, exactly 250 had said yes to the invitation!

The ethnic diversity at the party was obvious; not so apparent was the social diversity in the room. People who drove nails for a living sat next to techies who sat next to bus drivers. Mixed in were ministry colleagues, more than a couple dozen children, and fifty guests who come from a different faith tradition.

How could I best honor such a diverse gathering of friends and invite them to witness the transformational work of the gospel in my life?

The theoretical answer was simple: Let the party be a taste of heaven in which the guests can experience God's honoring acceptance, regardless of one's vocation, worldview, or sexual orientation. Let the desegregation and the plurality of the room be part of the good news. Let those who might feel like outsiders be lifted up. Let no one be defined by the nails they drive, the buses they operate, nor the people they marry, but by the dignity God has given every single person.

Let Honor Fall upon This Pluralistic Gathering of Friends

More specifically, I wanted my party to help invert power differences and lift up and honor those who might feel like outsiders. I envisioned my Hindu, Muslim, and LGBTQ guests being able to bring their whole selves. Dozens of children were coming. So were a large number of African American friends. Both of these populations (children and African Americans) represent only 6 percent of San Francisco, down from well over 20 percent in their heyday decades ago. I wanted to honor them too.

I intentionally gave the honored guests the most important roles that best suited them. The hosting role, the decorations, photography, event coordination, gifts, and money—were all handled by friends who would otherwise be the most socially marginalized in the room. I publicly thanked them all.

And the children? I provided two huge banquet tables filled with activities (manned by two adults) and beverage stations just for them. I didn't know it at the time, but honoring specific guests made a lasting impression. One guest noted that even the children were honored. "People don't have kids at these kinds of parties," another guest said. I couldn't have imagined it any other way.

Since the impetus of the party was my upcoming fiftieth birthday, I wanted to take full advantage of this marker in my life to deliver a gospel experience in the most engaging way possible. I asked the Lord, "What is the most loving, inclusive, inviting, gospel-infused event I could pull off with this unique gathering of friends?"

The answer was inspired by Hebrews 12:1–2.[4] Christ shunned the shame "for the joy set before him" (Heb 12:2). I wanted to share areas of my life in which my shame was similarly "reversed," along with the joy that came from the shame-reversal work of Christ in my life.

I adopted Richard Rohr's "falling upward" theme[5] to frame the storytelling piece of the party. "Falling" refers to my first-half-of-life journey of uncovering much of the shame I lived under. "Upward" refers to the second half of my life, in which I've learned to live from an identity of God the Father's *beloved*.

I wanted to use the party to share this "falling upward" shift in my life and how it had opened my soul to share what most deeply moves me for the sake of others.[6] My closest friends were concerned: Could I pull off something so innovative, yet be vulnerable in the context of a party? It was a risk worth taking.

Engaging My Pluralistic Culture with Today's Prophets

"Today's generation listens with their eyes and thinks with their feelings."
—Ravi Zacharias[7]

The utterly rational character from the classic TV show *Star Trek* inspired my nickname, "Mr. Spock," long before I received my engineering degree. In those days, I spoke and thought like Mr. Spock, meaning I suppressed my emotions and denied that feelings had any importance.

But as I've grown, I've learned to value my feelings. Moreover, I've learned to communicate gospel truth in a way that deeply engages people's feelings.

This is especially important in cities like San Francisco, where artists are the primary prophets engaging hearts and minds. Whether or not their ideas are true is another matter. And that's why Ravi Zacharias' quote, above, is so important.

In pluralistic contexts, how do we best engage people with the truth?

In light of this question, I recruited artists to help me tell my "falling upward" story in a way that would best engage the eyes and feelings of my guests.

We did this through five distinct but complementary segments. I commissioned five portraits and art installations, with an artist's statement for each segment, so that guests could access my story using their different senses.

Following are a series of pictures and a summary of each installation.

MisEducation
The story of how God transformed my pursuit of knowledge into the pursuit of "being known"

Wilderness
The story of personal and vocational loss without any end in sight

Authenticity
The story of how the need to prove myself began to lose its power

Husbandhood
The story of how my wife's year-long bedrest brought about the greatest surrender experience

Work
The story of how my blue-collar job transformed how I see work as a part of my worship

Each of these five segments began with an invitation and introduction from Kirk, the host and one of my closest prayer partners in San Francisco. Kirk then introduced a two-minute video to anchor each segment.

Another friend directed and produced the videos. He kept me to the commitment of keeping each video segment under two minutes. Saying less would say more.

A creative presentation that included musical and spoken-word performances followed each video. For example, in the "Wilderness" installation, Bruce Cockburn, an award-winning musician,[8] performed his yet-to-be-released song "Forty Days in the Wilderness."

Kirk invited the guests to interact with the art installations and with one another. I provided journals for guests to record or draw their thoughts. Many of my guests later told me how they saw their own story in mine through the combination of art, music, and video.

Honor—Deeply Memorable and Part of the Gospel

In the months following the party, some guests shared with me how it motivated them to take steps to honor their own loved ones. Still others have used my party as a template for their own events. I've documented parts of the party on a website and invite you to view it.[9]

Guests told me that the most powerful part of the evening was a round of toasts shared by my closest sojourners. Together, they gave testimony to aspects of my life no one else could have possibly articulated—the product of vulnerable prayer time together over five years.

One of my atheist friends later told me, "That was the best Christian witness I've ever experienced." I loved that the most powerful display of honor was not even something I had planned. I had asked these men to give toasts; I had no idea how profoundly their words would move my guests' hearts.

I envisioned that every aspect of the party—the toasts, music, art, choreography, food, flowers, the diversity of people in the room, and even the party's location—would all compound the effect of gospel storytelling in the most relevant and *vulnerable* way possible.

"If you did not hear the gospel at the party, you must have been asleep," said one of my pastor guests.

Even what I did *not* provide at the party—alcohol—told a story. I made it clear that the party would be "dry" to honor guests in recovery. One guest shared, "I've never been to a party, had fun, and not gotten drunk."

Altogether, I used my life to paint a picture of the gospel through every possible means, knowing that more in-depth conversations would follow in which I could engage with my friends on a deeper level. And that's exactly what I have been experiencing—months and months of deeper than ever before spiritual conversations with many of my guests.

Christians in particular have asked me how I got fifty people who don't share my faith to attend. The truth is that I invited a lot more than fifty people who don't share my faith. What's more, these relationships are the product of seeing myself as a carrier of Jesus' love—no matter my vocation over the many years of cultivation. The people I invited were neighbors, fellow musicians, people from my gym, even my Zumba teacher! Their presence was the result of years of bridge-building and relational cultivation.

Engaging My Pluralistic Cultural Lifestyle

I just read your beautiful post and visited your website. I listened to the tributes and the "Time after Time" song—incredible. And the art installations, wow! I feel so honored to know you, and blessed to count you as a friend.

—Rev. Alyson Jacks, Unitarian Church of San Francisco

Like others who could not attend, Rev. Jacks honored me by sending her sentiments. Well-wishes like these from friends outside my evangelical tradition touched me significantly. How blessed I am to have these friendships!

Rev. Jacks is just one of hundreds of people I invited to the party from relationships I have cultivated over time and with great intentionality. Yes, I've learned a lot from Scripture, classes, and books. But in applying this knowledge—learning to love people whose views differ from mine or who are just plain different from me—I have truly learned how to honor people as Jesus would.

My relationship with Rev. Jacks is one such unlikely friendship, not just because she is a Unitarian minister and I am an evangelical minister, but also because she is a lesbian and I am straight. Yet we've had the joy of deepening our trust and friendship through leading some innovative events together.

Luke 10 recounts the story of Jesus sending out seventy-two of his followers to minister on his behalf. The following four lifestyle principles from Jesus' instructions help frame how I share God's love in my urban, pluralistic context:

1. Break Your Comfortable Inertia

I met Rev. Jacks at an ecumenical interfaith meeting. I would not have known about this meeting nor considered going had it not been for my prayer group of fellow ministers. When we pray, we invite one another to spaces outside our comfort zones. In Luke 10:2–3, Jesus mentioned the idea of "go" three times, using three different Greek words. It seems that Jesus wants to intentionally break our inertia to move us beyond our comfortable relationships.

I would not have joined the interfaith group were it not for this men's prayer group and its consistent challenge to enter into uncomfortable spaces. But my initial discomfort was ultimately rewarded, as it was this very group who eventually toasted me at my party.

This rhythm of breaking our inertia changes how we see people, bringing our perspectives into greater alignment with God's view of people. I am uncomfortable with people who identify as LGBTQ (among others). Breaking my comfortable inertia and entering those spaces forced me to address my fears. Befriending many people like Rev. Jacks has been healthy for my soul. It has tightened my theology and taught me to see others as Jesus would.

2. Bring Peace Vulnerably

The interfaith group gathers in a large church hall filled with round banquet tables. The leaders are from a diversity of churches—many of them ecumenical, advocacy-oriented, and gay-inclusive. Some have been featured on national news for how they have pushed the boundaries of their respective denominations to be more progressive. We don't all share the same theology, but we come together to seek the greater good for San Francisco, even if we do it in different ways.

My younger self would have approached the room with a combative mentality, painting those outside my theology as "them." But I've recently learned how to embody the principle of vulnerability that Jesus communicated in Luke 10:4 (ESV): "Carry no moneybag, no knapsack, no sandals."

Jesus wanted the disciples to experience dependence on *him*—rather than on their default sources of security.

My "moneybag" would include my apologetics training, my well-rehearsed gospel-presentation training—anything that would allow me to stay in my head and not be present emotionally. Luke 10:4 is a beautiful call to be present, *vulnerably present.*

As I continue letting go of things that make me feel secure, I have found that I am able to *listen, feel,* and *engage* more easily with others. I have begun to listen better to others' desires and stories of pain—even if I disagree with some of their views or choices. My friendship with Rev. Jacks was birthed in this context.

3. Look for the People God Has Already Prepared

Jesus continued, "Whatever house you enter, first say, 'Peace be to this house!' And if a son of peace is there, your peace will rest upon him. But if not, it will return to you" (Luke 10:5–6 ESV). This kind of "person of peace" is *receptive* to the peace of God you bring. "And remain in the same house, eating and drinking what they provide" (Luke 10:7a ESV). When that peace is received, this "person of peace" will naturally want to *reciprocate* with forms of hospitality. "Do not go from house to house" (Luke 10:7c ESV). Why did Jesus include this instruction? Because a person God has prepared is well-connected to a *referral* network. In other words, the reciprocity developed with this person will spread to others, because such a person has a *reputation* in his or her context.

Receptivity, reciprocity, referrals, and *reputation* are exactly what I saw in Rev. Jacks. She received the peace I offered, and, in return, she offered hospitality through meals we've shared. Plus, both she and her church are well-connected to others in the interfaith community.

One day, Rev. Jacks asked me to consider joining her committee to help plan San Francisco's inaugural interfaith bike ride. I was excited because this group included the executive director of the interfaith committee, along with leaders from a diverse cross section of San Francisco's faith community and biking community.

4. Bring the Kingdom of God Near to Them

Twice in Luke 10:9–11 Jesus instructed his representatives to proclaim, whether or not the people received them, that "the kingdom of God has come near." The most frequent way I've brought God's kingdom near to people is by imagining and sharing, then offering a way to honor a given space.

Doing this for this interfaith bike ride committee provided a breakthrough in the course of our meetings. Momentum was already building. We anticipated a good crowd based on the sign-ups of dozens of riders from San Francisco's diverse faith communities, and we wanted to give them a good experience. Rev. Jacks posed the question, "What kind of ride would we want to offer these riders?"

I immediately responded, "We've got a unique set of riders who come from varied sacred spaces. Why not honor the riders who are members of a given space with a liturgy of blessing? And before we do that, since so many of these sacred spaces have a story all their own through their history and architecture, how about we honor that story at the beginning of each stop? And what if we end each site visit with a benediction for its members and our riders?"

The committee unanimously agreed and asked me to take the lead in this liturgy. I now had the green light to design a liturgy to honor the sacred spaces and the people who are part of them. I believe the Spirit inspired me to imagine this plan and the way I shared it. I did not offer to take this responsibility; the committee invited me to do so, which was far better. That was an honor for me. Bringing the kingdom of God near to them resulted in mutual blessing.

The Fruit of Applying Luke 10 Principles to the Interfaith Bike Ride

The green light I received from the interfaith bike committee meant I had a relational base from which I could visit other communities of faith to prepare the liturgy for this ride. I spent time researching each site's architecture, history, and faith backgrounds. And because I was an ambassador of both the interfaith community and the bike coalition, I had the "referral ticket" to correspond with different leaders, priests, pastors, and rabbis—seeking to honor each one with the way I then integrated their input into the ride.

This included faith communities that were gay-inclusive, Jewish, Buddhist, Unitarian Universalists, and more. As I listened to their stories and integrated them into the liturgy, I earned their trust that I would not slap evangelical dogma on top of their words. Building this mutual trust formed a vital foundation before the ride began.

When the day of the ride came, dozens of bikers from the neighboring faith centers showed up at my church to begin this liturgy. People who might never set foot in a Christian church experienced my church's Spirit-infused singing.

Likewise, these riders and I were escorted into the sacred spaces of other faith centers. During the ride, some riders were initially suspicious because they knew I was an evangelical Christian. Many people asked me questions like "Are you one of those dogmatic Christians?" But as the afternoon progressed and they witnessed me being a spokesperson for faith traditions that clashed with my faith tradition, I was accepted as a type of nondogmatic, nonjudgmental Christian.

By the ride's end, the wall of suspicion had broken down between the forty riders and me. It was replaced by hugs and a sweet spirit. The inaugural ride was documented online and shared with both the interfaith community and the San Francisco Bicycle Coalition. I invite you to read about it on my website.[10]

The next year, I led the ride again. But now, with trust and relationship under my belt, I took a different and more explicit approach to bring honor to the various faith communities. This time I wanted to tell the story of how churches in San Francisco helped advocate for the city's marginalized people.

With the riders, we stood in different sacred spaces—gardens and memorials—where ashes of AIDS victims and war refugees were scattered. Inside both modern and historical sanctuaries, amid stained-glass windows and altars, we listened to gripping testimonies of how congregations stood *with*—and advocated *for*—past and present victims of war, housing displacement, and local law enforcement.

Documenting this ride provided me another opportunity to honor all the people involved. Rev. Jacks again led the planning committee, who gave me the honor of presiding over the ride. I have deepened my friendship with them and other faith center and bike coalition leaders. I am honored to get to know other people of faith in San Francisco in the context of their places of worship.

Because I broke my inertia, was vulnerably present, and brought the kingdom near to them through honor, God has opened up more relational channels than I have time for.

Continuing the Mission

The interfaith bike rides have opened up other unique opportunities to share God's love among my neighbors. Through Rev. Jacks, I befriended a youth teacher and subsequently planned a joint Unitarian and evangelical Christian Sunday school for our respective youth groups to explore faith.[11] Plus, as of this writing, the bike coalition's board president, having read some of my bike posts, asked me to consider helping him organize a redlining bike tour to tell San Francisco's story of segregation.

To make room for these new initiatives, planning the party, starting a nonprofit, and more, I made the tough decision to step down from the interfaith bike committee after two years. Stepping down from committees is part of my rhythm to stimulate new growth. Such decisions are often hard for me. But I'm compelled to continue the mission. My story here is one of many that have led to hundreds of spiritual conversations within different circles in pluralistic San Francisco.

Engaging *faith in Jesus* in a pluralistic context with a framework of honor-shame is both innovative and effective. Here are a few tactics I encourage the reader to consider:

Discover the God of Shame-Reversal through the City

Study the city's history—its neighborhoods, its stories through books, tours, talking with other people, etc. Explore how the city reflects God's kingdom now, or how it can reflect God's kingdom if we seek its peace and flourishing (Jer 29:7).

Make walking, biking, or mass transit a part of your rhythm. I've had many spiritual conversations just from this rhythm alone.

Look for the people who are seeking God's peace in the city. This will help you see cities with an honor-shame framework in a way that engages others.

The interfaith liturgies and tours I've led are excavated *shame-reversal narratives* from the life of the city. When we discover a shame-reversal story, it is usually evidence that God has been at work.

The smells, sights, brokenness, and beauty of the streets have become my favorite backdrop to immerse people of all faiths into God's story. But for Christians, in particular, I imagine the psalmist opening the doors of the church and saying, to paraphrase Psalm 48:12–14, *Get out there and see if you can spot the beauty of God through the beauty of the city!*

Cities and their plurality of cultures are a frontier of missions. Using an honor-shame framework opens huge conduits for others to experience God's invitation to shame reversal.

Honor People through Prayer and Research

Paul's missionary preaching in Acts 14–17 illustrates how to honor the other person's narrative as long as possible, building trust before voicing disagreement. The accrued trust honors the other person, even when you feel you must disagree.

Paul was a master at drawing from his hearers' narratives in order to communicate a kingdom narrative that honors others. I have discovered that this sometimes requires researching what others have shared with me. They may share how a world event, an aspect of their worldview, or a song lyric has been transformational. I've had to research everything from "Why do Sikhs carry daggers?" to Marxism, to all kinds of music.

As I'm researching, I ask God what the good news of the kingdom would look like in this context. People often feel very honored when they learn that I've taken them seriously enough to make myself a student of their world. After reimagining it in God's kingdom and offering that picture, it's not uncommon for the other to eventually say, "I've never thought about Christ (or Christianity) that way."

Focus on "Shame-Reversal" Stories

These are the stories in which Jesus restores honor to someone steeped in shame. This motif is central in Scripture, climaxing in Jesus' crucifixion and resurrection. I exhort you to look for "shame-reversal" potential where you live, work, and play.

At my party, giving roles to those who had the most potential to be honored (like my LGBTQ friends) was a small but meaningful way to counter their perceived shame. *Pray and honor* these shame-reversal stories into reality.

In addition, identify whatever shame-reversal stories may be drawn from your own life. This requires knowing your own testimony from an honor-shame perspective. Sharing this with others is both powerful and disarming. This is foundational to all the missionary training that I lead. I believe it is also foundational to the emotional health of followers of Christ.

Find Authentic Disciples with Whom to Pray and Be Vulnerable

I've mentioned that I pray regularly with a group of men—the same group of men who gave the toasts at my party. They are all ministry leaders. What drew me to them was their authenticity and emotional maturity.

These traits allow me to share with them my whole self—my joys, disappointments, pride, and shame. Their prayers and their examples sparked the idea of throwing my fiftieth birthday party. Their inspiration led me to make the whole evening the most vulnerable, innovative, creative, and redemptive evening I've ever experienced. These are the fruits when shame meets acceptance.

My time with these men has transformed all the subsequent groups I have led. For example, a couple of years ago I led a small group in San Francisco in which the men, eventually, felt so much safety and acceptance that they all came out as gay. For some, it was the first time. I witnessed deeper transformation in that group than I had ever experienced in decades of small-group participation.

Conclusion

"People are looking for a demonstration, not an explanation. . . . One living sermon is worth a hundred explanations." —Robert E. Coleman[12]

Living sermons lead people to the King, whose kingdom is being brought near. This King is Jesus—the one who initiated, proclaimed, prayed for, and superbly demonstrated the kingdom in the most inclusive way.

People in dense, hyper-diverse, and globally influential cities like San Francisco are especially prepared to respond to Jesus because of the way these cities reflect God's kingdom. They are a sanctuary for refugees, orphans, widows, and all types of marginal peoples. San Francisco's music and murals already capture this fact. Additionally, it's not uncommon to read or hear news stories about instances of intentional acts of kindness between strangers, like a bike messenger stopping to help a homeless woman and her newborn baby.[13] *Beautiful.* The kingdom has surely drawn near to the city's people, setting the stage to lead them to the King himself.

I bring Jesus into conversations when I sense that the kingdom's peace has made an impact. Any earlier than that moment tends to suppress the real Jesus under some distorted picture of him based on bad experiences from Christian culture. Sometimes that moment can arrive in fifteen minutes; other times, hours and hours of conversation need to pass before I bring up Jesus. Sometimes the reaction to Jesus is wrought with emotion and tears (awkward in a public coffeehouse). In other instances, the reaction is strongly against Jesus. Sometimes people reject the name of Jesus; other times, people express that their view of Jesus has changed. I usually assume my conversations are just a part of many they need to have. Recently a gay friend began dropping in on public weekly discipleship meetings I was leading. He was soon baptized and is now a new disciple.

God will reach whomever he wants to reach. But the blessing of sharing God's love in a culture like San Francisco has invited me to excavate my own living sermon to new depths. And that's the basis of this chapter: God is using a Mr. Spock-ish guy from San Francisco, reversing his shame to honor. God is using him to equip many, bringing the kingdom near in their context—to the honor and glory of God.

For Further Reflection

1. The Gospels have many accounts of Jesus relating compassionately to the "other." As you have honored, valued, or appreciated people who are different from you in ethnicity, lifestyle, or values, how has God stretched you?

2. Hong uses Richard Rohr's notion of "falling upwards" to frame his life narrative. What shame-reversal stories from your own life give witness to your identity of honor as God's beloved? How might this authenticate the gospel for others in your ministry context?

CHAPTER 10 Endnotes

1   Dallas Willard, *The Allure of Gentleness: Defending the Faith in the Manner of Jesus* (New York: HarperOne, an imprint of HarperCollins Publishers, 2015).

2   Lesslie Newbigin, *The Gospel in a Pluralist Society* (Grand Rapids: Eerdmans, 1989), 15.

3   Steve C. Hong, "An Atheist and a Theist Blog Together about Life," Kingdom Rice, March 17, 2016, https://kingdomrice.wordpress.com/2015/10/20/an-atheist-and-a-theist-blog-together-about-life/.

4   See Steve C. Hong, "The Gospel: The Ultimate Covering for Our Shame," Kingdom Rice, August 2, 2016; https://kingdomrice.wordpress.com/2016/08/02/the-gospel-the-ultimate-covering-for-our-shame/.

5   Richard Rohr, *Falling Upward* (San Francisco: Jossey-Bass, 2013).

6   Dan B. Allender, *To Be Told* (Colorado Springs: Waterbrook, 2005).

7   Bethan Mingle, "Ravi Zacharias Interviewed in Baltimore: 'We Are Being Trapped in the Quicksand of the Absence of Objective Truth,'" RZIM, https://rzim.org/global-blog/ravi-zacharias-interviewed-in-baltimore-we-are-being-trapped-in-the-quicksand-of-the-absence-of-objective-truth/.

8   Bruce Cockburn website, https://brucecockburn.com/.

9   Steve C. Hong, "Art Installations and Videos—Falling Upward: The Journey Beyond 50," https://sites.google.com/site/stevefallingupward/Media.

10 Steve C. Hong, "Sharing Love with San Francisco's Interfaith Worshiping Communities," Kingdom Rice, July 30, 2015, https://kingdomrice.wordpress.com/2015/07/30/sharing-love-with-san-franciscos-interfaith-worshiping-communities/.

11 Steve C. Hong, "Unitarian Universalists Visit My Christian Church," Kingdom Rice, May 6, 2016, https://kingdomrice.wordpress.com/2016/05/06/unitarian-universalists-visit-my-christian-church/.

12 Robert E. Coleman, *The Master Plan of Evangelism* (Grand Rapids: Spire, 2010), 68.

13 Amy Graff, "Unknown bike messenger 'hero' as homeless woman delivers baby on street," SFGATE, November 30, 2015, https://www.sfgate.com/news/article/Homeless-woman-birth-Muni-stop-bike-messenger-hero-6657639.php.

DISCIPLESHIP IN ASIAN HONOR CULTURES

CRISTIAN DUMITRESCU

Discipleship is a familiar term in religious circles. Christians often quote Matthew 28:16–20 as a key text to support a biblical understanding of discipleship as mandated by Jesus: "Go and make disciples, baptizing and teaching them." In fulfilling the Great Commission, Christians are to make disciples as a result of their evangelistic and missionary enterprises.

A popular understanding of discipleship assumes that teaching and baptizing are its basic components, and most mission strategies focus on teaching new converts a set of beliefs and particular Christian traditions. The basic mission approach in this case is education. However, educational strategies seem to be limited in effect, and results are frequently unsatisfactory. Christian converts around the world often display syncretism in more or less visible ways. Christians from Hindu, Muslim, Buddhist, or animistic backgrounds often return to their previous faith communities, and Christians blame insufficient teaching and understanding or lack of spiritual growth for the discipleship failure.

The most important question, however, is *What is discipleship?* Many definitions could be summarized as "the process of helping someone establish a relationship with Jesus and instructing that friend in the life of faith."[1] Books, articles, roundtables, and blogs describe the process through which a person becomes a disciple. Alice Fryling emphasizes that "discipleship is relationship."[2] The process is often labeled as *mentoring,* and in business environments *coaching.* According to the Apostle Paul, discipleship is a multiplication process that is passed from one disciple to another (2 Tim 2:2) "to the end of the age" (Matt 28:20).[3] While disciples become disciplers, it is necessary to make sure that the Master remains Jesus.

Even with a proper definition of discipleship, attempts to practice it are often accompanied by frustration. For example, simply learning or reading *about* discipleship is not the same as actually discipling someone. Jesus barely taught about discipleship; he *demonstrated* how to do it by *doing* it. Plenty of resources on discipleship define, describe, and analyze this critical topic. The more we *talk about* discipleship, the more frustrated we often become because reality beats theory. Merely discussing discipleship cannot substitute for practicing discipleship.

Another reason for frustration in discipleship is our desire for effectiveness. We want numbers, and we want them quickly. Measuring discipleship quantitatively is often deceiving, because one never achieves full efficiency and never retains all those disciples. Perfectionism in discipleship kills the joy of it. In addition, one never fully arrives as a complete disciple because discipleship is a lifetime process.

Too often people are told that discipleship means to become strangers to their own culture. As Lamin Sanneh observes regarding European missions in late nineteenth-century China, "When someone wanted to become a Christian the missionaries told him or her that his or her customs were contrary to the gospel," and that it was necessary to abandon them before baptism. What Sanneh observed to be true about Western missionary efforts in the nineteenth century to varying degrees has continued in the world Christian movement.[4]

Finally, many sincere Christians believe that Jesus provided a specific model of discipleship and they try to imitate it or simply copy and paste it. Too often they give up because the "model"—or the way they understand it—doesn't work. What's wrong? Where's the problem? Since the problem can't be with Jesus, it must be our failure if we forget that "we are witnessing through our lives, attitudes, and behavior."[5]

In Matthew 28, Jesus indicates that the goal of mission is discipleship. Missionaries and pastors baptize many new converts, but the discipleship process is often lacking. Sincere people look to Jesus as a model, yet tend to ignore the social or cultural contexts in which they are working. As Darrow Miller contends, things don't just happen without attention to context: "Just as the soil in which a tree is planted will play a decisive role in the growth of the tree, likewise the values, attitudes, culture, and ethos of a people will determine whether its development is healthy, stunted, or nonexistent."[6]

In many places, discipleship programs are not contextualized for the specific people groups where mission takes place. Most discipleship resources offer strategies developed in and for the Western world. This chapter addresses avoidable frustrations in the discipleship journey in the Asian context.

Asian Cultural Values that Impact Discipleship

Culture is unavoidable. It constitutes the parameters that define our lives. Culture, therefore, is the context in which all discipleship takes place. Since a multitude of diverse cultures exist, discipleship programs should consider the values defining local culture. According to Sherwood Lingenfelter, it is common for a group of people to "use their cultural values and systems to critique those who fail to live up to their rules, to judge and condemn based upon appearances, and to punish failure to conform by inflicting emotional and physical pain."[7]

However, no culture is perfect, and while "the image of God can be found in every culture," says James Plueddemann, "the effects of our depravity are also evident."[8] Therefore, culture-sensitive discipleship must be open yet critical.

Honor/Face

The most important cultural value in many Asian countries is *honor*. The typical Asian is significantly concerned about saving and maintaining face and restoring honor. This can create challenges for the discipleship process, when honor concerns become more important than the Christian values of honesty, obedience to God, and love for one's neighbor.

It has been common, in my experience, to hear statements or answers that are obviously not true. Many Asian Christians, however, do not seem to have a problem with what Western missionaries would label as lying or deception. Since Asians tend to have a pragmatic worldview, truth and how they view truth can differ significantly from the typical Western view.

For example, some point to Exodus 20:16 and suggest that the ninth commandment is not a blanket prohibition against lying, but a specific concern for "false testimony *against* your neighbor." From this Asian perspective of integrity and honesty, when an untrue statement is necessary to save someone's face, the need to maintain honor and avoid shame justifies the lie. A typical Asian concern is social harmony—maintaining good relationships with the members of one's family and community. As a result, their behavior can contradict Western cannons of accuracy and truth, because social harmony trumps other values.

Another key difference between Asian and Western worldviews lies in the area of logic and language. Western thought typically operates in binary terms, which, by the use of antonyms, often pose values in opposites. Something must be right, or else it is wrong; it must be either true or false, black or white. There is little room for grey. Nothing can be a little false or less true.

Communication theorist Robert Logan concludes that the Greeks "became slaves to the linear, either-or orientation of their logic."[9] Western logic isolates the form of a word and presupposes that its meaning remains constant. As Richard Nisbett describes the process, "The attributes become the basis of categorization; ... the categories become the basis of rule construction; and events are understood as the result of objects behaving in accordance to rules."[10] This binary logic in which missionaries and evangelists present biblical teaching, extracting moral principles and doctrinal statements that fit determined categories, often conflicts with the Asian logic that takes context into consideration.

Asian languages are primarily contextual. Take, for example, the Chinese language, with its pictorial symbols. Each pictorial is made from a variety of symbols that together create a context. To speak Chinese does not mean to simply recognize the symbols, but to know how to identify the meaning of those symbols in the particular context. Nisbett contends that in East Asian languages, "Words (or phonemes) typically have multiple meanings, so to be understood they require the context of sentences."[11] Similarly, Hebrew written words are made of consonants. The meaning of a Hebrew word is decided by the vowels attached, and that choice is influenced by the context of the sentence, phrase, or the general context of the story. This fluidity of Asian languages allows for nuances.

For most Western missionaries, the Bible is the inerrant word of God. Inerrancy often stands upon a literal reading and interpretation of Scripture. However, Jesus and many other biblical authors used parables and figures of speech that were not intended to be understood literally. A metaphor may stand for more than one reality. Parables are often open-ended, and the lesson or meaning is left up to the listener or reader. More passages in the Bible are *descriptive* than *prescriptive*.

Many Asian converts find the worldview of the Bible resembling much more closely their own worldview than the ways Western missionaries present its teachings. For example, polygamy and having mistresses besides an official wife are quite prevalent in parts of contemporary Asia. Western missionaries require local converts and disciples to abandon their polygamous practices and mistresses. Monogamy is presented as part of the moral rules of God's kingdom. Asians, however, point to the biblical patriarchs and kings and to their polygamous families and are amazed that there is no injunction from God against Abraham, Jacob, David, or Solomon. In fact, there exists no clear commandment against polygamy.

The fact that God announces the ideal of one man and one woman and at the same time allows people to have more than one spouse creates a paradox that Western missionaries struggle with. Such missionaries uphold the ideal, considering everything else as a moral failure. However, Asian disciples often have no problem allowing a difference between the practical reality and the ideal. Using relational logic, they develop a pragmatic discipleship model that fits their worldview and the biblical record, allowing people to develop toward God's ideal over time.

Asians will often go to extraordinary lengths to avoid being ashamed, especially in public. This creates a problem for Western missionaries because, from their perspective, the gospel requires people to first admit their status as sinners. However, the Bible shows that shame is the consequence of sin. Asians generally refuse to publicly acknowledge any failure, mistake, or even a generic belonging to a fallen human race, because they will lose face. Public discussions of weaknesses can lead to the view that Christianity is a shameful religion. If the status of *sinner* is a problem, so too is the precise instruction on Christian life. At the level of practice, Buddhism, Hinduism, and Islam are ways of life that are mainly taught by example, in addition to the more or less regular instruction.

When Christians insist on the need for training in beliefs and in-depth instruction, Asians often balk and consider Christianity to be childish. That is, one tells only children exactly what they are supposed to do, what to believe, and how to behave. To honor someone means to treat that person as mature and responsible. As Jeanette Yep notes, "Losing face in a group-oriented culture changes our identity."[12] No wonder Christianity has such a limited appeal in Asia—these Western forms of discipleship often *shame and humiliate people otherwise considered honorable.*

Even for those Asians threatened by this type of shaming in Christianity, there is no question that sin exists—and communities have to deal with it. However, sin is often understood as a threat to the group rather than primarily as the misbehavior of an individual. A conflict always shames the community.[13] Preserving honor requires the community to deal with problematic issues internally.

My friends from a Romani church refused to bring individuals who failed morally to face the entire church. Though not Asian, Romani communities, like Asians, have their own honor courts where conflicts and problems are discussed and resolved.[14] Allowing individuals to go to public courts is considered a huge shame, indicating their failure to discipline and manage their group's members. When one of them is in trouble, the entire extended family or clan rallies behind the person. If an individual loses face, the entire community loses face.

Here is another discipleship challenge: Due to a significant desire to preserve face and honor, Asian disciples are apt to formally accept what Western missionaries teach them. In order not to lose face by implying that they have not understood a teaching, Asians often do not ask questions, since doing so calls into question the teacher's authority. By agreeing and not challenging (even if they disagree), Asian disciples are not only showing concern for their own honor but also trying to save face for the missionaries. Asking questions implies that the missionaries were not able to properly explain the biblical teaching.

Community

The strong *communal* aspects of Asian societies often lead to competition between discipleship norms and the demands of local groups. Due to strong worldview assumptions, many Asian disciples end up with a veneer of Christianity applied to the old values and assumptions. Syncretism is widespread among disciples in the East and Far East. Such syncretistic outcomes can often lead to crises among the young churches or Christian communities when group allegiances become dominant in an honor-based society.

It is not unheard of for a Christian-background person to "honor kill" another Christian because of the demand of the honor codes of their own group or society. Although the Philippines is a Christian country, the past few years saw a surge of honor killings related to drug trafficking or even drug use. Such practice was encouraged by the national leadership in the name of washing away the shame of public defilement and international accusations. Legal courts could not keep up with the deluge of cases, and people silently felt that honor was restored. Their allegiance to the greater Filipino ethos took priority over Christian moral principles. This allegiance to the group is shared by most communal societies.

In an African context, genocides, as the one in Rwanda in 1994, reveal that allegiance to the ethnic group was stronger than allegiance to Christ. Hutus killed Tutsis and even moderate Hutus in the name of restoring their own face and honor. The danger, as Duane Elmer points out, is that "living up to the expectations of one's significant others tends to be the dominant value even to the point where morality, ethics, and right/wrong are defined by one's dominant group or in-group."[15]

This is a significant discipleship issue in collectivist, high group-emphasis contexts. Communal ties are often unspoken and invisible to Western missionaries, who commonly report individual conversions only to admit later that the majority of new converts returned to their old faith communities. This reality raises serious concerns regarding missionary strategies in Asia.

First, Christianity is sometimes presented as a set of beliefs rather than a way of life. Too often the faith is presented as a list of doctrines or beliefs to acknowledge— mere mental assent. Adding to this the default cultural value of saving face allows converts to declare their allegiance to Jesus publicly without working out the necessary way-of-life changes relative to their family and community. What is the result? Often, a syncretistic disciple with little depth. All other non-Christian religions are *ways of life,* and new Christian disciples expect to be taught the Christian way of life that will replace the previous one.

A Muslim knows how many times to pray and when, and that happens every day. Christians pray only "when needed." A Buddhist can go to the temple and make merit any time because making merit is ongoing. Christians usually worship one day a week. Jesus stressed the importance of integrity in what one believes and how one behaves; Jesus is himself the ideal—perfectly integrating belief and behavior even unto death. Christian communities have to become models of a *new way of life* that new disciples can observe and embrace. For Asians, belonging to a community is not indicated by a membership card or their name registered in a record, but by sharing in the values and life of that community.

Another concern regarding Christian missionary strategies is the individualistic mindset Westerners often tacitly carry with them. Missionaries make individual converts, hoping they will later convert their communities. Unfortunately, individual converts often return to their community's religion and way of life because of lack of support in Christian churches. Western Christianity, with its strong emphasis on the individual, has in some ways lost its ability to think and live communally—and missionary strategies reflect this. Effective discipleship strategies for most Asian contexts need to seriously consider how to accommodate more communal relationships, which would include the practices of group conversion and group discipleship.

Respect/Hierarchy

Respect for authority and *hierarchy,* or deference, as Elmer calls it,[16] is another important value impacting discipleship in Asian contexts. Asian approaches to leadership are often at odds with Western perspectives. Leadership in Asia often does not emphasize personal achievements (like the Western merit-based approach), but comes from status, age, and heritage. The Western emphasis on giving leadership to young people and achievers can be seen as immaturity in Asia. A leader has to be married, have children, and have life experience expressed by age in order to be respected and recognized as a leader. A young person with initiative is often seen as a rebel—a shame for the community—and will not be followed. However, Asians will naturally follow a guru, teacher, or rabbi. The respect given to those with seniority and status is a critical issue to consider when Western missionaries train Asian leaders. Thus, when Jesus is introduced as Master, people find themselves attracted to him.

In addition, most Asian leadership selection is not decided by a democratic vote. People follow their respected elders, who in turn share their wisdom and experience with the members of the community. Western democracy is often not the best fit for Asian societies. Values such as consensus and harmony are more important than *Robert's Rules of Order.* In fact, it is easier to move forward with almost unanimous support rather than facing half a group opposing the voted decision. "The strength of a process that involves everyone is that everyone helps make the decision."[17]

However, Asians tend to follow leaders that, from a Western perspective, have failed morally or do not deserve to be in leadership positions. It is not uncommon in Asia to see people worshiping dictators. Strong Christian leaders often attract many followers and establish large congregations. The notion of respect is commonly associated with obligation. Obligation and uniformity support the idea of harmony. Although individual choice may be involved, the community may determine acceptance or rejection of a strong leader. The individual's identity is given by the group, and the group also sanctions discipleship choices. My observation is that Asians prefer autocratic leaders and power.

Patron-Client Dynamic

Patron-client relationships combine honor, respect, and obligation and underlie discipleship ties. It is not uncommon for a disciple to expect material help from his or her new faith community. This attitude reflects the usual structure of society where a patron who provides services or gifts to a client becomes responsible for the well-being of that client's entire family. Jayson Georges observes, "People grant leaders authority and prestige in return for provision and protection."[18]

Missionaries working in Asia have always been confronted with direct or indirect requests for long-term or lifetime help. Their suspicion that these disciples' motivation to be baptized is only for material gain ignores one of the fundamental social mechanisms of patron-client relationships.

Similarly, when a person blesses a client and accepts to become a patron, the client becomes indebted to the patron for life. Filipinos talk about *utang-na-loob* as a debt of volition, a voluntarily moral obligation to serve the patron indefinitely. What if relationship with Christ would be introduced to Asians not as the Western understanding of *friendship*—but as the classic Asian *patron-client relationship*? The result may be a stronger and longer-lasting discipleship.

Figure 3: A Biblically-based Conception of Patron-client Relationships

As figure 3 above shows,[19] the patron-client relationship is essentially reciprocal. Yes, patron-client relationships have pitfalls and are subject to abuse. But beautiful biblical values inherent in the patron-client relationship also abound. These include *allegiance, loyalty, blessing, covenant-faithfulness,* and *trustworthiness*. These positive values are building blocks for contextualizing the gospel, but they may be especially well-suited for contextualizing the discipleship journey.

Power

Power is sought not only by autocratic leaders but also by Asian Christian disciples. Filipinos traditionally have sought the protection of *anitos*, who represent the spirits of their ancestors, believing these *anitos* have power and wisdom available whenever someone performs the required rituals. Their lack of worldview change has led to syncretistic beliefs that God, though powerful, does not intervene directly in human affairs, but prefers to work through intermediaries vested with divine power. In times of crisis, Asian disciples tend to return to entities believed to have power over life and death, such as the witch doctor, called *albularyo* in the Philippines, or to spirits, who often bear the names of Christian saints.

Conclusion

Discipleship in Asia presents both challenges and opportunities. As an imitation practice based on relationship, discipleship finds a fertile environment in Asian communities. Although people may embrace Christ, time and again they find themselves in opposition to their own communities because the values of God's kingdom may differ from their local culture's values. The strong desire to save face and avoid shame leads disciples either to return to their faith communities or to live a syncretistic life. As Walter Liefeld notes, discipleship requires total commitment on the part of the disciple, a reordering of life priorities.[20]

The good news is that much of the Bible was written in Asian cultures, and the values specific to the Mediterranean context provide an excellent bridge to a contextual model for discipleship. Seeking honor and power, employing patron-client relationships, respecting authority, and obeying the rules of the community may not fit the Western discipleship model, but these values constitute effective channels to communicate the Master's desire to restore his relationship with people. The Lord desires to enter into a patron-client relationship with them in order to restore their honor and bring them into the community of God's kingdom.

Contextualizing discipleship for Asia is not only a necessity, it is also a rewarding experience that will bring satisfaction both to the discipler and to the disciples.

For Further Reflection

1. Dumitrescu argues that discipleship programs in many places are not contextualized for the people groups where mission takes place. Many discipleship resources developed for Westerners are *assumed* to be relevant among all peoples. How have you seen this, specifically as it relates to honor and shame?

2. How might typical Asian values (e.g., respect, hierarchy, obligation) overlap with the gospel? How might these same values make patron-client dynamics an important consideration for the discipleship relationship?

CHAPTER 11 Endnotes

1 Alice Fryling, ed., *Disciplemakers' Handbook* (Downers Grove, IL: InterVarsity, 1989), 18.

2 Ibid., 8.

3 Scott A. Moreau, Gary A. Corwin, and Gary B. McGee, *Introducing World Missions: A Biblical, Historical, and Practical Survey* (Grand Rapids: Baker, 2004).

4 Lamin Sanneh, *Disciples of All Nations* (New York: Oxford University Press, 2008), 221.

5 Jo Anne Dennett, *Thriving in Another Culture: A Handbook for Cross-Cultural Missions* (Melbourne: Acorn, 1998), 36.

6 Darrow L. Miller, *Discipling Nations: The Power of Truth to Transform Cultures* (Seattle: YWAM Publishing, 2001), 22.

7 Sherwood G. Lingenfelter, *Leading Cross-Culturally: Covenant Relationships for Effective Christian Leadership* (Grand Rapids: Baker, 2008), 50.

8 James Plueddemann, *Leading Across Cultures: Effective Ministry and Mission in the Global Church* (Downers Grove, IL: InterVarsity, 2009), 65.

9 Quoted in Richard E. Nisbett, *The Geography of Thought: How Asians and Westerners Think Differently … and Why* (New York: The Free Press, 2003), 11.

10 Ibid., 10.

11 Ibid., 157.

12 Jeanette Yep, ed., *Following Jesus without Dishonoring Your Parents* (Downers Grove, IL: InterVarsity, 1998), 76.

13 Sherwood G. Lingenfelter and Marvin K. Mayers, *Ministering Cross-Culturally: An Incarnational Model for Personal Relationships* (Grand Rapids: Baker, 2003), 70–71.

14 Delia Grigore, *Curs de antropologie și folclor rom* (București: Universitatea din București, Editura Credis, 2003), 153–54, 161. For a detailed description of the Romani court system, the *Kris*, see Rena C. Gropper, *Gypsies in the City: Culture Patterns and Survival* (Princeton, NJ: Darwin, 1975), 81–107.

15 Duane Elmer, *Cross-Cultural Connections: Stepping Out and Fitting In Around the World* (Downers Grove, IL: InterVarsity, 2002), 173.

16 Ibid., 13.

17 Duane Elmer, *Cross-Cultural Servanthood: Serving the World in Christlike Humility* (Downers Grove, IL: InterVarsity, 2006), 159.

18 Jayson Georges, *The 3D Gospel: Ministry in Guilt, Shame, and Fear Cultures*, Timē Press, 2014), Kindle edition, Kindle location 235. For a more comprehensive survey concerning patron-client relationships in Scripture and mission, see Jayson Georges, *Ministering in Patronage Cultures: Biblical Models and Missional Implications* (Downers Grove, IL, InterVarsity Academic, 2019).

19 This diagram was developed by Jayson Georges and Werner Mischke as a result of a group exercise conducted at the Patronage Symposium, Arab Baptist Theological Seminary, October 3–5, 2018.

20 Frank Gaebelein, ed., *The Expositor's Bible Commentary: Matthew, Mark, Luke*, Vol. 8, (Grand Rapids: Zondervan, 1984), 313.

AN HONOR-SHAME GOSPEL FOR SYRIANS DISPLACED BY WAR:
Jesus Christ as Good Shepherd and Honorable Patron

RICH JAMES

Safaa was in her first-year training as a doctor in Aleppo. She cannot forget the day that Mahmoud, her big brother, was killed by a stray shell. Mahmoud left behind his wife and their newborn son. They moved in with the rest of Safaa's extended family. The emotional pressure of all this weighed heavily on Safaa's mom; she became very ill. Eventually, Safaa fled with her mom and brother to a nearby country, where they now live in a small rundown apartment.

Safaa has stopped studying; all her educational records in Syria were destroyed when the record office was shelled. A year ago, they heard that a shell had hit their extended family home. Her late brother Mahmoud's widow and son were killed.

The conflict in Syria has displaced Syrians across the Middle East and into many Western countries.[1] How can we present the good news of Christ to Syrian refugees, like Safaa and her mom, in a way that is biblically faithful and culturally meaningful?[2]

We will see that patron-client relationships play a significant role in Syrian culture. Syrians use the metaphor of shepherding to describe them. We will explore how the metaphor of shepherding in Ezekiel 34 and John 10 can be used to help Syrians understand the gospel of Christ.

What Is Patronage?

Mustafa told me that when he was young and wanted a job, he, like many Syrians, approached a man with standing in the community to ask for assistance. This particular man was someone with whom Mustafa had a good relational connection. Mustafa told him his situation, and the man said he would get one of his other connections to offer him a job. Mustafa said the man did so because Syrians consider it honorable for someone with standing, money, and connections to use them to benefit others in their community. This is an example of a patron-client relationship, with Mustafa obviously the client.[3]

Syrians essentially understand relationships to be about reciprocal care. An Arabic proverb says, "Be generous to a generous person and you'll win him; be generous to a bad person and he will rebel against you." As my Syrian friends explain, when someone benefits you, you naturally wish to benefit them in return. Friends can do *like for like*, but in this case Mustafa could not benefit his patron with a *like* service. Mustafa had neither the same standing nor the resources. Therefore, he reciprocated with a different gift: gratitude. He generously thanked the man and gave his allegiance to him in front of the community. Mustafa made sure to do as the man wished. In these ways Mustafa showed that he respected and valued the patron. Everyone involved was honorable. The relationship continued to be reciprocal and meaningful.

Patronage—Concepts and Metaphors

Over the years, I have been blessed with the opportunity to train thousands of Arabs from many backgrounds to enhance their communication skills. I have learned from them that Arabs tend to think and talk about life in ways quite different from Westerners.

When we Westerners want to describe things in life, we tend to use theoretical concepts and theories to make sense of life. Accordingly, Western scholars use the abstract concept of patronage, or patron-client relationships, to describe the kind of relationship between Mustafa and the man he went to for help. We might say something like, "Patron-client relationships are asymmetrical relationships which involve the mutually beneficial exchange of goods, services, and allegiance which continue over time." Mustafa is the "client" and the man he went to is the "patron." Our term *patronage* has an abstract definition.

Syrians, however, prefer to describe things using concrete examples rather than abstract concepts. They skillfully use the concrete example as a *metaphor* to make implicit comparisons with other things in life—one thing understood *through* the other thing.

Jesus constantly used metaphors. As Kenneth Bailey has wonderfully explained, Jesus was a "metaphorical theologian."[4] Jesus spoke and taught in parables; he used proverbs, metaphors, and allegories. These were not merely simple stories, but complex ways of creating meaning and talking about life *through* concrete figures of speech. Many books of the Bible describe and explain life in this way. Much more could be said on this broad topic, but here's the point: Middle Easterners often think and speak in *concrete metaphors* rather than in *abstract propositions*.

How, then, do Syrians describe what Westerners abstractly call "patron-client relationships"? Syrians often use the concrete example of *shepherding;* they speak about the patron-client relationship using the metaphor of *shepherd and flock.* The shepherd represents the patron (*al-rāʿī*).[5] The flock represents the clients (*al-raʿiyyah*).[6] "Flock" is a collective plural—a group of people. Like a "shepherd," a patron is expected to lead, care, and provide for the flock. Syrians say the flock is expected to respond to their patron by "listening to the patron's voice." By this, Syrians mean *to obey and give allegiance* to the patron.[7]

Finally, Syrians talk about "loyalty" (*al-walā'*) and "trust" (*al-thiqah*) in the shepherding relationship. Shepherds/patrons trust that their flock will follow them—and as the flock obediently follows their shepherd, the clients (flock) trust their shepherd to provide and care for them. Ideally, both shepherd/patron and client/flock give loyalty and allegiance to one another for the relationship to hold. The diagram below shows the ideals of reciprocity—with loyalty and trust at the crux of the shepherd-flock (or patron-client) relationship. Either party can initiate the relationship by voluntarily providing a benefit to the other. The second party then voluntarily decides whether they wish to reciprocate.

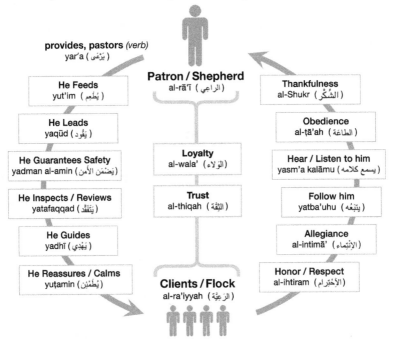

Figure 4: Elements of the Shepherd-flock (or patron-client) Relationship

Syrians tell me that "shepherd and flock" relationships permeate their society. These ways of relating are common among tribes, clans, and extended families, and also across the socio-political and even religious spheres of life.[8] Since Syrians are so accustomed to the wide-ranging role of these shepherd-and-flock (or patron-client) relationships, it is no surprise that many Syrians displaced by war evaluate their current dire circumstances through a patronage lens.

Here are a few quotes showing what Syrian refugees are wrestling with:

We used to be proud of being Syrian, but now we feel shame. We see ourselves as the lowest people. We are scattered in foreign lands with no "connections" and nobody to care for us anymore.

—Nour

We're all trying to get to the West. Those countries will provide us with protection, a living, and a new life. Some people think we will take this and give nothing back. We are good people; we will be loyal to them.

—Majid

We thought God would protect us. God has not. God has put us in terribly hard circumstances. He has destroyed our lives and scattered us over foreign lands with nothing. God is punishing us and testing us. Does God really care for us?

—Um Fadi

Each of these sentiments relates to patron-client relationships. *Who will provide protection, food, and safety?* The patrons they trusted previously have forsaken them and let them be scattered. They question whether God cares for them. They struggle with questions of loyalty and allegiance. *To whom can we turn as our patron?*

Two Different Shepherds in Ezekiel 34

The Bible uses the metaphor of shepherding to speak about human leaders and their followers (e.g., Ps 78:70–72; Ezek 34; Matt 26:31; Mark 14:27; John 10:12; Acts 20:28; Eph 4:11;[9] 1 Pet 5:1–4).[10] Leaders are called "shepherds." Those who follow them are called a "flock" or "sheep." The verb "to shepherd" is used to speak about leaders caring for their people. The metaphor of shepherd and flock as an apt description of patronage in the Ancient Near Eastern world has ancient roots.[11]

Moreover, the metaphor is also employed by biblical writers to speak about the relationship between Yahweh and his people.[12] This chapter will explore two passages, Ezekiel 34 and John 10.

Just as the Israelites are exiled, God uses the shepherding metaphor to speak of their leaders (Ezek 34:2). He describes them as terrible shepherds:

Woe to you shepherds of Israel who only take care of yourselves! Should not shepherds take care of the flock? You eat the curds, clothe yourselves with the wool and slaughter the choice animals, but you do not take care of the flock. You have not strengthened the weak or healed the sick or bound up the injured. You have not brought back the strays or searched for the lost. You have ruled them harshly and brutally. So they were scattered because there was no shepherd. (Ezek 34:2–65)

The good news is that the Sovereign Lord himself promises to come as a shepherd to save his sheep. He will search for them, rescue them from where they have been scattered and lost, gather them from the nations, provide them with security, feed them, give them peace, bind up the injured, and strengthen the weak (Ezek 34:11–16). The passage concludes with God speaking in covenantal language about an enduring patron-client relationship—reiterated though the metaphor of shepherding:

> Then they will know that I, the Lord their God, am with them and that they, the Israelites, are my people, declares the Sovereign Lord. You are my sheep, the sheep of my pasture, and I am your God, declares the Sovereign Lord. (Ezek 34:30–31)

Modern Syrians who encounter this passage understand the shepherding patronage metaphor. It is their everyday language. They often connect the passage to their own experience of being displaced and "scattered" by war.

The passage helps them see that what has happened to them is not God punishing them; rather, it is the result of the failings of human leaders. God did not send the bombs which destroyed their lives. This destruction was caused by fallen evil people. The horrible experiences of Syrians displaced by war are not what God wants! Rather, God is working to rescue them, to gather them. God wants to be their trustworthy and unfailing Patron/Shepherd.

The Good Shepherd in John 10

Patronage played an important role in the first-century Palestinian world of Jesus and his hearers.[13] They related to the motif of *God as shepherd*. In John 10, Jesus applies the shepherd motif to *himself*.

First, Jesus says that when someone is truly a shepherd, "his sheep follow him because they know his voice. But they will never follow a stranger; in fact, they will run away from him because they do not recognize a stranger's voice" (John 10:4–5). Jesus uses the concrete scenario of shepherding and pointing to patron-client relationships. He is saying that some falsely call themselves shepherds of God's people. These false shepherds make claims to be their leaders, their patrons, who care for them and should be followed. But Jesus says they are "strangers"—they are not true shepherds or patrons.

Anyone can *claim* to be a shepherd and patron of others. Ultimately, the allegiance and loyalty of the sheep (the followers) demonstrate whether someone is recognized as a shepherd/patron. Jesus says the sheep won't recognize the voice of those claiming to be their shepherds. There is no trust, no allegiance, no following—and therefore no shepherd-flock relationship. In stark contrast, Jesus claims that his sheep *do listen* to *his* voice. His sheep *do follow him.*

Moreover, Jesus uses the shepherding metaphor to speak about the character of those who are good and honorable patrons:

> The good shepherd lays down his life for the sheep. The hired hand is not the shepherd and does not own the sheep. So when he sees the wolf coming, he abandons the sheep and runs away. Then the wolf attacks the flock and scatters it. The man runs away because he is a hired hand and cares nothing for the sheep. (John 10:11–13)

False shepherds, patrons in name only, don't protect their flock when they themselves face danger. Instead, they abandon them. Jesus says these leaders reveal themselves to be mere hired hands, not true shepherds.

Jesus is the Good Shepherd. Good shepherds or good patrons live their lives to genuinely protect their flock. They are in it for the sheep. Jesus says his loyalty to his sheep and his qualities as a good patron will be proven: *He will lay his life down for them.* This is the extent of his commitment and care. Jesus can be trusted as the truest patron—the Good Shepherd.

We could call this "concrete metaphorical Christology." Jesus uses the metaphor of shepherding to discuss patronage, leadership, and *himself.* Jesus marginalizes fallen human shepherds. He declares himself *the* honorable patron who can be trusted.

The ancient Mediterranean world was a collectivistic culture. Collective groups used honor and shame as powerful tools to recognize, enforce, and reinforce values. Collective communities recognize those who embody the values as noble/honorable.[14] This is a pivotal aspect of the culture of Jesus' hearers and John's intended readers/hearers: They were honor-oriented.[15] The Greek word for "good" (*kalos*) typically refers to actions recognized by public opinion as worthy of honor.[16] Jesus is the "'good" or "honorable" shepherd in two ways: His actions in caring for the flock are morally good, and he is recognized as noble/honorable.

All these contours shape the phrase "good shepherd." Jesus clearly means noble/honorable as well as moral. Jesus doesn't just *claim* this view of himself; he gives *evidence.* He lays down his life to protect his flock—he is noble and trustworthy. What's more, people *recognize* that Jesus is honorable—they listen to his voice and follow him.

We Westerners may find the shepherding metaphor beautiful but vague. Hoping to clarify Jesus' identity and work when talking to Syrians, we may prefer to use abstract descriptions. We should recognize two things: First, this concrete Christological metaphor was common among those with whom Jesus spoke and deeply related to their collectivistic culture. Second, the metaphor is still part of the everyday language many Syrians use to describe protection, status, identity, and community care. The metaphor speaks loud and clear in Syrian culture—whether ancient or modern.

Syrians and the Shepherd Metaphor

The shepherd in Ezekiel is "the Sovereign LORD" (Ezek 34:11). Jesus places himself in the position of the Sovereign Lord. He is the shepherd of the Sovereign Lord's flock. Think about that. Jesus claims the position and role held by the Sovereign Lord in Ezekiel. This is not a conceptual, ontological Christology. It is metaphorical. Syrian refugees can explore who Jesus is—his divine identity, his exalted honor, his saving role as patron-rescuer—all through the metaphor of shepherding.

Syrians seek patrons whom they can *trust* to continue to care for them. Loyalty (*al-walā'*) and trust (*al-thiqah*) join patron and clients together in an enduring relationship. Jesus' death is the honorable death of a faithful and loyal shepherd who lays his life down to rescue his sheep. Jesus does this out of his firm allegiance to them. Jesus does not abandon his flock to save himself. Jesus is faithful—so much so that he says the close and faithful relationship between the Father and the Son is like the close and faithful relationship between the shepherd and his flock (John 10:14–15).

Syrians are seeking safety and security. Most patrons merely *claim* they are loyal. Jesus' faithfulness as a shepherd/patron is *demonstrated* as loyal. Therefore, the cross is not a sign of weakness, but rather it demonstrates that Jesus is faithful even to the point of death on behalf of his people.

Both patrons and clients can initiate the relationship in society. But Jesus is our initiator; he lays down his life for his sheep. This has already happened. Jesus searches for his sheep and calls them. Jesus wants to give his gift of life. Syrians understand that no one comes to Jesus with the hope of giving enough to initiate a patron-client relationship. Instead, they see that everyone comes to Jesus as a *response to the giving of himself to us.* Jesus proves his faithfulness on the cross; offering the "gift" of his life initiates the relationship. Jesus as shepherd/patron offers his life for salvation. The sheep/clients decide whether to accept his offer and place their trust in him.

The shepherding metaphor helps Syrians recognize that Jesus claims to be their patron. Many Muslims believe Jesus came only to the Jewish people. Jesus says, "I have other sheep that are not of this sheep pen. I must bring them also. They too will listen to my voice, and there shall be one flock and one shepherd" (John 10:16). Jesus claims to be the shepherd of other peoples too. All those who "listen to his voice" can respond and become his sheep.

Conversion to Christ includes complex political, social, cultural, and religious dynamics.[17] Jesus gathers us all into one new people. The flock of God is defined by *allegiance* (*al-intimā'*) to the person of Christ. In this way, the Good Shepherd/ patron metaphor, and the ensuing view of conversion as changing allegiance from other patrons to Jesus, can be a helpful avenue through which Syrians displaced by war can approach working out their identity in Christ. The question of allegiance helps to bring clarity in the midst of cultural, economic, and political complexities that easily cloud the issue of conversion.

"Flocks" are a people who belong to the same shepherd/patron. Syrians know that flocks give allegiance to their shepherd and to one another. By turning their allegiance to Jesus as their shepherd/patron, they understand that they also belong to his flock. They learn to accept all those whom Jesus has accepted. They become one collective people and identify with one another as the flock of Jesus. They are no longer scattered, and Jesus will not allow them to be scattered again.

The Arab patron-client metaphor and John 10 both use the language of "listening to the voice" of their patron. This motif can help Syrians displaced by war shift away from approaching prayer as a ritual activity. Instead, as clients coming to their patron/shepherd and listening to his voice, they gain his leading and guidance. As they prayerfully respond to his guidance, he builds them into a stronger flock.

Syrians tend to think and communicate metaphorically, different from Westerners' theoretical, conceptual approach. The metaphor of shepherding in Ezekiel 34 and John 10 can help Westerners present the good news of Christ in a more meaningful way. Syrians are comfortable with this metaphor; they use it every day to talk about patron-client relationships, care, loyalty, and allegiance. Naturally, this motif can be supplemented with wider biblical material.

Conclusion: One Step in the Journey

Patron-client relationships are prominent in Syrian culture. Everyone—from poor peasant farmers to politicians—understands patron-client relationships. Syrians use the metaphor of shepherd and flock to describe patron-client dynamics in everyday language. The biblical metaphor of God as the true and good Shepherd can help Syrians displaced by war to see that they have been failed by their human patrons.

The key passages of Ezekiel 34 and John 10 help Syrians see relationship with Jesus through the patron-client lens. They see Jesus claiming the role of Sovereign Lord. They see Jesus as Shepherd/Patron of God's flock. They see Jesus demonstrating that he is a faithful and loyal patron—giving his life for his sheep/clients in loyal allegiance to them. Moreover, Christ's death as the patron's self-sacrificial gift is a way of positively reframing the cross. What is normally a hindrance to belief due to the horrible shame of the crucifixion—may be reframed into one of sublime loyalty, generosity, and honor.

The good news is that God, their Shepherd/Patron, is seeking Syrians displaced by war—calling them, rescuing them, caring for them. Syrians recognize that Jesus initiates the patron-client relationship. They need not make themselves seem to be attractive clients to Jesus. Jesus seeks them and calls them to follow him. They can respond by accepting Jesus' call—turning their allegiance to him. In transferring their allegiance to Jesus, Syrians also transfer their allegiance to the whole flock of Christ. Syrians displaced by war can explore their new identity—their new source of honor—in Christ and in his body the church.

Because of the profound needs of Syrians displaced by war, they may be rightly understood as clients of the generous church/flock in countries where they reside today. But this is a long journey. Long-term, Syrians displaced by war are not to be perceived as only clients of the institutional church, but as full-fledged fellow members of God's global flock. They share allegiance to Christ with the rest of the flock. They belong to Christ and to one another. This carries reciprocal, honorable responsibilities. They are *cared for*—while they also *care for others*; they are *loved*—while they also *love others* in the flock. The whole flock enjoys the patronage of Christ together.

The shepherding motif can help us communicate the good news of Christ to Syrians displaced by war in a way that is biblically faithful and culturally meaningful.

For Further Reflection

1. Westerners often use theoretical language instead of metaphors. Reflect on how this has been the case in your own understanding of the gospel. How can you concretize the more abstract concepts of the gospel by using metaphors such as Jesus as Good Shepherd or Patron?

2. Consider the shepherd metaphor through the lens of honor-shame. How does this impact your understanding of Jesus? How might using an honor-shame framework similarly illuminate other biblical metaphors?

CHAPTER 12 Endnotes

1 *NOTE:* I want to give thanks to Syrian brothers and sisters who have helped me to explore some of this theme. They are due this honor, and I am grateful.

2 Syrians have been displaced by the consequences of war in many ways. Some are internally displaced in Syria, others have been displaced to surrounding counties, where they reside formally or informally. Some displaced Syrians hold a formal refugee status, others do not. Some Syrians have been granted asylum in other countries. It is helpful to remember this diversity when considering Syrians who have been displaced by war and their situations.

3 In technical discussions this man may best be called a "broker." He was a patron to Mustafa, providing a gift or service of "connection" rather than directly providing a job.

4 See Kenneth E. Bailey, *Finding the Lost: Cultural Keys to Luke 15* (St. Louis: Concordia Press, 1992), 15–22.

5 الراعي

6 الزَّعِيَّة

7 Some Arabs view patronage negatively. The issue here is not that reciprocity is viewed negatively, but rather in regard to the way it can be abused by the "haves" to oblige the "have nots" to obey them.

8 Of course, each relationship has subtleties and contextual and relational distinctives, yet similar dynamics are at play. For some examples, see Halim Barakat, *The Arab World: Society, Culture and State* (Berkeley and Los Angeles: University of California Press, 1993); Raymond Hinnebusch, "Syria's Alawis and the Ba'ath Party," in Michael Kerr and Craig Larkin, eds., *The Alawis of Syria: War, Faith and Politics in the Levant* (New York: Oxford University Press, 2015), 120; and Thomas Pierret, *Religion and State in Syria: The Sunni Ulama from Coup to Revolution* (New York: Cambridge University Press, 2013), 41.

9 The word commonly translated "pastors" in English is "shepherds" (*poimenas*) in the Greek.

10 The shepherding motif is used more widely to describe people in Matthew 9:36 and Mark 6:34.

11 "Shepherd of the people" was a metaphor used in classical antiquity to refer to leaders. See Johannes Haubold, *Homer's People: Epic Poetry and Social Formation* (Cambridge: Cambridge University Press, 2000), 17.

12 For a fuller examination, see Kenneth E. Bailey, *The Good Shepherd: A Thousand-Year Journey from Psalm 23 to the New Testament* (Downers Grove, IL: SPCK, 2015).

13 David A. deSilva, *Honor, Patronage, Kinship and Purity: Unlocking New Testament Culture* (Downers Grove, IL: InterVarsity, 2000), 121.

14 For a full discussion, see my forthcoming work, coauthored with E. Randolph Richards, *What Went Without Being Said: Cultural Values in the Biblical World* (Downers Grove, IL: InterVarsity).

15 Jerome H. Neyrey, *The Gospel of John* (Cambridge: Cambridge University Press, 2007), 16.

16 E. R. Dodds, *The Greeks and the Irrational* (Berkeley: University of California Press, 1963), 26 n. 109. This aspect is listed in *Strong's Concordance*.

17 For a good exploration of this complexity, see Warrick Farah, "The Complexity of Insiderness," *International Journal of Frontier Missiology* 32, no. 2: 85–91.

A GOSPEL THAT RECONCILES:
Teaching about Honor-Shame to Advance Racial and Ethnic Reconciliation

KATIE J. RAWSON

At an InterVarsity international student conference in the late 1990s, a group of Japanese Christian students publicly apologized to the students from other East Asian countries for the sins Japan committed against their nations during World War II. Greatly impacted by this apology, an Asian "seeker" in the audience made a commitment to follow Jesus. By recognizing and appropriately responding to acts of shaming, the Japanese students opened doors to reconciliation, and nonbelievers saw God's glory in Christ, which is what Jesus prayed for in John 17:20–21.

These students, having become aware of their nation's history, knew how to show honor as a response to shame. This powerful incident illustrates the main point of my chapter: *When followers of Jesus learn to recognize shaming dynamics in a situation, they can use honor to resolve conflicts started or aggravated by shame.*

Three critical factors enable the effective use of honor in Christian peacemaking and reconciliation: 1) personal and historical awareness of how ethnic identity and worldview have influenced would-be peacemakers; 2) cross-cultural understanding; and 3) an awareness of the biblical basis for this work. The Japanese students already had a level of understanding of honor-shame. They had learned the historical facts of those shaming events and, in a preceding conference seminar, had been exposed to the biblical example of Daniel confessing the sins of his ancestors (Dan 9:4–19). All three critical factors necessary for effective repentance were in place for their dramatic act. As someone committed to helping Christian international students learn how to catalyze change at every level of society, I believe all three of these factors are critical in discipling Christians as peacemakers and reconcilers.[1]

Personal and Historical Awareness

Awareness of how worldview, ethnic identity, and history have influenced us, our ethnic groups, and the nations is necessary for inter-cultural reconciliatory work. While developing this material during the past several months, I have personally discovered new aspects of my white, Western identity.

Western Thought	Non–Western Thought
Rules define reality	Relationships define reality
Universal focus	Particularistic (in–group) focus
Control internal and desirable	Control external
Analytical: see objects/categorize	Holistic: see the whole
History is less important	History is foundational

Figure 5: Comparison of Western and Non-Western Thought

When I included the figure above in my book on cross-cultural evangelism,[2] I was aware of differences between Western and non-Western thought, but I hadn't fully realized how Western thought patterns could feed racism. Both Western and non-Western thinking have strengths and weaknesses, and most of the characteristics I noted in the chart can be advantageous in some situations and disadvantageous in others.

When teaching about the Western worldview, I have always presented both its strengths and weaknesses. But I began trying harder to see the log in my own Western eyes as I read history I had never read or been taught before. After reading books like Jennifer Harvey's *Dear White Christians: For Those Still Longing for Racial Reconciliation*[3] and Ken Wytsma's *The Myth of Equality*[4] and learning how the concept of race developed in the United States, I realized some sobering truths: The analytical/categorizing characteristic of Westerners can lead to stereotyping and racism; the disregard of history can cause Westerners to ignore important history; and the drive to control can cause us to intervene in situations we don't understand. All these tendencies can contribute to conflict.

Reading books is not enough, however, to sufficiently understand the impact of history. I heard my African American colleague Fred Williams tell his story of growing up in racially segregated North Carolina. He described the challenges faced today by the African American teenagers and college students he knows. I started to understand more deeply the impact of shame. I began to feel shame as well.

What I experienced was *healthy shame;* I was properly ashamed of both my ancestors and myself for the racism I had unwittingly breathed in from them. This new awareness of my white, Western identity and its accompanying drive to control has made me more sensitive to people of color. In conversations with them, I now ask questions about history; and I try not to dominate decision-making in multiethnic groups. My journey to understand recent racial history and my ethnicity has only recently begun, but this journey has already brought about deeper relationships with African American friends.

Recognizing Shame-Promoting Dynamics

A nongovernmental organization (NGO) with Christian and Muslim staff serves at-risk youth—many of them refugees. They also serve Middle Eastern women who have experienced significant shame. The Islamic State (ISIS) had offered these at-risk youth and women the opportunity to join their militaristic movement; ISIS promised strong identity and honor. But the NGO kept them from getting involved in ISIS by providing mentoring and non-formal education for the youth and job training for the women. This is proactive peacemaking.

Around twenty-five years ago, the founder of this NGO recognized the conflict-promoting dynamics in the Middle East. He had a vision of reversing these dynamics by developing individuals as relational beings. In particular, his NGO labored to give women greater dignity. He learned history, language, and culture—and entered humbly into partnership with local Christians and Muslims to begin an organization based on "putting the last first."

By recognizing shame-promoting dynamics in a situation and responding in culturally sensitive ways, Christians can become reconcilers and peacemakers—both in the body of Christ and in the larger community.

An act of shaming almost always leads to a ruptured relationship and often to emotional distancing, violence, and even death. The first couple dishonored God. The human-divine relationship was ruptured. The corruption extended to all humans and their relationships—and even to the earth.

Psychiatrist James Gilligan interviewed 2,500 inmates of a maximum-security prison. When asked why they had murdered, the majority replied, "Because I was *disrespected.*"[5] The enemy uses shame to provoke or worsen conflict.[6] Shame that begins on an individual level can easily lead to systemic shame. Systems and structures that dehumanize people (e.g., slavery and incarceration) are shaming and can cause significant conflict.[7]

The actual terms *honor* and *shame* may not occur in such situations. Moreover, using the word *shame* can be shaming, and therefore the word itself should be avoided. There are often *verbal, bodily, and behavioral clues* that shaming is present. These clues often vary according to the culture. One easy way to spot shaming dynamics is to consider what causes "loss of face." Conversely, honoring behavior will "give face." The chart below offers clues for identifying shame.

Shame Dynamics
Use of words "disrespect," "respect," "face," "dignity"
Anger, acting out, agitation
Harming of self or others
Silence
Inappropriate laughter
Saying yes, then backing out, or being lukewarm about something
Systems that dehumanize people such as poverty, incarceration, or deprivation of education

Figure 6: Indications of Shaming Dynamics

Another way to discover shaming in a conflict is to look at *power-fear dynamics.* Satan holds people in bondage by the fear of death (Heb 2:14–15). Indeed, losing face or other forms of public shaming can mean social death. Satan can hold people in fear of physical death or fear of social death (shame) and use his captivity of people to cause conflict.

Additionally, fear of losing control (the loss of power) fuels many conflicts. White supremacist violence may come from the fear of relinquishing social status and control. Those in power or those seeking power (bullies and politicians, for example) often use honor and shame (national, group, or personal) to obtain or maintain power.[8] The horrible shame perpetrated through rape can be a weapon of control or war.

Westerners and white people (who are often those in power) can unintentionally incite conflict because of a failure to understand cultural dynamics. Missionary trainer Duane Elmer shares the story of a Westerner who let his views on a certain church vote be made known, causing everyone to vote with him to maintain his face. But later they showed only lukewarm enthusiasm for the plan they had voted for.[9] This was an indirect way of saying no.

African American pastor Leroy Barber tells about a group of people who came into his neighborhood one day with bags to collect garbage and with white paint to cover what they thought was graffiti on a wall. When a neighborhood youth became very agitated at the idea of painting over the wall, the members of the group should have realized something was wrong. Barber arrived just in time to explain that the "graffiti" was in fact a memorial to friends who had been killed. This example illustrates the necessity of *partnership with insiders* when entering new cultures.[10]

Using Honor to Prevent Conflict and Build Relationships

Showing honor or respect can deescalate conflict and build or restore relationships. Returning to Pastor Barber's story, the following week the outside group returned, and the youth who had been so upset explained the wall to them, telling them about departed friends. This act of listening (itself an act of honoring) helped undo the damage from the shaming of the previous week.[11]

Restorative justice programs keep juvenile offenders from incarceration and provide opportunities for them to regain face in the eyes of the community. These programs provide a powerful way to use honor to turn around shame. The Mennonite Central Committee partnered with the Reedley (California) Police Department, Community Youth Ministries, Reedley Peace Center, and the Kings Canyon Unified School District to launch the Reedley Peace Building Initiative. Juvenile offenders had the opportunity to restore relationship with those they had hurt through mediation and to do community service rather than go to jail. Only five percent of the youth reoffended.[12]

Worshiping communities that show respect for others are God's intended response to shame-infected systems.[13] God intends these communities to be safe places where people can share themselves without fear of being shamed, practice forgiveness, and learn to make peace in the broader world.

These principles work at home as well. Medine Moussounga Keener talks about evening praise and prayer with her family as she grew up in the Congo. These times together provided opportunities for family members to reconcile with one another. Medine's parents modeled the practice of asking for forgiveness and forgiving others. She never forgot those lessons. Later Medine and her husband, Craig, taught about ethnic reconciliation in Francophone Africa.[14]

In the 1990s, the Boyle Heights area of Los Angeles was filled with violence from rival gangs. After a Bible study about Jesus telling Peter to walk on the water in the midst of a storm, a group of Latina mothers decided to walk in the midst of *the storm in their neighborhood.* They sang folk songs, shared snacks, and talked with gang members.

The love of these mothers broke down barriers between the gangs, and eventually gang members began sharing their painful stories. Out of this interaction eventually grew a tortilla factory, a bakery, a childcare center, a conflict resolution class, and more. The women honored the neighborhood youth by listening to their pain and helping to start programs that dealt with shaming structures such as poverty. A community of believers applying the Scriptures in the power of the Spirit transformed the entire neighborhood.[15]

Biblical Basis for Disciples as Peacemakers/Reconcilers

God's "cultural mandate" in Genesis 1:28 included the command to rule over the entire earth—to fill the earth and govern it. This implies a diversity of cultures, each reflecting the image of God. But humans chose their glory instead of God's glory and wanted to remain monocultural (Gen 11:4). The division of languages at Babel was intended to ensure that the cultural mandate was obeyed.[16] The ethnocentrism of Babel dishonored God and refused the diversity he intended.

In Genesis 12:3 we learn that God promised Abraham that his family would bless *all* nations. One early example of this blessing is found in the story of Joseph (Gen 37–50). Joseph forgives his brothers for selling him into slavery and blesses many nations by his leadership in Egypt. God makes it clear that the *shalom* he intends for individuals and groups involves right relationships and justice (cf. Ps 85:10; Isa 58).

As seen in Jesus' teachings (e.g., Luke 4:14–28) and behavior (John 4:1–42), he did not tolerate ethnocentrism. God intends for his people of every color, ethnicity, gender, and generation to dwell together in unity. He also tells his people to forgive those who have sinned against them (Matt 6:1, 18, 21–35)—and he declares that peacemakers are "blessed" (Matt 5:9).

Both Jesus and the martyr Stephen forgave those who sinned against them. The ability to forgive others and love one's enemies is a virtue that speaks powerfully to Muslims both overseas and on American campuses. It was one of the major factors that propelled a group of Muslim students at a recent InterVarsity retreat to keep dialoguing about Jesus.

The Scriptures are a powerful tool in discipling for peacemaking. Role models—people obeying those Scriptures—are also vital (see chart on the following page.)

Contemporary examples of people forgiving their enemies include Christians in the Middle East who have endured persecution by terrorists—and the relatives of the people killed in the 2015 Charleston, South Carolina, church shooting.[17] A striking example of peacemaking from my childhood is the way my mother and Christian colleagues—white and black—helped our elementary school introduce racial integration in Mississippi in the 1960s.

Jesus' call in the Beatitudes for his followers to be peacemakers (Matt 5:9) could seem next to impossible in today's fractured world. Powerful forces of darkness are arrayed against those who would make peace. Restorative justice and other forms of showing honor don't always succeed. If, however, our disciple-making includes teaching and modeling the Scriptures on these subjects, helping disciples understand their ethnic identities and the histories of conflict in their nations, and recognizing and using honor-shame dynamics—then these disciples will be better equipped for reconciliation. They will know how to use honor to resolve conflicts started or aggravated by shame.

Genesis	• Gen 11:4 (Tower of Babel). The people seek their own honor ("let us make a name for ourselves") and refuse to obey God's command to fill the earth (1:28). The confusion of languages is God's way of ensuring that a diversity of cultures will develop. Babel both dishonors God and refuses the diversity God created to bring him more glory (11:9). • Gen 12:3 (God's call of Abraham). Abraham's family will bless all the nations. • Gen 37–50 (Story of Joseph). Joseph is called to forgive his brothers; he is a blessing to many nations.
Old Testament kings and prophets	• Solomon speaks of foreigners at the temple (1 Kgs 8:41) and demonstrates God's glory to the queen of Sheba (1 Kgs 10:1–9). • Elijah is cared for by a Sidonian widow (1 Kgs 17:7–24). • Elisha heals a Syrian general (2 Kgs 5:1–19). • Isaiah speaks of a Messiah who will be a light to Gentiles (Isa 42:1–8; 49:1–7) and foresees a house of prayer for all nations (Isa 56:6–7) • Other prophets speak of God's care for the nations (Amos 9:7, Ezek 39:21–24, Jonah 4:10–11). • Psalms call the nations to glorify God or speak of nations honoring him (e.g., Pss 67, 86:9; 96; 98). • Jeremiah instructs the Jewish exiles in Babylon to seek the peace of the city where they live (Jer 29:7). • Daniel's behavior in exile blesses other nations and glorifies God; Daniel identifies with the shame brought on his people because of their sins (Dan 9).
Gospels & Acts	• Jesus' "inaugural address" in Luke 4:14–28 declares a jubilee for the poor and portrays the Sidonian widow and Syrian general served by the prophets in a positive light (1Kgs 17:8–24 and 2 Kgs 5:1–19), angering his own townspeople who apparently wanted a Messiah just for Jews. • Jesus and the gospel writers portray Samaritans and Roman centurions in a positive light (Matt 8:10–12; Acts 10). • Jesus crosses ethnic, cultural, and gender barriers in relating to the Samaritan woman (John 4:1–42). • Jesus says peacemakers are blessed (honored) and will be called children of God (Matt 5:9). • God demonstrates to Peter that the gospel is also for Gentiles (Acts 10) and uses Paul to preach it to them (Acts 13–28).
Paul's Epistles	**Romans** • Paul explains to the Roman church containing both Jew and Gentile that Jews and Gentiles alike are justified by faith (1:14–17). • Paul describes salvation in terms of honor–shame (1:18–20; 3:23; 10:10–11). • Paul encourages believers from diverse groups to honor one other above themselves (ch. 12) and give up actions that could be a stumbling block to members of the other group (ch. 14–15). **Ephesians** • Paul teaches that Christ's blood reconciles humans to God—and Jews to Gentiles (ch. 2) into a new humanity (2:15) • Paul writes that the church reflects the multicolored wisdom of God to powers and principalities (3:8–10), instructing them to walk in forgiveness (Eph 4–5) and stand against spiritual enemies that are out to stop the mystery of God's reconciling gospel from being lived and preached (ch. 6). • There is a spiritual battle against the glory of God shown through reconciled peoples (6:10–20).
Revelation	• John sees people from every nation, tribe, people and language worshiping before the throne and the Lamb (Rev 7:9–16). • The nations bring their glory and honor into God's city (Rev 21:22–27). • Trees have leaves for the healing of the nations (Rev 22:1–2). • The glorifying of God through the diversity that people refused in Genesis 11:4 is brought to fruition through the work of the Lamb.

Figure 7: Selected Biblical Foundations for Peacemaking through Showing Honor

For Further Reflection

1. How can our responses to acts of shaming open doors to reconciliation and the gospel? How can we be an answer to Jesus' prayer in John 17:20–21?

2. What kinds of ethnocentrism or racism did you "breathe in" while growing up? What historical factors may be in the background of racial conflicts in your context?

CHAPTER 13 Endnotes

1 I am indebted to InterVarsity colleagues Eva Liu Glick and Fred Williams for some of the insights in this chapter. I partnered with them to present a seminar on honor-shame and reconciliation at our national staff conference in January, 2016.

2 I adapted this figure from Katie J. Rawson, *Crossing Cultures with Jesus* (Downers Grove, IL: InterVarsity, 2015).

3 Jennifer Harvey, *Dear White Christians: For Those Still Longing for Racial Reconciliation* (Grand Rapids: Eerdmans, 2014).

4 Ken Wytsma, *The Myth of Equality: Uncovering the Roots of Injustice and Privilege* (Downers Grove, IL: InterVarsity, 2017).

5 James Gilligan, *Violence: Reflections on a National Epidemic* (New York: Vintage Books, 1997), cited by Donna Hicks in *Dignity: Its Essential Role in Resolving Conflict* (New Haven, CT: Yale University Press, 2011), 38; emphasis added.

6 See Genesis 3–4. See also Rawson, *Crossing Cultures*, 160–64; and Hicks, *Dignity*, 11.

7 Kurt Thompson, *The Soul of Shame: Retelling the Stories We Believe About Ourselves* (Downers Grove, IL: InterVarsity, 2016), 145–46.

8 Rawson, *Crossing Cultures*, 94.

9 Duane Elmer, *Cross-Cultural Conflict: Building Relationships for Effective Ministry* (Downers Grove, IL: InterVarsity, 1993), 56–59.

10 Leroy Barber, *Embrace: God's Radical Shalom for a Divided World* (Downers Grove, IL: InterVarsity, 2016), 86–87.

11 Ibid.

12 Krystal Klaassen, "Second Chances for Juvenile Offenders," Mennonite Central Committee blog, November 1, 2015.

13 Thompson, *Soul of Shame*, 147–67. See also Philip Jamieson, *The Face of Forgiveness: A Pastoral Theology of Shame and Redemption* (Downers Grove, IL: InterVarsity, 2016), 136–39.

14 Craig Keener and Medine Moussounga Keener, *Impossible Love: The True Story of an African Civil War, Miracles and Hope Against All Odds* (Bloomington, MN: Chosen Books, 2016), 236–37; and private conversation with the author, April 17, 2017.

15 James Bryan Smith, *The Good and Beautiful God: Falling in Love with the God Jesus Knows* (Downers Grove, IL: InterVarsity, 2009), 131–32.

16 Brenda Salter McNeil, *Roadmap to Reconciliation: Moving Communities into Unity, Wholeness and Justice* (Downers Grove, IL: InterVarsity, 2015), 26.

17 On June 17, 2015, white supremacist Dylann Roof killed nine African Americans attending a Bible study at Mother Emmanuel AME Church in Charleston, South Carolina. The next day during a bond hearing, relatives of five of the victims told Roof they forgave him. See Elahe Izadi, "The Powerful Words of Forgiveness Delivered to Dylann Roof by Victims' Relatives," *Washington Post*, June 19, 2015, https://www.washingtonpost.com/news/post-nation/wp/2015/06/19/hate-wont-win-the-powerful-words-delivered-to-dylann-roof-by-victims-relatives/?utm_term=.a63017c08bef.

THE BOOK OF SAMUEL:
A Reconciling Narrative

NOLAN SHARP

History Is about Honor

On November 29, 2017, Bosnian Croat General Slobodan Praljak committed suicide in a courtroom in the Hague. For just a moment, the world media again took notice of the 1991–95 wars of Yugoslav succession. In 2013 Praljak was convicted of crimes against humanity and sentenced to twenty years in jail. Upon hearing in court that his appeal had been denied, he stood up and stated in a trembling voice, "Judges, Slobodan Praljak is not a war criminal. With disdain, I reject your verdict." And then he drank poison. Even though Praljak was unlikely to serve much more time in prison (he had already been in detention for thirteen years, and most prisoners had been released early), he chose a final, dramatic assertion of his own honor.[1] My Croatian friends were angry, believing his death was an injustice.

History provokes our sense of honor and shame. Our identity rests on enduring elements like nationality, religion, and race. The honorable or shameful acts of "our people" are our honor and shame as well. We read history with an eye to the honorable contributions of our heroes and recognition of our people's suffering.

Telling the stories of all sides in divided societies is a step in the right direction, but exhaustive accounts are tediously inaccessible and lack cathartic power. Despite the meticulous work of the International Criminal Tribunal for former Yugoslavia in uncovering and detailing what happened, I do not remember *ever* hearing someone from here praise its work.

Alternatively, trying to forget the past is a nonstarter. Public schools everywhere in the region continually rehash one-sided accounts of recent history. Conversations in cafés, even with close friends, frequently turn into arguments over when life was best, what went wrong, and which previous leaders are to blame for today's problems. Since society will continue to talk about the past, we desperately need a way to do so that moves toward reconciliation.[2]

Samuel as Reconciliatory History

First and Second Samuel provide a biblical pattern for reconciliatory history.[3] It is an epic and well-known tale, rich in secondary characters. Contemporary Western believers love Saul and David as case studies of godly and ungodly living and leadership. However, this text is not the product of an individualistic culture. The figures of Samuel, Saul, and David were as important to, and divisive among, its audience as Robert E. Lee for Americans, or Josip Broz Tito for people in former Yugoslavia. The successes and failures of these kings, judges, and prophets reverberated in the daily lives of the original audience of these two books. In writing one story addressing all sides, the stakes were extremely high for the author of Samuel.

The Enormous Challenge of Recounting Three Tumultuous Eras

Samuel is a compelling account of three different eras: Samuel's rule as a judge, Saul's rule as king, and David's rule as founder of a royal dynasty. The narrative weaves together a high view of God's sovereign control over the destiny of the nation of Israel, blunt honesty about the faults of each leader, and sensitivity toward the losses each group incurred. Robert Alter captures the subtlety of the author of Samuel, who believes in a morally imperative covenantal relationship between God and Israel; he believes in the authority of prophecy; and he believes in the divine election of the Davidic line. But one must hasten to say that he believes in all these things only with enormous dialectic complication, an order of complication so probing that at times it borders on subversion.[4]

The narrative of 1 and 2 Samuel is fair to all sides. It provokes sympathy for "losers" while taking "winners" to task. That such a critical, reflective document ever became part of the public record is astonishing. It succeeded in its task and endures as a model of reconciliatory history.

Recent evangelical scholarship has made a good case for dating Samuel's composition within the living memory of the events it portrays.[5] One part of its audience surely longed for the days of prophetic judges and blamed the institution of kingship as a fundamental rejection of God's direct rule. Another, the Benjamites, longed for the days when their tribe enjoyed preeminence under Saul. Lastly, the current regime wanted to see the legitimacy of the Davidic line defended. Each group knew the fatal flaws in the others' heroes. Yet a coherent national identity emerged that encompassed all these stories. The priests and prophets came to strongly support the Davidic line and the building of a national temple in Jerusalem. Benjamin became so strongly allied with Judah that, after Solomon died and the kingdom split, it alone of all the tribes remained allied to Judah.

Samuel, the Last of the Judges

The author of Samuel sensitively tells the story of each era, beginning with Samuel's mother, Hannah, and her desperate prayer for vindication as a barren wife. She dedicated her son to the Lord, and he grew up in priestly service under Eli, whose wicked sons ignored his rebuke (1 Sam 2:25). Eli was a powerless father and tragically died upon hearing of his sons' death in battle (1 Sam 4:18). His story foreshadows the tragedies of ruling families throughout the book of Samuel. However, Eli's foster-son Samuel grew up to be a prophet and a judge over Israel.

At that time, Israel lacked any formal political structure. In times of crisis, God raised up charismatic, heroic judges to guide the nation and fight off its enemies. For centuries, judges provided crucial but uneven leadership. Judges did not create lines of succession, levy taxes, or conscript men into a formal army. Samuel was a transitional figure out of the era of the judges. As both priest and hero, he saved the people from a Philistine threat and "judged" Israel for a generation (1 Sam 7:15).

Even though Samuel witnessed the tragic outcome of his loving foster-father's family, his own sons also turned out rotten. Furthermore, despite the fact no judge ever created a line of succession, Samuel, as an old man, pushed his evil sons forward to succeed him (1 Sam 8:1–3). It was only *in response to* this awful idea that the elders of Israel proposed that Samuel appoint a king instead. This "displeased" Samuel (1 Sam 8:6). However, the Lord told Samuel that this request for a king was a rejection of divine kingship (1 Sam 8:7). Samuel then warned the people of the harsh ways a king would rule over them (1 Sam 8:10–18).

The biblical view of a human king over Israel is complex. Deuteronomy 17 anticipates the installation of a king in Israel. And the only trace of authorial judgment over the chaotic days of the book of Judges is the statement, repeated four times, that "in those days Israel had no king" (Judg 17:6; 18:1; 19:1; 21:25). Two of those are also followed by "everyone did as they saw fit" (Judg 17:6; 21:25). But after saying that asking for a human king is a rejection of his (God's) kingship, God still tells Samuel to anoint a king and leads him to Saul. The book of Samuel shows shrewd awareness that every political system is a mix of positive and negative.

Samuel's bitterness over the rejection of his sons continued. He began his last great speech to the nation by pointing out, "My sons are here with you" (1 Sam 12:2). He claimed that the people asked for a king because of the threat of Nahash king of the Ammonites (1 Sam 12:12), covering up that he triggered the crisis by pushing his wicked sons forward. Despite the excellent mentoring he received as a foster-son, Samuel failed to mentor his own sons or the young men, Saul and then David, whom he anointed.

At this point in the story, loyalists to the tradition of judges and priestly leadership must concede that Samuel's story has been told truthfully, with tenderness and skill. Samuel's courage and his harsh prophetic criticism of kingship are clear. Yet his own flaws have been plainly retold as well.[6] However, no matter the flaws of kingship, a Samuel loyalist could not deny that God endorsed a human king over Israel.

Saul, Israel's First King

The second section of the story (1 Samuel 9–31) recounts the era of Saul's reign. Hesitant and insecure, Saul is one of the most tragic figures in the entire Bible. Samuel anointed Saul three times, each ambiguously, and did little to help him figure out how to lead. Despite early victories, Saul failed to obey God's direct commands, which resulted in his rejection as king (1 Sam 13:14; 15:10). He disgraced himself through murder and witchcraft and died a shameful death (1 Sam 22, 28, 31).

Despite these tragic flaws, Saul was a powerful leader who played a crucial role in establishing the kingdom of Israel. He won military victories, served as Israel's first king, and built a national government. He was God's answer to the people's prayers for a deliverer (1 Sam 9:16). He was humble (1 Sam 9:21) and changed in heart through the filling of God's Spirit (1 Sam 10). He possessed a gift to rally brave men (1 Sam 10:26) and rescued Jabesh Gilead (1 Sam 11). He and his son Jonathan defeated a massively superior Philistine army (1 Sam 13–14). He was earnest to obey the law (1 Sam 14:35) and fought and punished Israel's enemies on every side (1 Sam 14:47–48). *These* were the stories Benjamite elders told young children, and they have not been left out.

Saul reigned long enough that his son Ish-Bosheth was forty years old when he inherited the kingship (2 Sam 2:8).[7] As a Benjamite, Saul lifted the tribe and brought it prestige and wealth with his reign. An entire generation grew up enjoying Benjamite preeminence. When David (a Judahite!) threatened his reign and line, Saul turned on his own lieutenants in exasperation and said about David, "Listen, men of Benjamin! Will the son of Jesse give all of you fields and vineyards? Will he make all of you commanders of thousands and commanders of hundreds?" (1 Sam 22:7). The tribe of Benjamin lost tangible prestige and stature when Saul's line ended and naturally would have nursed resentment toward David's line.

David, a King from Judah

Saul's death cleared the way for the third era: the kingship of David of Judah. Biblically literate Christians know that David was a great man after God's own heart (1 Sam 13:14). It is not necessary here to recount all the positive aspects of David's leadership and heroism. Imagine, however, an old Benjamite who had served Saul as a young man as a "commander over hundreds." What might he have said about David? "This David is from an unimportant family (1 Sam 16). He is descended from a filthy Moabite.[8] He fled from Israel to a foreign country and went mad (1 Sam 21:23). He fought for the Philistines against Israel and lobbied to fight in the final battle against his own people (1 Sam 29:8). He sinned by taking Bathsheba and murdering her husband (2 Sam 11). His example came back to haunt him when his own son raped one of his sisters and triggered a civil war (2 Sam 13–18)."

It is shocking how plainly this book, clearly written to justify the Davidic line as God's sovereign choice for leadership over the nation, recounts David's murderous lust and betrayal of his own country. Consider how by such inclusions the author of Samuel gave potential ammunition to critics of David's line! We can hardly bring ourselves to integrate the flaws and successes of transformative leaders like Mahatma Gandhi or Martin Luther King Jr. because hateful critics use their flaws to undermine their legacy. We need our heroes, so much that we can hardly make space for a complete account of their lives. Yet the book of Samuel did just that while the unified kingship was still a tenuous institution.

Honor among Kings

Samuel also emphasizes the interpersonal honor shown between Saul, Jonathan, and David. Jonathan was one in spirit with David and made a covenant with the house of David (1 Sam 18:1; 20:16–17). He looked forward to serving David in his kingdom (1 Sam 23:17). Even Saul acknowledged (in lucid moments) that David treated him justly and would go on to "do great things and surely triumph" (1 Sam 26:25; cf. 1 Sam 24:20).

In return, David honored Saul, Jonathan, and the tribe of Benjamin. He pledged to Jonathan that he would always show honor to his family (1 Sam 20:15). He later honored that promise upon discovering and caring for Jonathan's lame son, Mephibosheth (2 Sam 9:1). He refused to hurt Saul or lead a rebellion against him (1 Sam 24:6, 11). He deeply lamented Saul's and Jonathan's deaths and honored their lives (2 Sam 1:27). These heroes were respectful of one another. No one can appeal to their personal example to reinforce hate.

The Power of an Artfully Told Story

Finally, Samuel compassionately portrays minor characters, especially those made casualties by the course of history. The author shows an awareness of the cost of *realpolitik* among political leaders.[9] Uriah's honorable loyalty cost him his life. Naively trusting David's story upon fleeing from Saul also cost Ahimelech his life (1 Sam 21:7). Michal loved David, one of the only plain references in the Bible of a woman's love for a man (1 Sam 18:20). Her loyalty saved David's life (1 Sam 19:11), but their marriage became a casualty of dynastic conflict. When David fled, Saul gave her as wife to a man named Paltiel (1 Sam 25:44). David later demanded her back to solidify his reign, and Paltiel followed after her, weeping (2 Sam 3:16). This tiny detail exemplifies the understated way Samuel acknowledges the heartbreaking complexity and cost of social cohesion and communal honor.

Long-term reconciliation and unification of Judah with Benjamin was by no means inevitable. David's initial hold on the kingship was quite fragile. For two years

Saul's son Ish-Bosheth ruled as a puppet king under Abner, one of Saul's generals, while David ruled only over Judah (2 Sam 2:1–8). War between these two houses "lasted a long time" (2 Sam 3:1). Generals on both sides murderously betrayed one another (2 Sam 3:27). Even upon taking the throne, David feared that scheming generals like Joab would betray him (2 Sam 3:39). Given this enduring tension and Benjamin's geographical location between Judah and the northern tribes, it is remarkable that Benjamin remained with Judah in the divided kingdom. The very tribe whose leader died in battle to make space for a man of Judah became its only permanent ally.

Applying Samuel to Honor-Bound Conflicts

It is incredibly difficult for nations, communities, and religious groups to simply acknowledge that their heroes are flawed, that even a just struggle can be tainted with injustice and cruel mistakes, and that losers and winners have only partial understanding and make ambiguous decisions. That Samuel does all of this is remarkable, and the book gives us practical lessons for working toward reconciliation.

Holistic Storytelling

First, evocative, accessible storytelling that encompasses multiple points of view is crucial to reconciliation. Reading Samuel aloud takes approximately four hours. In an oral society, the story held listeners' attention similar to the way we consume movies. Four hours is the length of *Gone with the Wind* or a two-part miniseries. This is not dry, lengthy history. Details like the outfits Hannah made for Samuel each year and Paltiel's weeping remind us that these were frail human beings like us.

Communal reception of such a compelling story can itself be part of a healing process. Samuel embarrasses each party at various times; but in the end, a fair audience must admit that the story left nothing out. Merely being willing to try to listen together to a common account is an essential first step. The shared experience of appreciating a compelling story itself opens the way for renewed common understanding.

Several times I have participated in a remarkable initiative in the Balkans called "Renewing Our Minds."[10] For nearly twenty years, ROM has gathered young people from the conflict areas of the former Yugoslavia (and other parts of the world) to spend several weeks together learning about peacemaking based on Jesus' example. The first third of the time largely emphasizes fun and team-building, helping young people learn to enjoy their contemporaries from adversarial countries. The second third is much harder: Leaders present the painful stories of each group through personal accounts and media. Attendees are often unaware of tragedies and atrocities that never appeared in their schoolwork. Then, toward the end, the leaders work to help attendees reintegrate a new understanding of themselves and their neighbors. Those who participate often view it as a life-changing experience because they learn that they can make space for others' stories without losing their own.

Institutional Honesty

Second, institutions can best ensure their endurance by combining confidence in God's sovereign choice to raise them up with complete transparency about their flaws, mistakes, and even cruel injustices. Desire for group honor is very deeply embedded in all of us. It tells us never to give an inch or admit a fault, lest our enemies use it to tear down something we love. But this is a lie. Great, enduring institutions develop the mechanisms and language to admit their sins honestly. In fact, the inability to admit faults and sins may be one of the strongest indicators that God's favor is being withdrawn from an institution or government.

It is not just that God *honors* honesty and transparency on the part of churches and Christian organizations—he *demands* it. When we bring the whole truth into the light, evil loses its power over us. How can we claim that we need to keep skeletons in the closet for the sake of God's work when his own Word so plainly speaks of the sins of the most important king in the Old Testament.

I wish for such a masterful short book or film for the six nations of the former Yugoslavia.[11] Each country is now independent and struggling to process its own enormously complex national history. Nations hailed the judgments of the International Criminal Tribunal for the former Yugoslavia when it found their adversaries guilty, but scorned it whenever their own people were indicted. Those old enough to remember the Yugoslav Wars generally recall what a dirty business it was, many having good friends who ended up on some other side; but youth receive a one-sided version of the story and are often more narrow-minded than their parents. Disappointment with slow economic growth and extremely high unemployment, even with entrance to the European Union, leaves politicians constantly tempted to resort to nationalistic baiting to turn attention away from their lack of success in building prosperous nations.

Communal honor and shame underlie and reinforce these conundrums. The Croatian Roman Catholic Church leadership and many politicians are working hard to convince the Vatican to elevate Alojzije Stepinac, the Archbishop of Zagreb in the World War II era, from beatification to sainthood. He is a complex character, who at times criticized the wartime fascist government but never broke with it. Because communist Yugoslavia eventually put him on trial, he became a symbol of Christian resistance. Beatification and possible sainthood increasingly remove him from honest conversation about his legacy.

Croatian history, like that of every nation on earth, is incredibly complex and full of ambiguous figures whose rise and fall were for the benefit or detriment of groups in their societies. Leaders bring both honor and shame to their people. The wounds of history keep reopening in Croatia, because honor demands that we not admit any wrongdoing. Cardinal Josip Bozanić, the current Archbishop of Zagreb, made this appeal in a sermon in the Zagreb Cathedral on March 11, 2017:

Brothers and sisters, we believers … consider our Homeland a gift. In caring for her as a gift we need to contribute to the renovation of the Croatian state, aware of all the sacrifices and sufferings that have had to be endured. It is not a small thing to us when someone *tramples* on that sacrifice, for what the Croatian people suffered during the last decades must not be *mocked* or *devalued*. Any attempt to attribute *shame* to that costly sacrifice cannot be justified by literary satire, irony, or metaphor. Even for the period of the Homeland War a strong light of truth is needed, just as for the period of the communist regime, because *insulting* Croatian victims grows from the same inspiration and has the same roots.[12]

Bozanić here is rejecting any complex account of the war. Even though Croatia won its independence, its religious and conservative leaders vigilantly undermine any reflection on its mistakes. This approach requires the truth to serve only one side; anything else is an unacceptable shame on the nation. Bozanić is criticizing journalists and artists who tell complex stories about Croatia. In contrast, even under communism, Croatian films like Antun Vrdoljak's 1971 *U gori raste zelen bor* movingly demonstrate the ambiguity of World War II in the region.

Confidence in God's Sovereignty

Third, Christians must demonstrate confidence that God does approve of, and support, nations and other institutions. The author of Samuel is clear that a kingdom under the line of David was God's will. The embarrassing stories of failure and defeat do not nullify that. Christian leaders have an indispensable part to play in directly telling reconciling stories, especially in a deeply religious country like Croatia. They must reassure believers that God is sovereign and that he is not threatened or diminished by the whole story of the fallible human actors he uses. They fail instead when they cannot bring themselves to risk honor by telling the whole story well.

There is a theological failure in this region to grasp that God's unimpeachable honor extends to support the existence and thriving of nations. An honorable nation then builds on its God-given confidence to tell the story artfully and without anxiety. Those who truly know the Prince of Peace will love and welcome all the diverse groups in their own society, and they will embrace their stories as well. Making space for those stories—especially from minorities and out-of-power groups—honors God and ultimately preserves the honor of the whole nation.

History Can Show Honor to All

For complex reasons, people all over the Balkans fought for and against fascism, communism, democracy, kingdoms, and empires. The characters at the center of these events were often tragically flawed. Years before Slobodan Praljak's suicide, Abdulah Sidran, one of his childhood friends, recalled in an interview how complex Praljak's childhood was. He grew up after World War II as the son of an officer in the Yugoslav Communist Secret Police (OZNA). Although they were a Croatian family, his father's job was to hunt down Croatian fascists in one of their former strongholds. As a result, Slobodan was hated in his own neighborhood as the son of an informer. Sidran commented that "a child who grows up carrying such a terrible burden on his back seeks for a solution in choosing his life's path."[13]

By choosing the side of Croatian nationalism, Praljak dramatically refuted his father's career. Such internal conflict is a constant in the stories of this region (e.g., nationalists whose mothers were from the "other" nation and fascists whose wives were Jews). The books of Samuel gently disclose these complexities of the human heart. When historical figures and movements cease to be complex, we feel justified making all-or-nothing judgments on those conflicts, and on those in which we ourselves participate.

The reconciling power of Samuel has one last fitting echo in the New Testament. The gospel of Jesus, the Lion of Judah and Son of David, was preached among the Gentiles by a man of Benjamin, whose parents named him after the greatest leader their tribe had ever known—namely, Saul.

God's choice of David as king was not an absolute rejection of Saul, his family, or Benjamin as a people. We recognize God's sovereignty over the long run of history, which is a great source of pride for many and a painful reality for some. But the lesson of Samuel is that within the recognition of that sovereignty, space must be given to all the tragic and hurtful episodes that make up that history. No one silences another's voice, nor hides the facts. This is how Samuel can serve as a pattern for reconciliation in honor-shame contexts.

For Further Reflection

1. Sharp argues that human identity rests largely on nationality, religion, and race. The honorable or shameful acts of "our people" often become our honor and shame at the personal level. How is this the case in your own context and life?

2. Consider how Sharp applies the book of Samuel to honor-bound conflicts. How might you incorporate his three specific suggestions to address the interpersonal or institutional conflicts where you live and serve?

CHAPTER 14 Endnotes

1 Associated Press, "'I am Not a War Criminal,' Convicted Bosnian Croat Crie as He Takes a Fatal Dose of Poison." *Los Angeles Times*, November 29, 2017, http://www.latimes.com/world/la-fg-croatia-slobadan-praljak-20171129-story.html.

2 In this chapter I focus on examples from former Yugoslavia because that is where I have lived and worked for the past seventeen years. Yet it is clear to me that America is also undergoing a similar fracturing under the weight of competing honor claims and, like the former Yugoslavia, desperately needs reconciling narratives.

3 In this chapter, I refer to the books of 1 and 2 Samuel as one collective text under the name "Samuel" or "the author of Samuel."

4 Robert Alter, *The David Story: A Translation with Commentary of 1 and 2 Samuel* (New York: W. W. Norton, 1999), Kindle Locations 205–8.

5 David Toshio Tsumura, *The First Book of Samuel* (Grand Rapids, Eerdmans, 2006), 31–32.

6 Robert Alter's remarks in *The David Story* opened my eyes to Samuel's flaws. As evangelicals, we have paid little attention to his flaws and the ways he contributed to Saul's failure.

7 There is a textual problem with 1 Sam 13:1, which should tell us how long Saul reigned but is garbled. See Tsumura, *First Book of Samuel*, 331.

8 The book of Ruth hints at its purpose in chapter 4 when it reveals that Ruth is the great-grandmother of David. This wonderful story has honor-seeking authorial intent—to neutralize any aspersion of David's mixed ancestry.

9 Moshe Halbertal and Stephen Holmes recently made the fascinating argument in *The Beginning of Politics: Power in the Biblical Book of Samuel* (Princeton, NJ: Princeton University Press, 2017) that Samuel is the first politically reflective work ever written.

10 More information on ROM can be found at forumforleadership.blogspot.hr.

11 This series of resource books for history teachers is filled with primary source documents reflecting all sides of the conflicts in the Balkans: *Teaching Modern Southeast European History: Alternate Educational Materials*, Christina Kouluri, series editor (Thessaloniki, Greece: Center for Democracy and Reconciliation in Southeastern Europe, 2009). This is the kind of work that can provide source material for such reconciliatory storytelling.

12 Quoted in Drago Pilsel, "Bozanić potiskuje kršćanstvo u svijet mita i osjećaja," *Autograf*, March 3, 2017, http://www.autograf.hr/bozanic-potiskuje-krscanstvo-u-svijet-mita-i-osjecaja; my emphasis added to honor-related terms. The "homeland war" Bozanić references is the war on Croatian territory from 1991 to 1995.

13 Mirjana Vermezović Ivanović, "Abdulah Sidran: Prošlost je pakao naših prostora," *Novi List*, December 11, 2011, http://www.novilist.hr/Kultura/Knjizevnost/Abdulah-Sidran-Proslost-je-pakao-nasih-prostora.

THE MUSLIM WOMAN'S JOURNEY FROM SHAME TO HONOR

AUDREY FRANK

> You were washed, you were sanctified, you were justified in the name of the Lord Jesus Christ and by the Spirit of our God. (1 Cor 6:11)

> Instead of your shame you will receive a double portion, and instead of disgrace you will rejoice in your inheritance. And so you will inherit a double portion in your land, and everlasting joy will be yours. (Isa 61:7)

The young woman's legs trembled as her body wracked with another contraction. She must keep her focus, continue to put one foot in front of the other. She was almost at the river. Its rushing waters could be heard over the frantic beating of her heart, the sound increasing along with the waves of pain in her body, demanding submission. The baby would not wait much longer.

As she reached a small clearing, a telltale rag tied to the low-hanging branches of a tree confirmed she was at the right place. She had marked it months before, carefully following the directions the old woman had given her. It was a place of sacrifice, a place of desperation. Women bearing the shameful burden of pregnancy outside of marriage came here to bear their children alone and dispose of them in secret.

The water gurgled and churned, singing happily, aloof to her pain. *I wish the water could wash away the dirtiness in my soul.* The thought flicked through her mind just as another splitting contraction brought her to her knees. Through a fog of pain and agony, a second thought rose up. Louder, stronger, more certain. *You will never be clean again.*

Aadil walked along the riverbank, deep in thought. He came here each week to pray and seek the Lord. As the Christian pastor of a small group of believers, his house was always brimming with visitors and those in need. The only way he could get alone with God was to take these long, solitary walks. Today he was meditating on Isaiah 45:3: "I will give you the treasures of darkness and riches hidden in secret places, so that you may know that it is I, the LORD, the God of Israel, who calls you by your name" (NRSV). Aadil wanted to find those treasures. He longed to be one with whom God shared his secrets. But the passage clearly said treasures are found in darkness. The dark passages of life, the suffering and pain his little flock faced as persecuted followers of Jesus in a Muslim country, were overwhelming at times. Could they persevere to find treasure there?

A cry like that of a wounded animal startled him out of his reverie. Pausing, he stood very still to listen. Again, he heard it. This time the noise was weaker. It sounded like a child.

Walking carefully toward the sound, Aadil moved branches out of his way and stepped over fallen tree trunks. There! It was getting louder. But he could see nothing but river, trees, and blue sky. Pushing through the thick grasses along the riverbank, he emerged onto a narrow pebble-strewn shoreline. Exposed on a rock, tiny arms punching the air in distress, lay a newborn baby.

Someone had taken care to clean the child and cut the umbilical cord. Crying pitifully, the baby girl was alone, with no blanket, no clothing, no comfort. There was no one else to be seen. Aadil tore off his shirt, gently lifted the baby, and wrapped her. He held the infant to his chest, trying to soothe her. Aadil looked around in distress, scanning the trees for the child's mother. Wading through shrubbery and climbing over rocks, he scoured the area. It was deserted.

Finally, he turned toward home, bearing the rejected child in his arms.

Over the years, Aadil and his wife found and adopted more than twenty abandoned babies from the riverside. Eighteen were girls. Their mothers remained hidden, anonymous. Shame had driven them to desperate acts of sacrifice and a false belief that they and their children had no value. Like the young mother who abandoned her daughter, each believed she could never be clean.

But for the children, there was hope. Isaiah 45:3 became a life verse for Aadil and those he rescued. There is a God who rescues the dirty and makes them clean, finds the shamed and gives them honor; and out of the darkness he brings forth treasures, like hope and a future (Jer 29:11).

The Pilgrimage to Purity

Dirty is another word for *shame*. *Clean* signifies *honor*. In many parts of the Muslim world today, women carry the burden of shame in silence. They don't know that Jesus Christ has abolished shame, giving honor instead. No one has ever told them that there is indeed Someone powerful enough, compassionate enough, and pure enough to make us clean and to keep us clean.

For Muslim women, the concept of purity is confounded by the cultural and religious beliefs of Islam surrounding women's nature and intrinsic value. Not only does she bear the responsibility of making herself pure, but she must also bear the burden of less worth compared to men. For example, the Qur'an uses similar language to describe both women and Satan when it states that women possess *kayd,* or maliciousness (Qur'an 12:28; 4:76). Furthermore, it teaches that women are incomplete beings, their inheritance only half of what a man receives (Qur'an 4:11, 176) and their testimony valued at half a man's testimony (Qur'an 2:282). Husbands have a legal right to their wives' bodies, even when intimacy is not consensual.

Keeping one's self clean through purification rituals is a constant burden that both Muslim men and women bear, but for a woman the task is overwhelming. During the month of Ramadan, she cannot complete a full cycle of fasting and prayer because of her menstrual cycle. Nevertheless, according to her religion she must make up those missed days if she hopes to be counted pure and have her prayers heard by God. Qur'an 2:222 holds forth this reminder: "Allah loves those who turn to Him constantly and He loves those who keep themselves pure and clean." If one cannot control her own personal purity, how can she be sure of Allah's love? This unanswered question leaves many Muslim women feeling not only dirty but also unloved.

We see a similar dilemma in the Gospel account of the woman who had been suffering from hemorrhages for twelve years.

> As Jesus was on his way, the crowds almost crushed him. And a woman was there who had been subject to bleeding for twelve years, but no one could heal her. She came up behind him and touched the edge of his cloak, and immediately her bleeding stopped.
>
> "Who touched me?" Jesus asked.
>
> When they all denied it, Peter said, "Master, the people are crowding and pressing against you."
>
> But Jesus said, "Someone touched me; I know that power has gone out from me."
>
> Then the woman, seeing that she could not go unnoticed, came trembling and fell at his feet. In the presence of all the people, she told why she had touched him and how she had been instantly healed. Then he said to her, "Daughter, your faith has healed you. Go in peace." (Luke 8:42–48)

Crushing crowds are the last place one would expect to see a woman such as this. She could not make herself ritually clean, for her bleeding condition was incurable, rendering her constantly impure. As a result, she was ostracized from society, her presence a source of impurity to others. She undoubtedly avoided people most of the time, and they, in turn, avoided her. In light of this seemingly implacable position of dishonor, her decision to enter the crowds and reach out to touch Rabbi Jesus is audacious and shocking. She demonstrated the desperate hope of a woman who has nothing left to lose.

In that moment of courage, she exposed the intersection of humanity's need for purity and God's provision of atonement through Jesus Christ. The Master and Teacher, the One who would a short time later shed his blood on the cross as the ultimate sacrifice for sin and shame, rising from the dead three days later, was completely and utterly pure. This woman had no power to defile him. Rather, his power went forth and healed her, making her clean and restoring her in every way. Her faith reveals to us a crucial element of the gospel for Muslim women suffering from the belief they can never be clean and loved by God. *Muslim women deserve to know the Messiah has secured their purity forever.*

Levitical law carefully prescribed steps to achieve spiritual purity from sin. On the Day of Atonement, the high priest offered two goats in an elaborate ceremony with a twofold purpose: One would be sacrificed, its blood symbolically cleansing God's people, the high priest, and the sanctuary. The other would bear the sins of the people and be sent outside the camp, providing a poignant illustration of their sin and shame being taken away (Lev 16:7–10).

Not long after his encounter with the unclean woman, Jesus would become the ultimate atonement sacrifice, his blood cleansing God's people forever as he hung on a cross outside the gate, bearing their sin and shame (Heb 1:3; 13:12).

For many women in the Muslim world, Jesus' power to make them pure has been central to their journey from shame to honor.[1]

The drums reverberated through the night sky, the simple harmonies of the worshippers rising to the twinkling stars. The heavens seemed to dance to the rhythms of praise emanating from the tiny village. Followers of the Messiah had traveled for days to gather here for a weekend of worship and fellowship. The hostess was a single mother, recently widowed. Her bright, joyful smile competed with the light from the moon as she walked among the throngs, handing out sweet bread and stoking the fires.

It was time for more tea. Bending low, Farhana stepped through the opening into her small mud hut. As she pushed open the corrugated steel scrap that served as a door to the back room, she smiled to herself. *No more jinn in here,* she thought. *No need to fear ever again.* When her husband was alive, she was forbidden to enter the room. It had been dedicated to his *jinn,* or the evil spirits he consulted with in his work. He made no decision without consulting the jinn. A powerful witch doctor, he had been highly sought after by people far and near. Everyone in the village remembered the day a Masai warrior from the far north had appeared, seeking her husband's strong magic against a tribal enemy.

Some witch doctors in her culture were healers. They provided charms and special incantations to heal the sick. But others, like her late husband, were killers. They were sought when boundaries had been crossed, women had disobeyed, or the evil eye had become too powerful for charms. Their magic was dark and had the power to kill.

Farhana remembered the first day she laid eyes on her husband. Her father came to her in the field where she was turning over the stubborn soil with a short-handled hoe. She looked up expectantly, wondering why he had appeared instead of her mother to fetch her for lunchtime. Motioning to Farhana, he simply said, "Come."

Farhana followed him to their small house beneath the banana trees. An old man wearing an embroidered robe and Muslim *kufi*, a brimless, round hat, sat drinking tea. He was seated on a woven mat reserved only for the most special, honored guests.

Farhana's heart caught in her throat as a terrifying thought ran through her head. *He has come to marry me.* In that split second, Farhana considered running as fast as she could, away from her future. But the look in her father's eyes riveted her in place, immobilizing her. Her family's honor was at stake, and her obedience would determine not only her future but everyone's.

Her mother, who had been standing quietly just inside the doorway, broke the heavy silence. "Daughter, go make yourself clean. You will become a woman today."

Farhana lived in a world of folk Islam, an eclectic mix of Islam and animism. Islamic law dictated a complex web of rituals and rules to keep girls and women clean and pure. Family honor was inextricably bound to female purity. Animism, on the other hand, filled families with fear of angering the spirits that controlled the harmony between the physical and the spiritual worlds. Girls like Farhana learned from an early age to walk a fine line between adherence to religious rules and placation of the spirits.

Although her father had converted to Islam as a young man, when trouble came he typically depended on the traditional beliefs of his tribe, seeking power over the spirit world through appeasement. The previous year, neighbors had violated the boundaries of his farm, planting corn on his land and refusing to relinquish what was rightfully his. As a result, he sought the help of a powerful witch doctor, the man now sitting drinking tea by his front door. The curse he procured had apparently worked; his neighbor's oldest son had died. Today the witch doctor had come for his payment. Farhana would be the ultimate compensation, a pure child bride at age fourteen.

Every night those first weeks of marriage, Farhana wept. She had made a choice to honor her father, so why did she feel so dirty and ashamed? Her new husband was cruel and abusive, and God was distant. He did not seem to care no matter how much she cried out to him. Farhana wanted to die. One night after exhausting herself with such thoughts, she had a dream. A man dressed in light appeared to her and said these astonishing words, "I am the way, the truth, and the life. Follow me. One day someone will come and tell you my name." She awoke filled with hope, wondering who this person was.

Several years later, a missionary moved to Farhana's village. As they talked one night by lantern light, the woman spoke the words of Jesus in John 14:6: "I am the way, the truth, and the life. No one comes to the Father except through me." Farhana gasped as she heard the very words the man in light had spoken to her. *This must be him! His name is Jesus!* Farhana prayed with the missionary to become a follower of the Messiah, and her life was transformed.

In the following months, fear was replaced with power as Farhana studied the Bible with her friend and learned to trust Jesus. The shame that once paralyzed her, whispering its lies that she did not matter, released its grip and Farhana began to believe she was honored, clean, and valuable in God's sight. She learned that through his death and resurrection, Jesus had accomplished her purity and honor permanently. Truth took root in Farhana's heart and she could not stop singing. God knew her, and not only that, he had come himself to prove to her that she mattered to him!

She served her husband and waited, praying he would see that Jesus was the only way to God. He listened intently to her, but when he consulted his jinn, they told him it was all a lie. One hot afternoon, he dropped dead.

A short time later, Farhana had another dream. In it, her little compound was filled with people worshiping God in the name of the Messiah. Light was bursting from the walls of her mud house. The room of jinn was swept clean, standing empty with the door wide open. When she awoke, a thought resonated in her mind, and she knew what she must do. Sending news by word of mouth throughout the tribe, she invited believers far and wide to her home for regular worship celebrations.

Now the sounds of worship filled the air as she poured water into a pan for her guests to wash their hands. Another thought came to her. *You have made me clean. And now I can help others become clean. Thank you, Jesus.*

The Burden of Honor

Across the Muslim world, women are vessels of family honor. Their behavior, like a mirror, reflects the image of the families to which they belong. Purity, righteousness, and obedience reflect honor. Disobedience to Islamic law or cultural mores reflects shame. Shame is put upon not only the one who committed an indiscretion but also on her family. It is imperative to Islamic social and familial infrastructure that women maintain honor, avoiding shame at all costs.

Some women make choices to rebel against the constraints of Islam, dangerously risking loss of honor and possibly even their lives. Others, through circumstances beyond their control, such as infertility or the birth of a child with a physical disability, find themselves expelled from the group in shame.

Regardless of how they were forced from the group, such women are placed in a position of extreme vulnerability. They feel rejected and ensnared. The way out can be grim: death at the hands of another, or death at one's own hand. Muslim women in a position of shame commonly believe God is a harsh and distant judge who deems them less valuable than their male counterparts. This belief fosters confusion about not only their own identities but also the identity of God himself. Such women are captives in a prison of broken relationships with people and with God.

From an early age, girls are carefully taught by their mothers how to avoid shame. Women are responsible for training young children to recognize what is shameful and how to carefully keep from bringing dishonor to their families. Consequently, some Muslim women appear to Westerners to be promoting the oppression of women.

A well-known and extreme example is female genital mutilation (FGM), a surgery which, according to the World Health Organization, is commonly believed to "ensure premarital virginity and marital fidelity."[2] Ironically, in some cultures FGM is also considered to make young girls clean and pure, a desirable bride. Mothers are most often the ones taking daughters for this controversial and inhumane surgery. This apparent perpetuation of shame by women themselves is confounding to the Western worldview of innocence and guilt, right and wrong. From an honor-shame worldview, however, the continuation of such practices is often an attempt to avoid shame and maintain honor.

As children emerge into adolescence and young adulthood, they and the family honor they represent are closely guarded by fathers, uncles, and brothers. Men are responsible for training this age group in what is honorable and how to maintain a position of honor in the family and community. The role of men in honor training sheds light on why brothers and fathers commit honor killings. Purging, or killing the one who has brought shame on the family, is an extreme and desperate act to restore honor. It is most often pursued after attempts at avoiding, covering, and denying the shame have failed. Purging is the last resort, although it is the most commonly reported, much to the horror and outrage of the international community.

The honor burden that women bear is the nucleus of all Muslim life. Women serve as vessels of honor and men guard and protect that honor. Although men and women play different roles in the honor-shame paradigm, they share the same need for the shame-abolishing, honor-bestowing gospel of Christ.

The Barrier of False Belief

If we could peer behind the façade of human hearts from any culture, we would find that the Muslim woman's customary belief that shame is permanent is shared by many people. The weight of shame can be suffocating and life-draining. The resulting isolation from others causes deep loneliness. When that belief is taken a step further and applied to one's relationship with God, it may lead to despair and even suicide. Muslim women imprisoned for shame crimes in Kabul, Afghanistan often reported that they faced death either way—return home to be killed by a father or brother, or stay in prison and kill themselves.[3] Germany reports that the suicide rate among Muslim women living there is twice that of native non-Muslim females.[4]

The conflict between Western, liberal culture and the conservative honor culture of home drives many Muslim women to duplicity and fear for their lives. Shame shouts its lie, "You are worthless," prodding its bearer toward the darkness.

The honor-shame worldview fosters this false belief for those who have not yet discovered the Messiah who gave his life to secure humanity's honor forever. Worldviews are imperfect human perspectives, resulting in broken systems. Each worldview is seeded with light and darkness: the light of what was intended by the loving Creator and the darkness of humanity's sinful response to that generous provision. Innocence was created; guilt was chosen. Power was granted; fear overshadowed its liberty. Honor was freely given; shame resulted when woman and man chose to sin. The interplay between light and darkness can be seen in all worldviews. Men and women the world over strive to overcome the darkness.

There must be a preeminent view, a system of principles that overarch the imperfect and fragmented systems of people. The human heart longs for higher truth, the possibility of redemption. This God-given longing is the smoldering wick of hope in a heart that believes it can never be clean.

The Good News

The belief that women must carry the burden of honor for society is counter to the gospel message and was never intended by the loving Creator. No man, no matter how carefully constructed his rules for living, regardless of the diligence with which he guards honor, can establish and maintain honor for the human heart. No woman, no matter how much she avoids shame and follows the rules, can abolish dishonor. Humanity has inherited shame from Adam and Eve, and it is a condition of the human soul shared by men and women alike. We have lost our position of right standing with God. Instead of belonging to God we are alienated. We slump in a posture of dishonor before him. Through sin, we were separated from him; and the rift is irreparable through human effort. "But thanks be to God! He gives us the victory through our Lord Jesus Christ" (1 Cor 15:57).

Women coming to Christ out of Islam frequently report that an encounter with the Bible changed their understanding of God and themselves. They discover a God who, rather than being distant and harsh, draws near to them in their struggle and gently heals their wounds. Instead of judging them inferior, the God of the Bible elevates women to a place of honor, even in the presence of men. They learn that man and woman were both created in God's image, of equal value to him. Furthermore, both stand equally in need of a Savior to restore them to a position of honor before God. Jesus Christ did that when, bearing the sin and shame of humanity, he died on the cross and was raised to life. He has soundly defeated all that would separate men and women from God.

Scripture is rich with promises for the dishonored, the rejected, and the abandoned. The Bible is one of the most powerful keys we hold to sharing the hope we have. Those from an honor-shame worldview read its promises through the lenses of honor and shame.

The majestic narrative of God's mission to bring his children back into relationship with him is a story not only of *sin forgiven* and *fear overcome*, but also of *honor restored*. When we share the Bible with Muslim women, pointing them toward the rich stories of Jesus' encounters with women in the New Testament, they discover this life-changing good news. Stories such as the hemorrhaging woman in Mark 5:24–34, the Samaritan woman at the well in John 4:1–42, and the widow of Nain in Luke 7:11–17 are examples of Jesus' compassion for shamed women.

The good news for Muslim women is that there is indeed a God who makes the dirty clean, honors the shamed, and—out of the darkness of suffering—brings the treasures of hope and joy. Through Jesus Christ, humanity is invited to be restored to a relationship of honor with God.

Conclusion

The young pregnant woman who trembled in fear by the riverside had no idea that she could be made clean. She was desperately trying to cover her shame. Though she left its tangible consequence on a barren rock, she crept away in shame's shadow, most likely laboring beneath its yoke the rest of her life. But because of God's mercy and grace, her child began a different journey that day. As Pastor Aadil carried the rejected child in his arms toward home, he drew us a picture of the Lord who rescues us from shame, bears us up in his arms, and brings us into his family through Jesus Christ. The little girl who was abandoned and rejected on a barren rock encountered Jesus; and today she belongs to the family of God, she is accepted, and she is honored.

Jesus came to Farhana in a dream and promised hope. As she studied the Bible, she learned that her purity depended on Jesus' death and resurrection, not on her own efforts or the decisions made by others for her. Farhana herself became a messenger of the honor-gospel that purifies and forgives, sharing the good news that had miraculously changed her life.[5]

A position of honor is reserved for all those who will place their trust in Jesus Christ. Purification is promised to all who put faith in the Messiah. This is the hope we can offer Muslim women.

Every Muslim woman is somewhere on the journey from shame to honor. Perhaps she is at the beginning, believing the age-old lie passed down from shame's inception: "God doesn't really love you. He can't really be trusted."

Maybe she is caught in the trap of denying or covering her shame, but inside she is desperate to escape its grip.

Maybe she is waiting for you or me to tell her that Jesus the Messiah came to remove her shame and establish honor for her—forever, guaranteed.

Wherever she is on her journey, she deserves to know the sacrifice given for her honor. Her shame was indeed purged and she was made clean at the cost of a precious life. The life given was that of the Son of God himself; and because of his obedient death on a cross, Muslim women can be free from shame forever.

For Further Reflection

1. Christ's atonement made "purification for sins" (Heb 1:3). Frank writes, "*Dirty* is another word for *shame. Clean* signifies *honor.*" How might a gospel that cleanses from sin's defilement be especially relevant to the female world and minority populations?

2. Think about the notion of "the burden of honor" (and the associated practices of shame avoidance). Why might a gospel message using the legal language of innocence/guilt fail to fail to connect with this burden? How can an honor-shame gospel address this burden?

CHAPTER 15 Endnotes

1 Werner Mischke asks, "Is there Someone who is powerful enough, compassionate enough, pure enough to make us clean, and to keep us clean?" in his riveting examination of the gospel dynamic of purity in *The Global Gospel* (Scottsdale, AZ: Mission ONE, 2015), 266.

2 "Female Genital Mutilation: Key Facts," World Health Organization, http://www.who.int/news-room/fact-sheets/detail/female-genital-mutilation.

3 Tanaz Eshaghian, "Love Crimes of Kabul," HBO video, 2011, https://www.youtube.com/watch?v=G_uqJ0s6jwE.

4 Balci, Güner, "Forbidden Love: Taboos and Fear Among Muslim Girls," *Der Spiegel*, January 6, 2011, http://www.spiegel.de/international/germany/forbidden-love-taboos-and-fear-among-muslim-girls-a-737683.html.

5 To read more about Farhana's story, see Audrey Frank, *Covered Glory: The Face of Honor and Shame in the Muslim World* (Eugene, OR: Harvest House, 2019), Introduction.

Adams, Carol J., and Marie M. Fortune. *Violence against Women and Children: A Christian Theological Sourcebook*. New York: Continuum, 1998.

Adams, Marilyn McCord. *Horrendous Evils and the Goodness of God*. Ithaca, NY: Cornell University Press, 1999.

Adams, Susan A. "Using Transactional Analysis and Mental Imagery to Help Shame-Based Identity Adults Make Peace With Their Past." *Adultspan* 7, no. 1 (2008): 2–12. doi:10.1002/j.2161-0029.2008.tb00038.x.

Alexander, T. Desmond. *From Eden to the New Jerusalem: An Introduction to Biblical Theology*. Grand Rapids: Kregel, 2008.

Alkire, Sabina, Gisela Robles, and Suman Seth. "Multidimensional Poverty Index Winter 2016: OPHI *Briefing 41*," University of Oxford. Oxford Poverty & Human Development Initiative. https://www.ophi.org.uk/.

Alkire, Sabina, and Maria Santos. "The Missing Dimensions of Poverty Data." Oxford Development Studies 35, no. 4 (2007): 347-359.

———. "Multidimensional Poverty Index." Oxford Poverty & Human Development Initiative. 2010. http://www.ophi.org.uk/.

Alter, Robert. *The David Story: A Translation with Commentary of 1 and 2 Samuel*. New York: W.W. Norton, 1999. Kindle.

Ambrose. *Select Works and Letters*. Translated by H. De Romestin. Grand Rapids: Eerdmans, 1983.

Appiah, Kwame Anthony. *Honor Code - How Moral Revolutions Happen*. New York: W.W. Norton, 2011.

Ashford, Bruce Riley, and David P. Nelson. "The Story of Mission: The Grand Biblical Narrative." In *Theology and Practice of Mission: God, the Church, and the Nations*, edited by Bruce Riley Ashford. Nashville: B&H Academic, 2011.

Associated Press. "'I am Not a War Criminal,' Convicted Bosnian Croat Crie as He Takes a Fatal Dose of Poison." *Los Angeles Times,* November 29, 2017. http://www.latimes.com/world/la-fg-croatia-slobadan-praljak-20171129-story.html.

Athanasius. *On the Incarnation*. Translated by Archibald Robertson. Miami: HardPress, 2012.

Augustine. *Against Julian*. Translated by Matthew A. Schumacher. Washington, DC: Catholic Univ. of America Press, 1981.

Bauckham, Richard. B*ible and Mission: Christian Witness in a Postmodern World*. Grand Rapids: Baker Academic, 2003.

———. "Reading Scripture as a Coherent Story." In *The Art of Reading Scripture*. Edited by Ellen F. Davis and Richard B. Hays. Grand Rapids: Eerdmans, 2003.

Bell, Rob. *Velvet Elvis: Repainting the Christian Faith*. Grand Rapids: Zondervan, 2005.

Borges, Jason. "'Dignified': An Exegetical Soteriology of Divine Honour." *Scottish Journal of Theology* 66, no. 1 (2013): 74–87.

Bourdillon, Michael, and Jo Boyden. "Reflections: Inequality, School, and Social Change." In *Growing Up in Poverty: Findings from Young Lives*, ed. Michael Bourdillon and Jo Boyden, 269–80. New York: Palgrave Macmillan, 2014.

Bradshaw, Bruce. *Change across Cultures: A Narrative Approach to Social Transformation*. Grand Rapids: Baker Academic, 2002.

BrainyQuote. "Aristotle Quotes." http://www.brainyquote.com/quotes/quotes/a/aristotle148503.html.

Butler, Joel. *Jesus in the Gospels*. Unpublished document.

Chase, Elaine, and Grace Bantebya-Kyomuhendo. "Poverty and Shame: The Future." In *Poverty and Shame: Global Experiences*, ed. Elaine Chase and Grace Bantebya-Kyomuhendo. Oxford: Oxford Scholarship Online, 2014.

Chiang, Samuel E., and Grant Lovejoy, eds. *Beyond Literate Western Contexts: Honor & Shame and Assessment of Orality Preference*. Hong Kong: Capstone Enterprises, 2015.

Childs, Carla P., and Patricia Greenfield. "Informal Modes of Learning and Teaching: The Case of Zinacanteco Weaving." In *Studies in Cross-cultural Psychology*, ed. Neil Warren. Vol. 2. London: Academic Press, 1980.

Cicero, Marcus Tullius. *Pro Rabirio Perduellionis*. Translated by H. G. Hodge. Loeb Classical Library 19. Cambridge, MA: Harvard University Press, 1927.

Cloud, Henry. *Changes That Heal: How to Understand Your Past to Ensure a Healthier Future*. Grand Rapids: Zondervan, 1992.

Crouch, Andy. "The Return of Shame." *Christianity Today* 59, no. 2 (March 2015): 32–41.

Culture Learner website. "Culture Learner." August 31, 2015. http://wernermischke.org/.

Daigle, Lauren. *How Can It Be?* Centricity Music. Franklin, TN. 2014.

Davidson, Richard. *Flame of Yahweh: Sexuality in the Old Testament*. Peabody, MA: Hendrickson, 2007.

DeSilva, David Arthur. *Honor, Patronage, Kinship and Purity: Unlocking New Testament Culture*. Downers Grove, IL: InterVarsity, 2000.

Dictionary of Sociorhetorical Terms. http://www.religion.emory.edu/faculty/robbins/SRI/defns/.

Dossa, Nissou I., Marie Hatem, Maria V. Zunzunegui, and William Fraser. "Social Consequences of Conflict-Related Rape: The Case of Survivors in the Eastern Democratic Republic of Congo." *Peace and Conflict: Journal of Peace Psychology* 20, no. 3 (2014): 241–55.

Dunn, James D. G. *The Oral Gospel Tradition*. Grand Rapids: Eerdmans, 2013.

Duvall, J. Scott., and J. Daniel Hays. *Grasping God's Word: A Hands-on Approach to Reading, Interpreting, and Applying the Bible*. Grand Rapids: Zondervan, 2012.

Erickson, Millard J. *The Evangelical Left: Encountering Postconservative Evangelical Theology*. Carlisle, UK: STL, 1997.

Eusebius. *The Ecclesiastical History*. Edited by Kirsopp Lake, J. E. L. Oulton, and Hugh Jackson Lawlor. Cambridge, MA: Harvard University Press, 1992.

Bibliography

Fackre, Gabriel. "Narrative Theology." *Union Seminary Review* 37, no. 4 (October 1983): 340–52.

Fee, Gordon D., and Douglas K. Stuart. *How to Read the Bible for All Its Worth.* Grand Rapids: Zondervan, 1993.

Fikkert, Brian, and Russel Mask. *From Dependency to Dignity.* Grand Rapids: Zondervan, 2015.

Fingeret, Arlene. "The Illiterate Underclass: Demythologizing an American Stigma." PhD diss., Syracuse University, 1982. UMI No. 8301638.

Fodor, Jerry A., and Ernest Lepore. *Holism: A Shoppers Guide.* Cambridge, MA: Blackwell, 2004.

Foster, George M. *Tzintzuntzan: Mexican Peasants in a Changing World.* Boston: Little, Brown, 1967.

Fuller, Daniel P. *The Unity of the Bible: Unfolding God's Plan for Humanity.* Grand Rapids: Zondervan, 1992.

Gardner, Jane F. *Women in Roman Law and Society.* Indianapolis: Indiana University Press, 1986.

Gates, Bill. "Remarks of Bill Gates, Harvard Commencement." *Harvard Gazette,* June 7, 2007. http://news.harvard.edu/gazette/story/2007/06/remarks-of-bill-gates-harvard-commencement-2007/.

Georges, Jayson. "From Shame to Honor: A Theological Reading of Romans for Honor-Shame Contexts." *Missiology: An International Review* 38, no. 3 (2010): 295–307.

Georges, Jayson, and Mark Baker. *Ministering in Honor-Shame Cultures: Biblical Foundations and Practical Essentials.* Downers Grove, IL: InterVarsity, 2016.

Gingrich, Roy E. *Old Testament Survey.* Memphis: Riverside Press, 2001.

Goheen, Michael W. "The Urgency of Reading the Bible as One Story in the 21st Century." Lecture, Regent College, Vancouver, BC, November 2, 2006.

Goldingay, John. "Biblical Story and the Way It Shapes Our Story." *Journal of the European Pentecostal Theological Association* 17, no. 1 (1997): 5–15.

Goodman, Madeline, Robert Finnegan, Leyla Mohadjer, Tom Krenzke, and Jacquie Hogan. *Literacy, Numeracy, and Problem Solving in Technology-Rich Environments among U.S. Adults: Results from the Program for the International Assessment of Adult Competencies 2012.* National Center for Education Statistics, Institute of Education Sciences, U.S. Department of Education report. Washington, DC, 2013.

Greer, Peter. *For the Least of These: A Biblical Answer to Poverty.* Edited by Anne Bradley and Arthur Lindsley. Grand Rapids: Zondervan, 2014.

Gregory of Nazianzus. *Select Orations, St. Gregory of Nazianzus.* Vol. 107 of Fathers of the Church. Translated by Martha Pollard Vinson. Washington, DC: Catholic University of America Press, 2003.

Halbertal, Moshe, and Stephen Holmes. *The Beginning of Politics: Power in the Biblical Book of Samuel.* Princeton, NJ: Princeton University Press, 2017.

Hays, J. Daniel. *The Message of the Prophets: A Survey of the Prophetic and Apocalyptic Books of the Old Testament.* Grand Rapids: Zondervan, 2010.

Hellerman, Joseph H. *Embracing Shared Ministry: Power and Status in the Early Church and Why It Matters Today.* Grand Rapids: Kregel, 2013.

Hicks, Donna. *Dignity: Its Essential Role in Resolving Conflict.* New Haven, CT: Yale University Press, 2011.

Hofstede, Geert, and Gert Jan Hofstede. *Cultures and Organizations Software of the Mind: Inter-cultural Cooperation and Its Importance for Survival.* 2nd ed. New York: McGraw-Hill, 2005.

International Orality Network and Lausanne Committee for World Evangelization. *Making Disciples of Oral Learners.* Lima, NY: Elim Publishing, 2005.

Ivanović, Mirjana Vermezović. "Abdulah Sidran: Prošlost je pakao naših prostora." *Novi List.* December 11, 2011. http://www.novilist.hr/Kultura/Knjizevnost/Abdulah-Sidran-Proslost-je-pakao-nasih-prostora.

Jackson, Bill. *The Biblical Metanarrative: One God - One Plan - One Story.* Corona, CA: Radical Middle Press, 2014.

Jagerson, Jennifer. "Hermeneutics and the Methods of Oral Bible Storytelling for the Evangelization and Discipleship of Oral Learners." *Great Commission Research Journal* 4, no. 2 (2013): 251–61.

Jerome. *Commentary on Jonah.* Translated by Timothy Michael Hegedus. Ottawa: Bibliothèque nationale du Canada, 1992.

———. *St. Jerome: Letters and Select Works.* Translated by W. H. Fremantle. New York: Christian Literature Co, 1893.

Johnson, Diane E. "Considering Shame and Its Implications for Student Learning." *College Student Journal* 46, no. 1 (2012): 3–17.

Juvenal. *Satires.* Translated by Susanna M. Braund. Loeb Classical Library 91. Cambridge, MA: Harvard University Press, 2004.

Kelly, J. T., T. S. Betancourt, D. Mukwege, R. Lipton, and M. J. Vanrooyen. "Experiences of Female Survivors of Sexual Violence in Eastern Democratic Republic of the Congo: A Mixed-methods Study." *Conflict and Health* 5, no. 1 (2011).

Kelly, Jocelyn, Justin Kabanga, Will Cragin, Lys Alcayna-Stevens, Sadia Haider, and Michael J. Vanrooyen. "'If Your Husband Doesn't Humiliate You, Other People Won't': Gendered Attitudes towards Sexual Violence in Eastern Democratic Republic of Congo." *Global Public Health* 7, no. 3 (2012): 285–98.

Koulouri, Christina, ed. *Teaching Modern Southeast European History: Alternative Educational Materials.* Thessaloniki, Greece: Center for Democracy and Reconciliation in Southeast Europe, 2009.

Lewis, C. S. *The Four Loves.* New York: HarperOne, 2017.

Livius, Titus. *History of Rome 1.* Translated by B. O. Foster. Loeb Classical Library 114. Cambridge, MA: Harvard University Press, 1919.

Loewen, Arley. *Rethinking Shame and Honour.* Carlisle, UK: Micah Global, 2017.

Longenecker, Bruce W. *The Cross before Constantine: The Early Life of a Christian Symbol.* Minneapolis: Fortress, 2015.

Lyotard, Jean-Francois. *The Postmodern Condition: A Report on Knowledge.* Minneapolis: University of Minnesota Press, 1986.

Bibliography

Matthews, Michael. *A Novel Approach: The Significance of Story in the Hermeneutic of Reality*. Victoria, BC: Tellwell Talent, 2017.

Maximus. *On Difficulties in Sacred Scripture: The Responses to Thalassios*. Translated by Maximos Constas. Washington, DC: The Catholic University of America Press, 2018.

Mischke, Werner. *The Global Gospel: Achieving Missional Impact in Our Multicultural World*. Scottsdale, AZ: Mission One, 2015.

Neyrey, Jerome H. "Despising the Shame of the Cross." *Semeia* 68 (1996): 113–37.

Nagasawa, Mako. "Why God is Not Evil, Not One Bit: According to Irenaeus of Lyons." http://www.newhumanityinstitute.org/pdfs/article-irenaeus-on-gods-goodness-&-human-evil.pdf.

Nichols, Bruce. "The Role of Guilt and Shame in a Theology of Cross-Cultural Mission." *Evangelical Review of Theology* 25 (2011): 231–41.

Nida, Eugene A. *Customs and Cultures: Anthropology for Christian Missions*. Pasadena, CA: William Carey Library, 1975.

O'Connor, Flannery. *Mystery and Manners Occasional Prose*. New York: Farrar, Straus & Giroux, 1969.

Ong, Walter J. *Orality & Literacy: The Technologizing of the Word*. London: Methuen & Co., 1982.

Orenstein, Myrna. "Picking Up the Clues: Understanding Undiagnosed Learning Disabilities, Shame, and Imprisoned Intelligence." *Journal of College Student Psychotherapy* 15, no. 2 (2000): 35–46. doi:10.1300/j035v15n02_05.

Ovid. *Fasti*. Translated by James G. Frazer and G. P. Goold. Loeb Classical Library 253. Cambridge, MA: Harvard University Press, 1931.

Paauw, Glenn R. *Saving the Bible from Ourselves: Learning to Read & Live the Bible Well*. Downers Grove, IL: InterVarsity, 2016.

Participate. *People's Experiences of Living in Poverty: Early Findings for High Level Panel Deliberations*. Report. Monrovia, Liberia: Institute of Development Studies and Beyond, 2013.

Peterson, Eugene H. *Leap over a Wall: Earthy Spirituality for Everyday Christians*. New York: HarperCollins, 1997.

Pilch, John J., and Bruce J. Malina. *Biblical Social Values and Their Meaning: A Handbook*. Peabody, MA: Hendrickson, 1993.

Pilsel, Drago. "Bozanić Potiskuje Kršćanstvo U Svijet Mita I Osjećaja." Autograf. March 3, 2017. http://www.autograf.hr/bozanic-potiskuje-krscanstvo-u-svijet-mita-i-osjecaja.

Pitt-Rivers, Julian. "The Place of Grace in Anthropology." *HAU: Journal of Ethnographic Theory* 1, no. 1 (2011): 423–50. doi:10.14318/hau1.1.017.

Roberts, Alexander, and James Donaldson, eds. *Gregory Thaumaturgus, Dionysius the Great, Julius Africanus, Anatolius and Minor Writers, Methodius, Arnobius*. Peabody, MA: Hendrickson, 1994.

Ryken, Leland. *Words of Delight: A Literary Introduction to the Bible*. Grand Rapids: Baker Academic, 2005.

Schmutzer, Andrew J. *The Long Journey Home: Understanding and Ministering to the Sexually Abused: A Collaborative Address from Psychology, Theology, and Pastoral Care.* Eugene, OR: Wipf & Stock, 2011.

Scholz, Susanne. "Was It Really Rape in Genesis 34: Biblical Scholarship as a Reflection of Cultural Assumptions." In *Escaping Eden: New Feminist Perspectives on the Bible,* ed. Harold Washington, 183–98. Sheffield, England: Sheffield Academic, 1998.

Scroggie, W. Graham. *The Unfolding Drama of Redemption: The Bible as a Whole* (Three Volumes Complete and Unabridged in One). Grand Rapids: Zondervan, 1976.

Sen, Amartya. "Capability and Well-Being." Edited by A. K. Sen and Martha Nussbaum. *The Quality of Life*, 1993, 30–53. doi:10.1093/0198287976.003.0003.

Snowden, Mark, ed. 2016. Orality in America: Orality Sphere–Love 2020 Coalition. Mission America Coalition. https://orality.net/wp-content/uploads/2016/07/Orality-in-America.pdf.

Steenberg, Matthew C., and Dominic J. Unger. *St. Irenaeus of Lyons: Against the Heresies.* Vol. 3 of *Ancient Christian Writers.* New York: Newman Press, 2012.

Steffen, Tom A. *Business as Usual in the Missions Enterprise?* La Habra, CA: Center for Organizational & Ministry Development, 1999.

———. "Discoveries Made While Reconnecting God's Story to Scripture and Service." *Christian Education Journal: Research on Educational Ministry* 14, no. 1 (2017): 160–83.

———. *The Facilitator Era: Beyond Pioneer Church Multiplication.* Eugene, OR: Wipf & Stock, 2011.

———. "Pedagogical Conversions: From Propositions to Story and Symbol." *Missiology: An International Review* 38, no. 2 (2010): 141–59.

———. *Reconnecting God's Story to Ministry: Cross-cultural Storytelling at Home and Abroad.* Bletchly, UK: Authentic Media, 2005.

———. "Saving the Locals from Our Theologies." Unpublished paper. n.d.

———. *Worldview-based Storying: The Integration of Symbol, Story, and Ritual in the Orality Movement.* Richmond, VA: Rainmaker, 2018.

Stivala, Joan. "Death before Dishonour! Suicide of Christian Victims of Rape." *Eras* 13, no. 1 (2011): 1–17.

Strauss, Robert. *Introducing Story-strategic Methods: Twelve Steps toward Effective Engagement.* Eugene, OR: Wipf & Stock Publishers, 2017.

Tanner, Kathleen. "Adult Dyslexia and the 'Conundrum of Failure.'" *Disability & Society* 24, no. 6 (2009): 785–97. doi:10.1080/09687590903160274.

Tennent, Timothy C. *Theology in the Context of World Christianity.* Grand Rapids: Zondervan, 2007.

Thigpen, L. Lynn. "Connected Learning: A Grounded Theory Study of How Cambodian Adults with Limited Formal Education Learn." PhD diss., Biola University, 2016. Cook School of Intercultural Studies. ProQuest no. 10245810.

Tracy, Steven R., Celestia G. Tracy, and Kristi Ickes Garrison. *Mending the Soul: Understanding and Healing Abuse.* Grand Rapids: Zondervan, 2005.

Tracy, Steven, and Celestia G. Tracy. *By His Wounds: Trauma Healing for Africa.* Phoenix: Mending the Soul Ministries, 2014.

Tsumura, David T. *The First Book of Samuel.* Grand Rapids: Eerdmans, 2009.

Tucker, Ruth A. *The Biographical Bible: Exploring the Biblical Narrative from Adam and Eve to John of Patmos.* Grand Rapids: Baker, 2013.

Vanhoozer, Kevin J. *The Drama of Doctrine: A Canonical-linguistic Approach to Christian Theology.* Louisville: Westminster John Knox Press, 2005.

Walker, Robert, Grace Bantebya Kyomuhendo, Elaine Chase, Sohail Choudhry, Erika K. Gubrium, Jo Yongmie Nicola, Ivar Lødemel, Leemamol Mathew, Amon Mwiine, Sony Pellissery, and Yan Ming. "Poverty in Global Perspective: Is Shame a Common Denominator?" *Journal of Social Policy* 42, no. 2 (2013): 215–33. doi:10.1017/s0047279412000979.

Welch, Edward T. *Shame Interrupted: How God Lifts the Pain of Worthlessness and Rejection.* Greensboro, NC: New Growth Press, 2012.

Wells, David F. *No Place for Truth, or, Whatever Happened to Evangelical Theology?* Grand Rapids: Eerdmans, 1993.

Wiher, Hannes. *Shame and Guilt: A Key to Cross-Cultural Ministry.* Bonn, Germany: Verlag Für Kultur Und Wissenschaft, 2003.

Willis, Avery, and Mark Snowden. *Truth That Sticks: How to Communicate Velcro Truth in a Teflon Word.* Colorado Springs: NavPress, 2010.

Wright, Christopher J. H. *Mission of God: Unlocking the Bible's Grand Narrative.* Downers Grove, IL: InterVarsity, 2006.

Wright, N. T. *Paul and the Faithfulness of God.* Minneapolis: Fortress, 2013.

Wu, Jackson. "Have Theologians No Sense of Shame? How the Bible Reconciles Objective and Subjective Shame." *Themelios* 43, no. 2 (2018). http://themelios.thegospelcoalition.org/article/have-theologians-no-sense-of-shame.

———. "Rewriting the Gospel for Oral Cultures: Why Honor and Shame Are Essential to the Gospel." In *Beyond Literate Western Contexts: Honor & Shame and Assessment of Orality Preference,* ed. Samuel E. Chiang and Grant Lovejoy, 61–76. Hong Kong: Capstone Enterprises, 2015.

Yancey, Philip. *The Bible Jesus Read: Why the Old Testament Matters.* Grand Rapids: Zondervan, 1999.

CONTRIBUTORS

CRISTIAN DUMITRESCU (PhD, Andrews University) is professor of intercultural studies, missiology, and research at the Adventist International Institute of Advanced Studies in the Philippines and editor of Journal of Adventist Asia Seminary (JAAS). Cristian also pastors a church located inside the Taal Volcano on the island of Luzon, where he tests his missiological approaches from an honor-and-shame perspective.

CHRISTOPHER FLANDERS (PhD, Fuller Theological Seminary) is associate professor of missions at Abilene Christian University. He served as a missionary in Thailand for eleven years. His current research focuses on face and honor-shame issues. Christopher is the author of *About Face: Rethinking Face for 21st Century Missions.* He is also assistant editor for *Missio Dei: A Journal of Missional Theology and Praxis* (missiodeijournal.com).

AUDREY FRANK (MA, Appalachian State University) is the author of *Covered Glory: The Face of Honor and Shame in the Muslim World.* She has spent over twenty years serving in honor-shame contexts and teaches regularly on the impact of honor and shame on the Muslim woman's journey to Christ.

JAYSON GEORGES (MDiv, Talbot) has served in Muslim contexts for fifteen years. He is the founding editor of HonorShame.com. Jayson's books include *The 3D Gospel* and *Ministering in Patronage Cultures.*

STEVEN HAWTHORNE (PhD, Fuller Theological Seminary) coedited, with Ralph Winter, *Perspectives on the World Christian Movement: A Reader* and authored the *Perspectives on the World Christian Movement Study Guide.* He works with WayMakers, a mission and prayer mobilization ministry. Steven travels widely to help the *Perspectives* course get underway in strategic settings.

STEVE HONG envisions mission organizations, churches, and seminaries fully engaged with our globalizing, urbanizing world. He founded the nonprofit Kingdom Rice to help bring this vision to reality through San Francisco-based immersive teaching experiences and through coaching influencers to propagate this reimagined framework.

Contributors

RICH JAMES (BTh, University of Wales, DELTA, Cambridge Examinations) has worked as a trainer in inter-cultural communication in the Arab world for a decade. He helps lead teams of Christians ministering in the Middle East and is involved in projects relating to interfaith dialogue and Arab contextual theology.

VELI-MATTI KÄRKKÄINEN is professor of systematic theology at Fuller Theological Seminary and has served as a missionary in Thailand. He recently completed a five-volume systematic theology entitled *A Constructive Christian Theology for the Pluralistic World*. Veli-Matti's expertise is in pneumatology, ecclesiology, ecumenics, Pentecostal-charismatic theologies, theology of religions and missions, inter-cultural theologies, and comparative theology.

ARLEY LOEWEN (PhD, University of Toronto) directs Pamir Ministries, a media and discipleship ministry for Afghan people. Arley's desire is to see Jesus followers in honor-shame societies living honorably in their faith. He also trains professionals and students in Central Asia. Arley and his wife, Janice, have served with Operation Mobilization since the early 1980s.

WERNER MISCHKE (DD, *Hon. Causa*, HBI, Chennai, India) is vice president of Mission ONE, a partnership and training ministry advancing the gospel through the global church. He authored *The Global Gospel: Achieving Missional Impact in Our Multicultural World*. Werner has provided training in regard to honor, shame, and the gospel in many nations for a variety of organizations.

MAKO NAGASAWA (MTS, Holy Cross Greek Orthodox Seminary) directs The Anástasis Center for Christian Education and Ministry. He contributed to the NIV *God's Justice Bible* (Ezekiel) and coauthored the *Lazarus at the Gate* economic discipleship curriculum. Mako is part of the elder team of Neighborhood Church of Dorchester, Massachusetts.

KATIE J. RAWSON (DMiss, Fuller Theological Seminary; PhD, University of North Carolina) is international student ministry senior resource developer for InterVarsity Christian Fellowship. She has ministered among international students for over three decades. Katie authored *Crossing Cultures with Jesus: Sharing Good News with Sensitivity and Grace*, a guide to cross-cultural evangelism.

E. RANDOLPH RICHARDS (PhD, Southwestern Seminary) is professor of biblical studies and provost at Palm Beach Atlantic University. He formerly served as a missionary in Indonesia. Randolph has authored or coauthored numerous books and articles, including *Misreading Scripture with Western Eyes* and a forthcoming book on collectivist values in the biblical world.

NOLAN SHARP (MDiv, Bethel Seminary) has been a missionary with Cru in Zagreb, Croatia, for eighteen years, focusing on marketplace leaders. Nolan used to be an engineer in Silicon Valley, and he currently serves as an elder in a Croatian Baptist church.

TOM STEFFEN (DMiss, Biola University) is professor emeritus of inter-cultural studies at Biola University. He specializes in church multiplication, orality, honor-shame, and business as mission. He and his family spent fifteen years in the Philippines with New Tribes Mission before coming to Biola. Tom's books include *Reconnecting God's Story to Ministry: Great Commission Companies* (with Steve Rundle); and *Worldview-based Storying: The Integration of Symbol, Story, and Ritual in the Orality Movement*.

LYNN THIGPEN (PhD, Biola University) is a missionary with International Mission Board and an adjunct professor at Liberty University. Her dissertation, "Connected Learning: A Grounded Theory Study of How Cambodian Adults with Limited Formal Education Learn," is forthcoming in the American Society of Missiology Monograph Series.

STEVE TRACY (PhD, University of Sheffield) is professor of theology and ethics at Phoenix Seminary and founder/president of Mending the Soul Ministries. He is the author of seven books and numerous journal articles, most on sexuality and abuse. Steve is heavily involved in trauma ministry in East Africa, particularly the Democratic Republic of Congo.

JACKSON WU (PhD, SEBTS) is a theologian-in-residence with Mission ONE and has served in East Asia for almost fifteen years as a church planter and professor to Chinese pastors. Jackson has written *Saving God's Face, One Gospel for All Nations, and Reading Romans with Eastern Eyes*. His articles and resources can be found at jacksonwu.org.

Scripture Index

HEBREWS

1:3   110, 196, 202
1:1–8   47
2:9–10   14
2:10   10
2:14–15   178
2:17   108
4:14–16   108
4:14–16   94
5:8, 5:9   94
7:7   12
8:7–12   91
10:22   110
11   42
12:2   143
12:1–2   94, 143
13:12   196

JAMES

3:16   134

1 PETER

1:7   3, 8
1:4–5   8
1:21–22   47
1:7   103
2:9   107, 129
2:12   65
2:17   111
3:16   65, 69
4:12–13   8, 108
4:14   8
5:3   127
5:4   103
5:9   9
5:1–4   168
5:2–6   134

2 PETER

1:4   27
1:17–18   15

1 JOHN

3:2   27
3:8   90
4:10   106

REVELATION

7:9–16   182
18:3, 5, 7, 10   12
21:5, 9, 11   12
21:22–27   182
21:23, 26   12
21:26–27   52
21–22   41
22:1–2   182

CPSIA information can be obtained
at www.ICGtesting.com
Printed in the USA
FSHW021233230121
77926FS

9 781645 082804